Transforming Digital Learning and Assessment

Transforming Digital Learning and Assessment provides vital guidance to higher education institutions on how to develop faculty capacity to teach online and leverage the affordances of an ever-increasing array of new and emerging learning technologies. It offers higher education leaders with the context they need to position their institutions in the changing online environment, and with guidance to build support in a period of transition.

"Maki and Shea brilliantly combine foundational educational theory with a practical collection of resources and case studies on digital teaching, learning, and assessment. Evidence-based strategies guide administrators, faculty, and instructional support staff on how to navigate rapidly evolving educational technologies and enable customized learning for individual students. Comprehensive chapters by experts provide roadmaps for successful development and implementation of teaching, learning, and assessment technologies, not just for today, but far into the future."—***Monica Devanas***, *Director, Teaching Evaluation and Faculty Development, Center for Teaching Advancement and Assessment Research, Rutgers University*

"This timely book proves essential for educational technologists, transformative for instructors, and critical for higher education's online learning leaders. Covering rich and relevant topics, the editors have crafted a book that captures the expansive opportunities, real challenges, and dynamic contexts for implementing emerging technologies with a solid mixture of theory, analysis, and examples."—***Lance Eaton***, *Educational Programs Manager, Berkman Klein Center for Internet and Society, Harvard University*

"This book provides an extraordinarily rich and compelling view into the emerging landscape of digital assessment, showing us how learning technologies, artificial intelligence, and learning analytics can enhance university learning ecosystems. It deftly weaves in assessment-related, research-informed learning science, including concepts such as self-regulated learning and feedback. The examples and case studies elaborate concepts through deep dives into the specifics of technology integration, including change management approaches to collaboration across and within academic silos."—***John McCormick***, *Associate Director of Learning Design, Brandeis University*

"This volume compromises a pragmatic approach relevant to campus leaders, administrators, learning designers, and faculty looking to successfully embrace the application of learning technologies. The chapters are a direct and applied source of implementation instances at course and institutional levels. The reality is that assimilating new and dynamic learning technologies can be messy, this volume gives you insights on how to tackle the messiness in a coherent manner!"—***Enilda Romero-Hall***, *Associate Professor of Education and Graduate Coordinator of the Instructional Design and Technology Program, University of Tampa*

"*Transforming Digital Learning and Assessment* thoughtfully addresses the pressures facing higher education today. In order to survive, institutions need to give next generation learners access to a ubiquitous and affordable quality education. With integration of emergent instructional strategies, some discovered during the COVID-related "Great Digital Migration of 2020," this book is a key resource for higher education administrators and faculty navigating a 'new normal.'"—***Kim Round***, *Instructor, Chair, Harvard Extension School, Western Governors University*

TRANSFORMING DIGITAL LEARNING
AND ASSESSMENT

TRANSFORMING DIGITAL LEARNING AND ASSESSMENT

*A Guide to Available and Emerging Practices
and Building Institutional Consensus*

Edited by Peggy L. Maki and Peter Shea

Foreword by Bryan Alexander

1996-2021 25ᵀᴴ ANNIVERSARY

Stylus
PUBLISHING, LLC.

STERLING, VIRGINIA

COPYRIGHT © 2021 BY STYLUS PUBLISHING, LLC.

Published by Stylus Publishing, LLC.
22883 Quicksilver Drive
Sterling, Virginia 20166-2019

Library of Congress Cataloging-in-Publication Data
Names: Maki, Peggy, editor. | Shea, Peter, 1963- editor.
Title: Transforming digital learning and assessment : a guide to
    available and emerging practices and building institutional
    consensus / edited by Peggy L. Maki and Peter Shea.
Description: First edition. | Sterling, Virginia : Stylus Publishing,
    LLC., [2021] | Includes bibliographical references and index.
Identifiers: LCCN 2020058169 | ISBN 9781620369869
    (hardback) | ISBN 9781620369876 (paperback) | ISBN
    9781620369883 (pdf) | ISBN 9781620369890 (ebook)
Subjects: LCSH: Web-based instruction. | Web-based instruction--
    Evaluation. | College teaching--Methodology. | College teaching--
    Evaluation. | Educational technology. | College teaching--Aids
    and devices.
Classification: LCC LB1044.87 .T73 2021 | DDC 371.33/44678-
    -dc23
LC record available at https://lccn.loc.gov/2020058169

13-digit ISBN: 978-1-62036-986-9 (cloth)
13-digit ISBN: 978-1-62036-987-6 (paperback)
13-digit ISBN: 978-1-62036-988-3 (library networkable e-edition)
13-digit ISBN: 978-1-62036-989-0 (consumer e-edition)

Printed in the United States of America

All first editions printed on acid-free paper
that meets the American National Standards Institute
Z39-48 Standard.

Bulk Purchases

Quantity discounts are available for use in workshops and for staff development.

Call 1-800-232-0223

First Edition, 2021

To our families' enduring patience

CONTENTS

PART THREE: ADOPTION AND INTEGRATION OF LEARNING TECHNOLOGIES ACROSS THE INSTITUTION: CASE STUDIES

Where is digital learning headed?

To answer that question, we can start with recent history. Digital learning had been growing at a steady pace during the first 2 decades of the 21st century. Every year colleges and universities offered more classes online, recorded more lectures, helped more faculty members design digital classes, and flipped more classes. Students, faculty, and support staff used more technologies in their professional lives, from campus-hosted tools to the galaxy of applications and content accessed through the ever-expanding internet. Incrementally, bit by bit, semester by semester, higher education became more digitized.

Then COVID-19 struck the world. Among its myriad side effects and terrible costs, digital learning took off at its fastest pace ever. If we liken digital education's growth from 2000 to 2019 to a calm, steady fire, growing in size ember by ember, the COVID-19 pandemic poured accelerant all over the smoldering flames.

In a matter of weeks, even days, nearly every single campus in the United States shunted their entire educational enterprise online. This literally unprecedented move took place in an emergency, without time or resources for thorough planning. Faculty members redesigned classes in mid-stream. Instructional designers, academic technologists, librarians, and other support staff labored outrageous hours to make this migration happen. Suddenly, higher education was completely online.

Over the months that followed, many academics found their attention split. On the one hand, we had to look forward to summer and fall, to applying the spring's hasty lessons toward a reimagined fall term. On the other hand, we tried to reflect on that extraordinary, sudden, and underappreciated leap online, grappling with what it told us about academia's strengths, weaknesses, and emergent possibilities. In fact, we may be revisiting spring 2020 for many years to come, even as COVID-19 eventually recedes into epidemiological memory.

The great crisis of 2020 temporarily suspended our consideration of the broader challenges and possibilities facing higher education, or threw those topics into harsh new lights. The urgency of events soaked up our attention.

Considerations of demographics, which saw the teenage population plateau or decline in many regions, were outshone by the terrifying demographics of hundreds of thousands killed by the virus in the United States alone. The complex problem of college and university financing, including declining state support to public institutions, ballooning student debt and anxieties thereof, rising discount rates, and an overall sense that the campus business model of the 20th century was not fit for purpose in the 21st—all of this was thrown into overdrive as pandemic caused recession and clobbered academic finances across the board. The dual problem of the adjunctification of the professoriate and the growth of administrative staff became something different as paused searches gave way to early retirements, furloughs, layoffs, and program cuts. The slow drip of decreasing enrollment, starting in 2012, broadened into a current threatening to bear away entire campuses.

American academia struggled with the pandemic while at the same time grappled with an increasingly frayed social fabric. Traditional and social media amplified an ever more intensive partisan divide. A brutal recession threw tens of millions out of work in the worst unemployment crisis since the Great Depression. The sadistic murder of George Floyd sparked a nationwide wave of protest aimed at police reform and racial injustice, driving a reckoning over racism's horrific legacy and lived present. The overarching menace of climate crisis loomed large, eliciting denial opposed by often youthful outrage.

Under such pressures, higher education continued to do its educational work. As disinformation soared, we strove to teach and learn. While distrust and rancor grew, we sought to grow learning communities. In a sense, academia is very much about nurturing the exquisite art of conversations among and between learners and experts, and we stuck to that mission even as the world seemed to prefer screaming acrimony. Every classroom, virtual and otherwise, represented a commitment to that careful, necessary, and increasingly rare purpose.

We certainly possessed the tools to host conversations. Since the 1960s, the internet has served as a connective platform. While some modern digital platforms became intent on emphasizing fury, they also retained discursive functions. Humble blogging and old email lists continue as of this writing. So do podcasts, YouTube videos, Telegram groups, Twitter exchanges, and so on. Some take care to conduct or foster discussions across these sites. My Future Trends Forum, a weekly videoconference conversation about where academia may be headed is one example. Thousands of people have participated since 2016. I find people are hungry for conversation, amidst the shouting.

This is the immediate context for our exploration of digital learning's transformation. This is the situation within which the present volume appears. But as crucial as the events of 2020 are, as necessarily compelling to our attention, we must examine digital learning in the context of the unfolding future.

Pre-2020 trends are still in play and raise strategic questions about how we teach digitally and support that enterprise. The demographic transition, for example, is a deeply structured process, one which seems likely to survive the pandemic (Kearney & Levine, 2020; Vollset et al., 2020). This means that we should expect many populations to produce fewer children, while at the same time including greater numbers of senior citizens. Therefore, the traditional age undergraduate pipeline will narrow, driving up inter-institutional competition and making collaboration more challenging. It also opens up possibilities for academia to focus efforts on teaching more elders. How should we structure online learning for a population less likely to be immersed in the digital world? Should we increase international outreach to enroll a global audience?

Higher education's troubled sustainability is clearly a problem that isn't going away. One established response is to ramp up digital teaching in the (usually false) hope of lowering costs, in reaching out to people accustomed to the online world, in connecting with busy would-be learners who might find in-person education too challenging to undertake, or in some combination of these. Overall, increasing institutional facility in offering online classes will support this strategy. Additionally, I suspect that after COVID-19 recedes we will see greater demand for online learning as some learners come to appreciate the experience for various reasons.

If 2020's mobilization against racism persists, we should expect social justice to inform our digital teaching choices. The well-known ability of data gathering, data analytics, and artificial intelligence to reproduce various forms of inequality and inequity is something we must oppose, from course design to enterprise system selection and implementation. The representation of underrepresented minorities among digital support staff, decision makers, and instructors needs to be redressed, and the problem of unequal digital access suffered by Black and Latinx people has to be taken seriously.

Looking further ahead to how climate change might impact higher education, the digital teaching and learning world should face a variety of choices. First, if more people decide to cut back on carbon-intensive travel, campus IT may have to support an expanded range of services for remote learners. Second, institutional IT may come under scrutiny for its own carbon usage, and should be prepared to adopt low-carbon technologies and practices. Third, college and university operations may change in other ways, from shifting curricula to renovating or even moving campuses, all of which alter the nature of digital support. Fourth, an open question is how will the climate crisis change pedagogy? Digital teaching will play a key role in whatever transformation occurs.

Meeting all of these challenges will require a great deal of creativity from the faculty who teach digitally and the staff who support them. Innovation can mean exploring the emerging technologies explored in this book, including 3d printing, adaptive learning software, learning analytics, and various forms of artificial intelligence. It can mean identifying what works in massively open online classes (MOOCs) and making them well fit for pedagogical purpose. It can also mean using established technologies, including learning management systems (LMSs) and ePortfolios, as well as making familiar pedagogies even more effective, such as simulations. This creative teaching also involves applying the underappreciated findings of cutting-edge learning science and social network analysis. At the same time the innovative process requires supporting the human beings who make it all work, from faculty through educational technologists. All aspects of higher education are in play, from general education to assessment.

If we seize these opportunities ambitiously and energetically, the next decade and beyond may become known for continuous and successful innovation. The chapters that follow will help point the way.

Bryan Alexander
Senior Scholar
Georgetown University
Author of Academia Next: The Futures of Higher Education

References

Kearney, M. S., & Levine, P. B. (2020). Half a million fewer children? The coming COVID baby bust. *Brookings.* https://www.brookings.edu/research/half-a-million-fewer-children-the-coming-covid-baby-bust/

Vollset, S. E., Goren, E., Yuan, C.-W., Cao, J., Smith, A. E., Hsiao, T., Bisignano, C., Azhar, G. S., Castro, E., Chalek, J., Dolgert, A.J., Frank, T., Fukutaki, K., Hay, S. I., Lozano, R., Mokdad, A. H., Nandakumar, V., Pierce, M., Pletcher, M., Robalik, T. (2020). Fertility, mortality, migration, and population scenarios for 195 countries and territories from 2017 to 2100: a forecasting analysis for the Global Burden of Disease Study. *The Lancet,* 396(10258), 1285–1306. https://doi.org/10.1016/S0140-6736(20)30677-2

ACKNOWLEDGMENTS

Ve express our deep gratitude to each of our contributors, all overly committed professionals willing to take on yet another responsibility: developing a chapter for this collection. Collectively our seasoned contributors offer guidance to those who will transition into the digital teaching, learning, and assessment environment by sharing their expertise, experiences, perspectives, and even lessons learned.

We also wish to acknowledge the following individuals and organizations for granting permission to include their work in the following sections:

Introduction:

George Veletsianos for permission to quote from his definition of emerging technologies in "The Defining Characteristics of Emerging Technologies and Emerging Practices in Digital Education," in his edited book, *Emergence and Innovation in Digital Learning: Foundations and Applications* (2016), page 3.

Chapter 1:

Luke Hobson, program manager at Massachusetts Institute of Technology for reviewing and making suggestions for the Taxonomy of Current and Emerging Learning Technologies, Appendix 1A, pages 64–76.

Lauren Anstey and Gavan Watson for permission to include "A Rubric for eLearning Tool Evaluation," Appendix 1B, pages 71–81.

Donald Clark for permission to quote from his March 7, 2019 "Plan B" blog, page 44.

EDUCAUSE for permission to quote from M. Brown (2015, June 3). The LMS of the future: Exploring the next generation digital learning environment. *Transforming Higher Ed Blog. EDUCAUSE Review*, page 28.

EDUCAUSE for permission to quote from T. Mitchell (2019, March 11). Changing demographics and digital transformation. *EDUCAUSE Review, 54*(1), page 58.

Michael Feldman for providing additional information about the Empirical Educator Project (EEP) in a personal email to Peggy Maki on February 2020, page 82.

Will Thalheimer (2020), on behalf of the eLearning Manifesto Organizers, for permission to include the table comparing "typical elearning and SERIOUS eLEARNING" from the Serious eLearning Manifesto, page 52

Bertram Bruce and James Levin for email exchanges Peggy Maki had with them in March 2019, about their pioneering efforts to develop an educational taxonomy at the end of the 20th century, page 51.

Chapter 2:
   Gartner (2020) for permission to include the Gartner hype cycle, Figure 2.1, page 93

Chapter 5:
   Blackboard Inc. for permission to include three screenshots: Figure 5.1, page 148; Figure 5.4, page 163; and Figure 5.5, page 164.

Chapter 10:
   Jeffrey Yan, CEO of Digication, for permission to include the screenshots used for Figure 10.2, page 262, and Figure 10.4, page 264.

INTRODUCTION

Peggy L. Maki

Before the unexpected need for colleges and universities to shift suddenly to teaching online as a result of the COVID-19 pandemic, annual trends in online enrollment had been increasing in comparison with annual declining postsecondary enrollments for traditional face-to-face delivered courses. Specifically, enrollments for spring 2019, reported by the National Student Clearinghouse Research Center (2019), documented that overall traditional postsecondary enrollments decreased for the eighth consecutive year, down 1.7% from the previous spring. Overall enrollments for fall 2019 dropped 1.3% from the previous year; however, as *The Chronicle of Higher Education* reported, there were institutions in the mix that experienced enrollment growth while others experienced declines greater than the average decline (Conley, 2019; Piper, 2019). Doug Lederman (2018), coeditor of *Inside Higher Ed*, concluded that "without online education, college and university enrollments would be declining even more" (para.1). Julia E. Seaman, director and coauthor of the 2018 Babson Survey Research Group's report on online enrollment trends, described growth of distance enrollments as "relentless. . . . They have gone up when the economy was expanding, when the economy was shrinking, when overall enrollments were growing, and now when overall enrollments are shrinking" (Radicioni, 2018, para. 3).

Given this trend in online enrollment, more institutions will deem it necessary to establish an online presence or expand their current offerings of online courses, programs, degrees, certificates, or microcredentials to

- stabilize enrollment, given the current decline in traditional-aged student enrollment and, at some institutions, even a decline in students over 25—of which many elect to work instead of attend college (Bauer-Wolf, 2019);
- offer less expensive nonresidential programs;
- reach underrepresented populations or geographically bound students such as rural or Native American students by making quality broadband access a national priority in those "education deserts" (Meyers, 2018);

- accommodate working students' schedules;
- keep pace with employees' needs to advance themselves in an existing or emerging field—a commitment increasingly assumed by alternative providers as well; or
- in collaboration with other institutions, offer students in a program of study access to a broader range of course options than a home institution can offer, such as the Council of Independent Colleges' (CIC) Consortium for Online Humanities Instruction (launched in 2014). This collaboration among some of CIC's member institutions extends students' upper level humanities course options beyond those offered at their home institution (Griffiths et al., 2015).

Motivated by these or other internal or external catalysts, such as reduction of funding for public institutions, colleges and universities will need to recruit more full- and part-time faculty to transition into the digital environment. The experience of the COVID-19 pandemic that pressed faculty to either offer their face-to face courses remotely or attempt teaching online for the very first time only emphasized the importance of developing a coherent and integrated plan for facilitating learning online and developing a robust infrastructure to support it. In an interview with Doug Lederman (2019), Flower Darby, author of the 2019 book *Small Teaching Online: Everyday Lessons From the Science of Learning*, identified what lies behind faculty reluctance to teach online. Writing from the depth and breadth of her experiences as a senior instructional designer, faculty developer, and online teacher at both a community college and her university, she describes online teaching and learning as "relatively unfamiliar territory" (Lederman, 2019, para. 12) for faculty. Faculty members she supports, "like many others at institutions large and small, feel unprepared to teach online" (Lederman, 2019, para. 11) principally because they do not bring the "depth of experience" (para. 12) that they have built up from their years of teaching in the physical classroom. Just as crucial, many first-time faculty may not know what it is like to be a student in an online class. As a result, their preferred methods of teaching are likely to be influenced by their own experiences as a student in a traditional classroom rather than by research on principles of effective teaching online.

Making matters even more difficult for faculty new to teaching online and professionals on campus who guide and support this transition into the digital environment, such as individuals in educational technology or instructional design, is the fact that the landscape of learning technologies in the 21st century is rapidly evolving.[1] There is now a bewildering number of learning technologies from which to choose. Older learning technologies are being enhanced while technologies with new capabilities are simultaneously emerging. These emerging learning technologies are designed and built based on (a) the learning sciences, a multidisciplinary field dedicated to research on teaching and learning and (b) new applications of algorithms in artificial intelligence (AI) or its subfields, such as machine learning. Given new design principles and algorithm-based software, emerging learning technologies represent an evolution in learning technologies that enables educators to focus on the processes of teaching and learning made visible through the connective role of technology-enabled real-time assessment data. This focus is raising the bar for developing evidence-based, research-informed teachers and reflective, self-regulated learners. In time, as well, institutions that realize the potential of emerging learning technologies will distinguish themselves in their ability to continuously address the specific learning needs of individual students along their educational pathways.

In his edited book, *Emergence and Innovation in Digital Learning: Foundations and Applications*, Veletsianos (2016) offers the following characteristics of *emerging technologies* and *emerging practices* that develop as these technologies are adopted into different contexts and for different purposes. Based on his research on usage of these terms, Veletsianos identifies the following four characteristics:

Emerging technologies and *emerging practices*:

(1) are not defined by newness [they may or may not be new; they can be recent developments in older technologies, for example]
(2) are evolving organisms that exist in a state of "coming into being"
(3) are not yet fully understood or researched
(4) have promising but as yet unfulfilled potential (Veletsianos, 2016, pp. 7–10)

Veletsianos's characteristics describe the emerging learning technologies and practices presented in this book, technologies and practices that are coming into being, particularly over the last decade, facilitating, contributing to, or supporting teaching, learning, and assessment of student learning. They may be altogether new based on their purpose and underlying principles of design or may represent older technologies that now offer new capabilities for faculty and students. Indeed, they are not yet fully understood across all of our colleges and universities at this point in time. They do not have a mature higher education research history similar to that of face-to-face educational practices. Although there is a growing body of research on the use of emerging learning technologies, articles and reports often appear in technology-focused journals that faculty and other educators may not initially access as part of their research. Scholarly publications, such as journals on teaching and learning, often feature research on the integration of emerging learning technologies into courses. Widely read higher education publications such as *The Chronicle of Higher Education, Edsurge, EducationDive, EDUCAUSE Review,* and *Inside Higher Ed* regularly report on developments in emerging learning technologies and ways in which faculty and others across an institution are implementing them and harnessing the affordances these technologies offer. EDUCAUSE is the central higher education repository of research articles, resources, guidelines, studies of faculty or institutional implementation of specific emerging learning technologies, and the annual *Horizon Report.* That report documents technology usage trends; faculty and institutional needs as colleges integrate emerging learning technologies, such as faculty development; and projects the expected time period when widening use of specific emerging learning technologies is likely to occur.

Although, as Veletsianos (2016) states, emerging learning technologies have "promising and yet unfulfilled potential" (p. 10), a major significant innovation in emerging technologies, learning analytics (LA) integrated into LMSs and courseware, is already fulfilling its potential to provide educators real-time evidence of students' learning along the trajectory of a course. LA software mines student performance data and reports each student's performance patterns on assigned tasks, providing unique insights valuable to both instructor and student. LA is now built into most learning management systems (LMSs) to report test, quiz, poll, survey, questionnaire, or rubric scoring results in real time, as well as to report patterns of student behavior related to students' academic work, such as the amount of time a student contributes to an online discussion group. LA is also now increasingly being integrated into etextbook exercises or activities, courseware, other digital options, and even in interactive video presentations, providing continuous evidence of students' learning as it unfolds within the contexts of teaching and learning. Thus, to best prepare individual faculty and campus teams to transition effectively into the 21st-century digital landscape, this book is anchored in the evolving learning technology landscape that extends from current to emerging learning technologies.

Audience and Purpose of this Book

As many colleges and universities realized in their sudden shift to offer courses online during the coronavirus pandemic, transitioning an institution and its faculty into the digital teaching and learning environment benefits from the collaborative contributions of multiple campus constituencies. This book, by offering an overview of the rapidly evolving digital learning landscape and introducing readers to current and emerging learning technologies and how they will transform future practice, is intended for the following campus constituencies:

- Campus leaders and administrators who oversee campus teams charged with identifying learning technologies to meet an agreed-on program- or institution-level educational need and who are responsible for developing policies, practices, and the institutional consensus necessary to build a successful and sustainable commitment to digital teaching, learning, and assessment of student learning
- Campus experts who assist faculty and campus teams identify and effectively integrate learning technologies into courses, across programs, or across the institution; namely, instructional designers; individuals in educational, instructional, and information technology; and assessment and professional development directors
- Early-adopter full- and part-time faculty who are faced with designing their first online or hybrid course and may be unfamiliar with the range of major learning technology options that exist within and outside of an LMS

Harnessing the experiences, guidance, and perspectives of experts on the forefront of the 21st-century digital teaching, learning, and assessment environment, this collection aims to prepare two audiences to transition into that environment. The first critical audience is campus leaders, administrators, and the range of experts on campus who support individual faculty and campus teams as they identify learning technologies to facilitate, contribute to, or support teaching, learning, and assessment of student learning. These experts, who also may be new to or newly hired into their roles, include individuals in information, educational, and instructional technology; instructional design; assessment; and professional development. The second critical audience is full- and part-time faculty designing their first online or hybrid course or serving on a campus team charged with identifying a learning technology that meets a shared program- or institution-level need or goal.

To assist campus leaders or administrators, specialists in technology, instructional designers, directors of professional development, and assessment professionals who may be new in their campus technology roles this book does the following:

- Widens the canvas of major learning technology options you may suggest that faculty or campus teams consider so that they develop a more comprehensive understanding of the technological capabilities available to them.
- Provides a resource to learn more about educational technologies that foster communication and collaboration, critical thinking, creativity, and lifelong learning by way of an online professional development hybrid massive open online course (MOOC) developed through the State University of New York (SUNY) system. This MOOC includes a wiki component, a socially curated discovery search engine that identifies a range of digital tools, websites, mobile apps, tutorials, and resources. The search engine continues to expand new categories of technology options and online resources based on participants' contributions.
- Identifies collaborative processes related to engaging and supporting campus teams in identifying, adopting, leveraging the affordances of, and piloting or implementing an agreed-on program- or institution-level learning technology option or options to address a shared educational need.
- Includes case studies illustrating those processes that address the realities of confronting sticky issues along the way.

For individuals who may be seasoned in their leadership or support roles, chapters may contribute new strategies or processes to existing practices or provide new information about emerging technologies.

To assist full- and part-time faculty transitioning into the digital environment, this book does the following:

- Provides an overview of major current and emerging learning technology types across the evolving digital landscape as a foundation to assist faculty new to teaching online identify technologies with capabilities that effectively facilitate, contribute to, or support teaching, learning, and assessment of student learning. Particular attention is focused on the following emerging learning technologies that have the potential to transform those processes: (a) LA and adaptive-based learning technologies; (b) developments in immersive environments and 3D technology and tools that provide enhanced opportunities for students to assume different learner roles, teach themselves, construct meaning, represent their creativity, or demonstrate their learning in safe practice environments that may also build in feedback; and (c) AI-driven tools and AI assistants that contribute to or have the potential to contribute to teaching, learning, and assessment of learning.

- Deepens understanding of how representative emerging learning technologies are developed based on research on teaching and learning and new applications of algorithms that are at the core of AI.
- Helps faculty explore an ever-changing digital world by introducing them to a hands-on online professional development opportunity consisting of two components: (a) a hybrid MOOC that is also an open educational resource (OER), developed through the SUNY and (b) its affiliated wiki. The hybrid MOOC is designed for faculty, students, and others interested in learning about developments in educational technologies that contribute to collaboration and communication, critical thinking, creativity, and lifelong learning. In addition, through the affiliated socially curated wiki, participants can explore specific technologies, such as digital tools, websites, mobile apps, tutorials, and related resources. This online opportunity represents one of the types of "untethered" professional development alternatives that Pacansky-Brock (2019) proposes should evolve in higher education, stating that "face-to-face events don't foster digital literacy as effectively as learning in an online environment" (para. 9). Thus, she calls for professional development opportunities that are self-paced, collaborative, and flexible to meet the needs of individuals, particularly part-time faculty who usually cannot attend so-called tethered campus-based professional development times. Online professional learning opportunities also expand the range of colleagues with whom an individual can interact.
- Includes case studies, scenarios, and examples of how faculty are using current and emerging learning technologies.

To address our audiences, we invited a range of experts on the forefront of digital teaching, learning, and assessment to contribute to this book. Why? Altogether these voices from the vanguard offer seasoned perspectives, first-hand experiences, realistic guidance grounded in those experiences, resources, and campus scenarios or case studies that are, in themselves, instructive. Our contributors include the following:

- Campus leaders—deans, directors, and faculty who oversee their institutions' digital transition
- Technology innovators and designers who apply research ranging from the multidisciplinary field of the learning sciences to computational sciences, specifically AI and its subsets such as machine learning and natural language processing

- Campus specialists with learning technology expertise in areas such as information technology, educational technology, media, eLearning or distance education, or LMSs and instructional designers who provide professional development and support for faculty as they design online or hybrid courses (three of our contributors are also doctoral candidates researching new applications of learning technologies)
- Directors of assessment and professional development who have an educational background in or conduct research on learning technologies

With the experiences of the challenges faced by institutions and faculty as they shifted overnight into remote teaching or teaching online, driven out of necessity by the COVID-19 pandemic, the contents of this book provide the needed context and perspective to build on or advance institutions' transition into the digital teaching, learning, and assessment environment. At the very least, as Barbara Oakley, professor of engineering at Oakland University and teacher of a popular and free online MOOC, Learning How to Learn, recently stated, online learning "should be part of our educational arsenal—a safeguard against future crises" (Young, 2020, para. 24).

Organization and Sequence of Chapters

Although some readers may want to read all chapters in this book, in order, we have identified specific readers for whom the content may be most directly relevant. Those readers are identified at the end of each chapter summary.

Part One: An Introduction to Current and Emerging 21st-Century Learning Technologies

Part one takes a big-picture approach to the evolving learning technology landscape represented inside and outside an institution's LMS, where first-time faculty will likely design their first course. A chapter on how principles of research on learning and the engine of algorithms work together in the design of emerging learning technologies deepens readers' understanding of how the capabilities of some emerging learning technologies are developed. An online professional development hybrid MOOC and its associated wiki provide an opportunity for faculty; campus leaders; administrators; instructional designers; and experts in technology, professional development, and assessment to explore and even try out learning technologies, some of which are the focus of several campus scenarios. The final chapter in Part One provides overall guidance for the "messy middle" processes of integrating and successfully using a learning technology across the institution after one has been selected.

Chapter 1: "The Evolving Landscape of 21st-Century Learning Technologies" provides readers with an overview of the evolving landscape of learning technology options that reside within and outside of an institution's LMS. In particular, this chapter focuses on capabilities of emerging learning technologies that have the potential to transform the processes of teaching, learning, and assessment of student learning. Evidence-based learning technologies, LA-based and adaptive learning-based platforms, represent the first type of emerging learning technologies that continuously generates technology-enabled real-time assessment data about student learning, developing (a) faculty potential to become adaptive, evidence-based, and research-informed teachers and (b) student potential to become self-regulated learners. A second type is immersive environments with 3D technology that expand opportunities for students to learn first-hand, construct meaning, create, or practice and demonstrate their ability to integrate knowledge, skills, behaviors and habits of mind in a range of safe environments that ready them to deal with challenges and situations they likely will face after graduation. 3D tools enable students to translate their concepts, ideas, and creativity into dimensional representations. A third type of emerging technology is AI-driven tools and AI assistants that mimic human capabilities, such as decision-making, that have the potential to contribute to teaching, learning, and assessment of student learning. *Relevant to all readers.*

Chapter 2: "The Learning Sciences and Educational Technology" provides readers a window into the thinking and planning processes of two individuals who design emerging learning technologies based on research on learning. The contributors introduce readers to major principles that anchor the architecture and design of their learning technologies, illustrated in scenarios. Specifically, they identify three concepts from educational research used to develop effective digital learning experiences: principled assessment design, effective feedback, and metacognition leading to self-regulated learning. They then discuss how these concepts, integrated into learning technologies, can improve learner outcomes. This chapter also prompts readers to learn more about the science of learning and software applications that underlie specific learning technologies they may be considering. *Relevant to all readers.*

Chapter 3: "Empowering Faculty to Design Technology-Enriched Student Learning: A Constructivist and Connectivist Hybrid Massive Open Online Course" is the collaborative work of diverse experts knowledgeable about learning technologies. This chapter begins with a rationale for how and why a hybrid MOOC serves as a unique professional development opportunity for faculty who may feel reluctant to integrate learning technologies into online, hybrid, and even face-to-face delivered courses in substantive ways. Contributors then proceed to describe and illustrate the contents of this online professional development opportunity, also a type of OER, developed through the SUNY system.

The first component, #EmTechMOOC (Exploring Emerging Technologies for Lifelong Learning and Success) serves as a means of learning about, exploring, and experimenting with educational technologies in courses that foster students' communication, collaboration, critical thinking, creativity, and lifelong learning. The second component, #EmTechwiki, is a socially curated technology resource site that helps participants gain more in-depth knowledge about specific types of technologies or online resources based on search engine categories. The site continues to expand based on participants' contributions, such as added tutorials, material about a specific technology, or ratings of a particular product. In some cases individuals can try out a specific technology option before deciding to use it in a course. The chapter ends with several scenarios describing how instructors from a variety of disciplines have used the #EmTechMOOC to identify tools and resources to integrate into their courses. Scenarios include instructors' and students' perceptions of the effectiveness or usefulness of a selected technological option. Additionally, readers will learn that this hybrid MOOC also can assist students with tools, information, and strategies to navigate the digital world. *Relevant to faculty, instructional designers, individuals in educational and instructional technology, and assessment and professional development directors.*

Chapter 4: "A Guide for Successful Integration and Support of Learning Technologies" identifies core guidelines for teams of faculty, administrators, instructional designers, and technology experts to integrate an agreed-on learning technology into a campus culture. It draws on the expertise of the contributors who collectively have many years of experience in piloting innovative academic technology adoption. This chapter provides checklists for the members of an educational technology adoption team to help with their project management plan. It also identifies some potential problems and issues that institutions may encounter and suggestions about how to address them. *Relevant to campus leaders and administrators, faculty, experts in instructional design, and experts in educational and information technology.*

Part Two: Some Representative Examples of Course-Based Use of Emerging Learning Technologies

Part Two consists of four chapters that illustrate either the development or integration of course-based emerging learning technologies that facilitate, contribute to, or support teaching, learning, and assessment of student learning. Two chapters illustrate how data stored in an LMS can be mined to learn about patterns of students' learning behaviors and their performance levels. Two designers of learning technology platforms—one, an automated human-quality feedback platform; the other, a professional immersive environment scenario—illustrate how principles of or research on learning, the importance of real-time feedback, and applications of AI are integrated into the design and capabilities of these platforms.

Chapter 5: "Applying a Learning Analytics Approach to Improve Course Achievement: Using Data Stored in Learning Management Systems" provides an overview and examples of formative, summative, or predictive uses of LA based on student data stored—or that can be stored—in an institution's LMS. This chapter also includes a guide for how to use the LA software bundled in an LMS along the progression of a course. It closes with an engineering case study that identifies, first, how faculty have used predictive LA to identify student risk factors in one component of an engineering course and, second, how they have used formative LA to monitor the short- and long-term severity of those risks if students are unable to address them based on faculty interventions. *Relevant to faculty; administrators; instructional designers; experts in educational technology, instructional design, and instructional technology; and assessment and professional development directors.*

Chapter 6: "Data-Informed Online Discussion Facilitation: Using Data From a Social Network Analysis App to Improve Students' Online Interactions" describes how an in-house developed social networking app applied to data in an LMS visually represents students' levels of engagement and interaction in course discussion forums, leading faculty to develop interventions to improve those levels. With input from her faculty, a learning analytic and LMS specialist describes how the Social Networking Analysis (SNA) app she developed applies measures of student engagement in course-based discussion forums to student data stored in the college's LMS. Results of students' levels and patterns of engagement, heretofore invisible to faculty, are represented visually. Based on the visual representation of data, faculty have been able to develop timely interventions aimed at improving students' contributions to collaborative learning and community building, demonstrated in postintervention results. *Relevant to faculty; administrators; experts in instructional technology, instructional design, educational technology, and information technology; and assessment and professional development directors.*

Chapter 7: "Teaching, Technology, and Building Trust: What I've Learned About How Artificial Intelligence Can Improve Student Writing" is written from the perspective of a designer of a digital platform that provides real-time, human-quality feedback to students as they write their first draft.

The contributor describes the learner-centered motivation behind the design of the platform, the sound pedagogical practices that underlie the design, and the integration of an application from one of the subbranches of AI. The technology is a time-saver for faculty, especially those who teach large courses or say they do not have time to read drafts of student work. It is also a confidence builder for students because it provides a safe digital environment to get critical feedback in a timely manner. Further, as students write more, teachers get accurate baseline data about students' performance patterns. Armed with these data, faculty can direct time toward addressing students' individual underperformance patterns before they write their next draft or prepare a final copy of their paper. *Relevant to administrators; faculty; experts in instructional design, instructional technology, and educational technology; and assessment and professional development directors.*

Chapter 8: "How We May Learn: Cybersecurity Awareness Training as a Model for Future Learning Platforms" describes the ways in which learning technology used for cybersecurity awareness can provide a useful template for technology intended for teaching, learning, and assessment in other domains. Frequently, the most sophisticated learning technology available is found in domains where people are trained to deal with significant risks (aviation, medicine, military, cybersecurity). In this chapter, contributors examine a set of cybersecurity awareness training games called *Agent Surefire.* The contributors describe how *Agent Surefire's* immersive learning environment, capabilities of adaptive learning, and performance data capture are anchored in research on learning and algorithm-based software. They also suggest ways in which cybersecurity awareness training can serve as a model for learning tools that address academic subjects. *Relevant to administrators; faculty; experts in instructional design, instructional technology, and educational technology; and assessment and professional development directors.*

Part Three: Adoption and Integration of Learning Technologies Across the Institution: Case Studies

Part Three consists of three chapters that focus on the challenging processes of integrating learning technologies across institutions, thus requiring broad stakeholder buy-in. The first chapter identifies a framework that guides collaborative processes institutions can use to engage campus stakeholders in identifying an agreed-on assessment technology system that reports student assessment performance levels at the program or institution levels. Two institutional case studies in that chapter illustrate how institutions have used this model to attain agreement about the system they are currently piloting. The second chapter provides a campus leader's firsthand reporting of the processes that led to his campus adopting both ePortfolios and an assessment portal that provides faculty data about students' demonstration of general education outcomes. The third chapter in Part Three illustrates how transitioning from traditional curricula to learning technology–driven curricula has created a continuous and sustainable commitment to assessing medical and dental students' performance. That commitment includes nimble adaptation or refinement of learning technologies and teaching practices based on continuous reporting of students' performance to faculty, students, and even campus decision makers.

Chapter 9: "Enabling a Solution for Assessment and Technology" presents an assessment technology adoption framework (ATAF) that identifies major practices to guide campus stakeholders in collaboratively identifying an assessment technology system that facilitates or manages program- and institution-level assessment processes to meet various external and internal audiences' requirements or needs. Based on two institutions that are using the ATAF, contributors discuss how partnership-relationships based on collaboration, trust, and respect for others' expertise in each of the four quadrants of the framework—assessment, academics, educational technology, and the technology solution—effectively contribute to the process of achieving agreement about adopting a technology. *Relevant to campus leaders and administrators, faculty, experts in information and educational technology, and directors of assessment.*

Chapter 10: "Advancing General Education Assessment Through Faculty and Student Engagement With College-Wide Electronic Portfolios and an Assessment Portfolio" describes the practices and collaborative processes that enabled a community college to promote its student learning outcomes through the adoption of ePortfolios in conjunction with an assessment portal external to its LMS. The chapter contributor, also the leader of this initiative, describes the technological and cultural challenges that emerged in (a) the stages of identifying, adopting, implementing, and sustaining a commitment to an agreed-on assessment portal and (b) the development of agreed-on procedures for students to submit work that demonstrates general education outcomes. Key processes mirror those identified in chapter 4, with particular focus on the importance of: (a) engaging students as well as faculty in piloting a potential technological option to learn about its capabilities as well as the inherent challenges it may present to them and (b) developing rounds of workshops to assist both faculty and students becoming comfortable using it. *Relevant to campus leaders and administrators; individuals in educational and information technology; faculty; and assessment and professional development directors.*

Chapter 11: "Assessment and Technology Use at Graduate Health University" provides an in-depth look at how faculty across three schools within A.T. Still University have transitioned from traditional curricula to technology-based curricula that generate real-time assessment results about dental and medical students' progress toward mastering professional competencies and intraprofessional and interpersonal behaviors. In addition to benefiting students along their educational pathway, continuous assessment results benefit (a) faculty who then adapt pedagogies, simulations, and digital scenarios in real time to improve students' learning along their educational pathway and (b) campus leaders who are focused on designing or redesigning students' learning environments to improve professional outcomes that prepare their graduates to address 21st-century patient needs. *Relevant to campus leaders and administrators; faculty; experts in instructional design and educational technology; and assessment and professional development directors.*

The Human-Technology Relationship

Arguably, the greatest force in shaping the direction of educational practices over the past 25 years has been technology, specifically technologies related to the internet. The invention of the world wide web in 1989 created a communications platform the likes of which we had never seen before. That, in turn, fueled the creation of an ever-increasing number of learning technologies that took advantage of the possibilities for communication and collaboration via the web. Throughout this book, contributors focus on the human-technology relationship, describing the ways technology can support student learning. One overarching theme that emerges from these chapters is how the relationship between educators and students and learning technology has grown more complex than what it was only a few decades before. Of all the challenges, few seem more pressing than the issue of managing the data created when students interact with these technologies.

Both the amount and variety of student data that learning technology can obtain have increased as technology has become more sophisticated. However, as several contributors point out in this book, how individuals or institutions use the data technology generates raises ethical issues. For example, who has access to or owns generated data? How might data be used to form a stereotypical view of certain students and their likelihood of success, rather than used to help individuals realize their potential? Writing about responsible use of learning technologies in higher education, Maren Deepwell (2019), chief executive of the Association of Learning Technology in the United Kingdom, identified a driving question for our institutions:

"How can we empower faculty and students alike in acquiring the data and digital literacy skills required to make informed decisions about using technology intelligently and responsibly and ethically" (para.13)?

Another measure of how complex learning technology has become is the way in which algorithm-based software has come to play a dominant role in the learning technology industry. The design of the algorithms that shapes the technology is crucial. Consequently, when selecting a learning technology, it is important to identify not only the affordances a learning technology offers but also its limitations. For example, what is the relevance of the sampled population used to train a technology's algorithm in relation to the specific student demographics of a course into which that technology will be deployed? As Jamey Heit writes in chapter 7:

> There will always be higher-order tasks that are part of the learning process that cannot be reduced to an algorithm. Effective technology requires a design that acknowledges the limits of what that technology can do. The tradeoff is that humans should return the favor and acknowledge what technology is capable of doing and embrace that capability as a learning resource. (p. 197, this volume).

Whatever problems are posed by this new generation of learning technology, they seem small when compared to the extraordinary opportunities this technology offers in regard to solving challenges that once seemed intractable. The increasing capacity of emerging learning technologies to generate continuous real-time evidence of student learning has the potential to transform teaching and learning into dynamically interrelated activities that keep both faculty and students continuously focused on student learning along the trajectory of a course. Closing traditional time gaps among teaching, learning, and assessment, the continuous process of documenting student learning patterns through LA, in particular, draws immediate attention to the relationship between teaching practices and student learning.

Faculty can learn about the efficacy of their practices from those data, prompting them to adapt their practices or materials to meet the various needs of students. Identifying content and materials that meet individual student needs leads toward the development of evidence-based teaching practices and conversations with individual students that probe the causes of and ways to improve their underperformance patterns. In the words of the late Canadian teacher, Joe Bower, "Assessment is not a spreadsheet; It's a conversation" (Brown-Martin, 2016).

Students also simultaneously learn about their performance levels from those data. In the company of faculty, students become actively involved in investigating the reasons for—or causes of—their difficulties. In addition, real-time data provide students the opportunity to take responsibility for monitoring their progress toward overcoming their difficulties. Teachers become evidence-based course designers who also develop their teaching practices based on research on learning; students become reflective, self-regulated learners with the guidance of their faculty mentor.

The potential to improve students' learning across our student demographics is now within reach based on the capabilities of LA to continuously generate real-time formative assessment data about each student in a class. The central role that LA will play in the evolution of learning technologies in the coming years should not be underestimated. Effective learning technology has always been intended to support student learning outcomes. Along with the promotion of learning, this new generation of learning technologies will likely be designed to place equal importance on the aggregation and display of complex learning data about students from multiple contexts to support real-time assessment and the adoption of timely instructional interventions to promote greater degrees of student success. Let us suggest a new phrase, *teaching and data aggregation* (TADA), to denote the defining quality of next-generation learning technology.

The other phenomenon likely to have an enormous effect on the direction of learning technology is AI. The increasing adoption of AI has been a source of anxiety because it is seen by many people as a tool for making human workers obsolete. However, when discussing the future of AI in education, Holmes et al. (2019) do not see a future in which it replaces teachers. They do see "a future in which the role of the teacher continues to evolve and is eventually transformed; one where their time is used more effectively and efficiently" (p. 159). For example, AI, rather than replacing human instructors, has the potential to provide faculty members with their own teaching assistant.

The future of technology in education is much like its past. What will matter most is not the tools, but how humans use them. Before we use new tools, it is always best that we think about them carefully and then share our thoughts. This book aspires to contribute to that very important conversation.

Note

1. Throughout this collection, contributors use the terms *learning technologies* and *educational technologies* interchangeably to refer to those current and emerging technologies that facilitate, contribute to, or support the processes of teaching, learning, and assessment of student learning or provide new

sources of data about teaching and learning that have been heretofore invisible or inaccessible to faculty and even students. Some readers may be more familiar with the term *educational technologies,* instead of *learning technologies*; however, often that term serves as an umbrella for the broader range of technologies institutions use to meet their educational needs. That range is outside the scope of this book. For purposes of clarity, then, we use the two terms interchangeably as stated.

References

Bauer-Wolf, J. B. (2019, December 17). Adult learner enrollment keeps sliding, new data shows. *EducationDive.* https://www.educationdive.com/news/adult-learner-enrollment-continues-to-contract/569285/

Brown-Martin, G. (2016, December 19). Assessment is not a spreadsheet: It's a conversation. *Medium.* https://medium.com/learning-re-imagined/assessment-is-not-a-spreadsheetits-a-conversation-3d743c754809

Conley, B. (2019, September 6). The great enrollment crash. *The Chronicle of Higher Education.* https://www.chronicle.com/interactives/20190906-Conley

Darby, F. with Lang, J. M. (2019). *Small teaching online: Applying learning science to online classes.* Jossey-Bass.

Deepwell, M. (2019, October 14). Learning technology as a professional practice: Developing a critical perspective. *EDUCAUSE Review.* https://er.educause.edu/articles/2019/10/learning-technology-as-a-professional-practice-developing-a-critical-perspective

Griffiths, R., Brown, J., & Mulhern, C. (2015, October 10). *CIC Consortium for online humanities instruction: Evaluation report for first course iteration.* Ithaka S&R. http://www.cic.edu/p/Online-Humanities/Documents/Online-Humanities-Evaluation-October-2015.pdf

Holmes, W., Bialik, M., & Fadel, C. 2019. *Artificial intelligence in education: Promises and implications for teaching and learning.* The Center for Curriculum Redesign.

Lederman, D. (2018, November 7). Online education ascends. *Insider Higher Education.* https://www.insidehighered.com/digital-learning/article/2018/11/07/new-data-online enrollments-grow-and-share-overall-enrollment

Lederman, D. (2019, June 26). Small teaching online. *Inside Higher Education.* https://www.insidehighered.com/digital-learning/article/2019/06/26/bringing-small-teaching-online-classroom

Meyers, B. (2018, July 17). Who lives in education deserts? More people than you think. *The Chronicle of Higher Education.* https://www.chronicle.com/interactives/education-deserts

National Student Clearinghouse Research Center. (2019, May 30). Current spring enrollments—2019. https://nscresearchcenter.org/?s=Spring+2019+enrollments

Pacansky-Brock, M. (2019, January). Untangling academic transformation through untethered equitable professional development. *EDUCAUSE Review.* https://er.educause.edu/blogs/2019/1/untangling-academic-transformation-through-untethered-equitable-professional-development

Piper, J. (2019, December 19). Enrollment dropped 1.3% this fall from a year ago. But not every state tells the same story. *The Chronicle of Higher Education.* https://www.chronicle.com/article/Enrollment-Dropped-13-This/247719

Radicioni, B. (2018, January 11). New study: Distance education up, overall enrollments down. Babson College. *Centennial.* https://www.babson.edu/about/news-events/babson-announcements/babson-survey-research-group-tracking-distance-education-report/

Veletsianos, G. (2016). The defining characteristics of emerging technologies and emerging practices in digital education. In G. Veletsianos (Ed.), *Emergence and innovation in digital learning: Foundations and applications* (pp. 3–16). AU Press. https://doi.org/10.15215/aupress/9781771991490.01

Young, J. R. (2020, March 27). *How a pandemic could change higher education.* *EdSurge.* https://www.edsurge.com/news/2020-03-27-how-a-pandemic-could-change-higher-education

PART ONE

AN INTRODUCTION TO CURRENT AND EMERGING 21ST-CENTURY LEARNING TECHNOLOGIES

THE EVOLVING LANDSCAPE OF 21ST-CENTURY LEARNING TECHNOLOGIES

Peggy L. Maki

> *Different kinds of experience lead to different meanings, which, in turn, make different forms of understanding possible. (Eisner, 1993, p. 6)*

Twenty-first-century learning technologies (technologies that facilitate, contribute to, or support the processes of teaching, learning, and assessing student learning) are rapidly expanding. Individual faculty transitioning into the digital environment to design their first online or hybrid course or identify a digital component for an in-person course face the daunting task of selecting learning technologies from a dizzying array of options. Campus teams transitioning into the digital environment to identify the "best" platform or device to address a program- or institution-level educational need or goal face the same dilemma. Further complicating that selection process is the rapid pace at which 21st-century emerging learning technologies are being developed. Capabilities of emerging learning technologies are informed by and designed based on two major components. The first component is research on teaching and learning conducted in multiple disciplines under the umbrella of the learning sciences, represented, for example, in the fields of design studies, psychology, sociology, cognitive science, mathematics, computer science, and statistics. The second component is new applications of algorithmic models, techniques, and approaches developed in subfields or sub-branches of artificial intelligence (AI), such as using statistical tools that learn from data in machine learning. Algorithms are at the core of AI-driven tools (Holmes et al., 2019).

Given the fast-paced expansion of learning technology options in this century, this chapter provides an overview of the major current and emerging learning technologies. It serves as a framework within which the following campus constituencies can initially identify and then narrow down learning technologies based on how they facilitate, contribute to, or support the processes of teaching, learning, and assessment of student learning at the course, program, or institution level:

- Campus leaders and administrators who (a) help campus teams identify learning technologies to meet a shared program- or institution-level educational need as well as (b) develop policies, practices, and the institutional consensus necessary to build a successful and sustainable commitment to integrate those technologies into institutional culture
- Campus experts (e.g., instructional designers; individuals in educational, instructional, and information technology; and assessment and professional development directors) who (a) help faculty and campus teams identify learning technologies that enable students to equitably attain desired learning outcomes or enable the institution to achieve a specific need (e.g., documentation of student academic progress) as well as (b) guide faculty into the 21st-century digital environment
- Early-adopter full- and part-time faculty who will benefit from a broad view of major learning technologies and their capacities as they design their first online or hybrid course. Specifically, that broad view enables faculty to select technologies that address pedagogy and instructional strategies, provide opportunities for students to actively engage in their learning, offer experiences and activities that support the diverse learning needs of students, and generate evidence of students' equitable progress toward achieving desired learning outcomes

To contribute to these constituencies, this chapter consists of four parts. First, "Contexts for Selecting Learning Technologies at Individual and Campus Team Levels" provides an overview of how the context within which individual faculty or faculty collaborators design online or hybrid courses—from learning management systems (LMSs) to alternative digital learning options—shapes their process of selecting learning technologies. It also provides an overview of the wider set of representative contextual or cultural issues that campus leaders, administrators, technology experts, instructional designers, and assessment and professional development experts encounter as they assist campus teams in identifying a learning technology to achieve an agreed-on program- or institution-level educational need.

Second, "The Evolving Learning Technology Landscape" provides an overview of major types and contributions of current learning technologies to teaching, learning, and assessment of student learning followed by a more in-depth discussion of major types and potential transformative contributions of emerging learning technologies. These emerging learning technologies include (a) evidence-based learning analytics (LA)-based technologies that have the capability to mine students' learning and performance behavior patterns on tasks and report those patterns in real time and adaptive learning-based technologies that continuously adjust instruction and support to meet individual student learning needs and report students' performance levels in real time; (b) immersive learning environments and 3D technology and tools that provide students firsthand learning experiences to actively engage in learning, demonstrate their learning in interactive situations, or represent their creativity; and (c) AI-driven tools and AI assistants with the potential capabilities of customizing support for teachers and students.

Third, "A Taxonomy of Major Types of Current and Emerging Learning Technologies" describes the continuum of major current and emerging learning technology types in order to illustrate evolving capabilities. As a reference for campus leaders, administrators, faculty, and others who support and guide faculty and campus teams, the taxonomy contributes to initial discussions focused on identifying learning technologies that facilitate, contribute to, or support teaching, learning, and assessment of student learning.

Fourth, "The Potential of Emerging Learning Technologies: Major Projects, Initiatives, and Digital Growth in Publishing Companies" identifies some major developments across the higher education landscape focused on advancing the use of emerging learning technologies.

Part One: Contexts for Selecting Learning Technologies at Individual and Campus Team Levels

Contextual factors play a role in the process of selecting learning technologies. Specifically, the environment within which individual faculty choose to design online or hybrid courses shapes the process of selecting learning technologies. Campus teams face broader contextual factors, such as cultural resistance to technology in the process of selecting a digital platform or other options that meet a shared program- or institution-level educational need.

Course-Level Context

The most common context within which faculty design an online or hybrid course or integrate a digital option into a face-to-face course, such as an online discussion board, is an institution's LMS.

An LMS

For the majority of faculty across American higher education, an institution's LMS is the platform of bundled software that serves as the hub for developing content for, delivering, and managing (a) online courses, programs, or online components of a face-to-face delivered course; (b) resources, materials, and interactive opportunities that support students' equitable progress toward achieving expected learning outcomes; and (c) formative assessments along the trajectory of students' learning, now typically reported on faculty and student dashboards. According to Brown et al. (2015), by 2015 nearly 99% of our colleges and universities had an LMS. Someone newly entering the digital teaching, learning, and assessment environment should take an overview of the LMS's current core software options—often by reviewing an index of tools provided in the LMS. Keep in mind that LMS vendors periodically update their systems and are integrating more of the transformative developments in technologies.

Typically, an integrated software package bundled into an LMS includes many types of current learning technologies and some emerging technologies, as identified in Box 1.1. Altogether this integrated software package makes it possible to accomplish a range of tasks.

BOX 1.1.
Typical LMS Integrated Software

- Author your online course or an online portion of a hybrid course; host third-party digital platforms or courseware (some of which can be customized); or integrate a digital component into a face-to-face delivered course, such as an online discussion forum. Bundled courseware outlines or rubrics guide the design of your content and course, requiring alignment of the following components with your course overview and student learning outcomes: individual course modules, methods of assessment, instructional and support materials, means to engage students in their learning and with peers, and required technology students need in the course.

  Some institutions or individual faculty prefer to use national standards for designing online courses such as The Virtual Learning Leadership Alliance and Quality Matters' National Standards for Quality Online Learning, recently revised for Quality Online Teaching, Quality Online Programs, and Quality Online Courses. The Open SUNY Course Quality Review Rubric (OSCQR) was recently developed to

(Continues)

BOX 1.1. (*Continued*)

"assist instructional designers and online faculty improve the quality and accessibility of online courses" (Muller et al., 2019, p. 5). Most important, this rubric draws from several frameworks: Quality Matters; principles of effective teaching practice, such as for adult students; and research on learning (Muller et al., 2019).

- Adapt course materials used in face-to-face delivered courses or materials you are currently developing into online formats and/or integrate third-party platforms, applications, or add-ons into your course design, given developments in interoperability standards that developers of software usually specify in their products' description.
- Generate a gradebook, assignments, tests, and quizzes.
- Use faculty and student dashboards to assess and report on individual student performance levels on tests, quizzes, and results of applying rubrics generated by built-in LA software (capable of mining and reporting students' performance patterns), often referred to as *analytics* in LMSs.
- Provide real-time or near real-time feedback to students based on their performance levels through preprogrammed feedback generated from automatically graded multiple choice or fill-in-the-blank test or quiz results, email, interactive video, audio, or digital insertion of comments into students' online submissions. Fiock and Garcia's (2019) advice guide is an impressive resource for identifying online means and tools to give students feedback. Their article focuses on the importance of using methods that are appropriate for specific contexts.
- Run reports, also generated by integrated LA software, about student behaviors (e.g., log-in times or amount of time spent using online resource materials) at the individual and group levels or about students' overall performance on specific questions on a test or quiz, including a question's level of difficulty. (For a more detailed discussion of the data LA software can mine, see chapter 5.)
- Recognize students' academic accomplishments by way of awarding badges.
- Detect plagiarism or proctor exams. Virtual proctoring is usually arranged with a third-party provider such as ProctorU (www.proctoru .com).

(*Continues*)

BOX 1.1. (*Continued*)

- Provide students 24/7 access to course materials and resources, increasingly using mobile devices.
- Establish communication channels (a) with your students for individual as well as group communication such as through videoconferencing and (b) among students for social interaction and knowledge building, such as through discussion forums, chat rooms, wikis, or hangouts.
- Provide collaborative means for students to work together to promote knowledge building or collective contribution to solving a problem or creating a product.
- Connect students either to in-person or online platforms, tools, or virtual assistants for the following:
  - Academic support services, such as tutoring, technology assistance, library and information resources
  - Student support services, migrating toward being offered in online platforms that integrate interactive chatboxes or virtual assistants, such as in the Upswing platform (Upswing.io)
- Provide access to all of previous items to students with disabilities by way of assistive technology tools integrated into an LMS (see also the assistive category in Appendix 1A). Awareness of the learning needs of all students is increasing focus on using principles of universal design for learning (UDL) in the design of online courses, preparation of course materials and resources, assurance of full participation in course activities, and provision of options for assessing students' learning (Tobin, 2019).

Alternatives to an LMS

Designing online or hybrid courses within an LMS environment is a safe haven for full- and part-time faculty who are transitioning into the digital learning environment. William Beasley (2012), a professor of instructional design who focuses on online pedagogy and online course design, describes LMSs as "powerful organizational tools" (para. 3). However, the desire for greater customization in course and content design, flexibility in teaching methods across disciplines, and open access to tools and options outside of those provided in an LMS has led and is leading innovators to design digital learning environments as alternatives to current LMSs.

For example, some faculty have developed their own course toolbox outside the LMS. These toolboxes consist of specific digital options that support their pedagogical preferences and disciplinary needs, such as web 2.0 tools and apps (e.g., wikis, blogs, social networking sites), media options available in the cloud, and third-party or institutionally developed applications. Faculty may also desire the flexibility of adding digital tools to an online or hybrid course as they are actually teaching the course, especially if they identify newly released software that they want students to learn how to use immediately or they realize a pressing need to integrate a more effective digital tool than was originally planned to assist students in mastering a difficult concept. Other faculty have chosen to design their courses from scratch, using the capabilities of a specific digital learning platform, such as one that adapts content to meet the needs of individual learners. They then integrate or add additional apps that best serve disciplinary needs. For example, pages 41 to 42 describe the collaborative efforts of faculty at Arizona State University (ASU) to design an astrobiology course built on an adaptive learning platform. In "7 Things You Should Know about LMS Alternatives," the EDUCAUSE Learning Initiative (2010) explained that "underlying this approach [to designing an online course outside of a LMS] is the belief that students should become more familiar with today's technology tools because these skills will be useful in the workplace" (para. 1). Typical alternative environments for hosting self-designed courses include an internally built institutional system or a mash-up of web applications assembled by a faculty member and hosted from a blog platform or a social networking site (EDUCAUSE Learning Initiative, 2010).

Critics of LMSs have long lamented the limitations imposed on faculty as they design online or hybrid courses within an LMS environment. Specifically, they argue, faculty are forced to design courses based on digital tools and options available in a given LMS, rather than granted the autonomy to customize courses based on disciplinary practices and personal pedagogical styles. Beasley (2012) referred to LMSs as *walled gardens* that "provide substantial control over the environment in which learning activities take place" (para. 1). In essence he argued that the LMS should open itself to other means of social engagement or learning experiences outside of those typically bundled into the system, such as opportunities for students to witness an external conversation on a relevant topic (Beasley, 2012). In 2014, the Bill & Melinda Gates Foundation provided EDUCAUSE with a grant as a result of the ongoing criticisms about LMSs. EDUCAUSE launched the Next Generation Digital Learning Environment (NGDLE) initiative to describe the characteristics of a digital learning environment that would (a) identify what faculty specifically need to design learner-centered courses across different disciplinary practices and personal pedagogical styles and

(b) tailor course materials, resources, and learning opportunities via continuous access to environments outside of an LMS and broadly integrate them into course design. In 2015, Malcolm Brown, director of EDUCAUSE'S Learning Initiative, identified the following LMS characteristics, many of which are now possible given national attention to principles of Universal Design for Learning (UDL) and the affordances of emerging learning technologies:

1. Interoperability. The linchpin of the NGDLE, this is the capacity to easily integrate tools, exchange content, and collect learning data. Interoperability enables everything else.
2. Personalization. This is the customization of the environment to support needs at the individual, discipline, and institutional levels.
3. Analytics, advising, and learning assessment. This is the analysis of all forms of learning data, resulting in actionable information.
4. Collaboration. It is vital to support collaboration at a variety of levels, and to make it easy to move between public and private digital spaces.
5. Accessibility and universal design. All participants must be able to access content and have the means to produce accessible content. This must inform the design of all NGDLE components. (para. 8)

Duke University's Kit system is an institutional example of an NGDLE built outside an LMS that addresses disciplinary, pedagogical, and student needs. Now an open source project, the Kit system is designed based on a user interface that stores cards (kits) for each course to which instructors add apps (Tingen, 2019).

Program- and Institution-Level Context

Campus teams focused on identifying a learning technology that meets an agreed-on program- or institution-level educational need or goal may face broad, often entrenched cultural issues in that process. This is especially true if the selection process marks the first time faculty at large—many of whom may have already voiced resistance to technology—will transition into the digital environment. Campus leaders, experts in educational and information technology, and instructional designers need to be tuned in to these kinds of resistance, often emerging from anxiety related to fear of the unknown, fear of loss of autonomy, a long-held belief that teaching with technology is not as effective as face-to-face delivery of courses, or that technology itself will "take over" higher education. Those leading the charge to select a shared learning technology need to help those new to the digital environment understand the affordances of learning technologies under consideration. For example, consider addressing the following common questions and concerns faculty often have:

- How do digital courseware options help faculty save time on tasks such as marking quizzes or tests and identifying patterns of underperformance that need to be addressed?
- How does a specific platform collect and analyze heretofore invisible or inaccessible data about student learning? How can faculty use those data to continuously improve currently enrolled students' performance levels?
- How does a specific platform collect, analyze, and widely disseminate data about students' performance levels across a program so that faculty continue to address patterns of underperformance along students' pathways?
- How do learning technologies benefit faculty as well as students and campus decision makers? (See chapter 11 for more information about the mutual benefits of learning technologies to students, faculty, and decision makers.)
- How will students and faculty learn to access and successfully use features of a technology?
- How well is the institution prepared to support and sustain a commitment to an option?

The range of these kinds of issues—from technical to philosophical, but absolutely important to consider—is further discussed in chapter 4. Specific processes involved in selecting institutional assessment systems that store, aggregate, and disaggregate assessment results and report them for internal or external audiences (i.e., within the LMS or outside the LMS) are described in chapters 9 and 10 and illustrate that range of wider issues several institutions have had to address.

Part Two: The Evolving Learning Technology Landscape

Pivoting the evolution of learning technologies, particularly during the last 10 years, has been the coupling of research on teaching and learning with AI applications in the design of learning technologies. Beginning with an overview of current learning technologies, this part describes how the new capacities of emerging learning technologies have the potential to deepen student and faculty engagement in the processes of teaching, learning, and assessing student learning as dynamic and interrelated processes in real- or near real-time.

Current Learning Technologies

Current learning technologies have continued to address the importance of establishing faculty and student presence online, evident in the communicative and collaborative technologies typically available within an LMS. Technologies have also continued to develop options for (a) teaching online (beyond the use of PowerPoint); (b) learning online, recognizing the diverse needs of our learners; and (3) assessing student learning online beyond traditional approaches. Importantly, faculty have also developed a range of ways to use current technologies to engage students in their learning, as discussed next.

Communicative

A deeply rooted faculty criticism of online teaching and learning is that the sense of presence and interpersonal dynamics achieved in face-to-face delivery contexts cannot be effectively achieved in an online mode. Although the modes of delivery do differ, continuous advances in learning technology capabilities, together with the ways faculty successfully use those capabilities, have contributed to deepening faculty and student presence. It is now possible for faculty to engage actively with students, students to engage actively with other students, and students to engage actively with other students or professionals across the globe to learn, collaborate, and even build knowledge in virtual learning communities.

Communication between faculty and students and communication between and among students is possible, for example, by way of

- discussion forums, chat rooms, or hangouts that promote student-to-student engagement and may also involve faculty participation;
- tools such as blogs, wikis, discussion forums, chat room forums, and hangouts;
- messaging systems that post student comments or views or post faculty course updates or announcements, such as reminders of assignment due dates;
- video presentations that have built-in student comment or response boxes or a "hand up" symbol, which signals a student's need to ask a question; and
- online poll or survey tools, such as Poll Everywhere (polleverywhere .com). Faculty can effectively use this option to determine students' prior knowledge of, experience with, or anxiety about the topic or particular unit of the course or levels of misunderstanding or confusion during or after a lesson.

Collaborative

Collaboration between faculty and students or among students is possible, for example, by way of the following options:

- Google Docs: students invite peers or interested others to edit a presentation or document
- Video web conferencing: faculty or other students deliver feedback to students about their work (Fiock & Garcia, 2019)
- Collaborative learning technologies: students engage in online discussion and group work using tools that promote collaborative learning and interactions, such as group brainstorming with platforms like Adobe Connect (www.adobe.com/products/adobeconnect.html), Blackboard Collaborate (www.blackboard.com/teaching-learning/collaboration-webconferencing/blackboard-collaborate), or Kaptivo (https://kaptivo.com/kaptivo-overview/); Mallon and Bernsten (2015) list a host of other digital options that support collaborative learning processes.
- Wikis: sites where students may choose to embed their work and request others to build on it
- Virtual worlds: a medium of faculty-student communication that has evolved over the past decades, particularly useful for virtual online labs for STEM

Faculty have also developed productive ways to integrate communicative and collaborative technologies in their online courses. For example, contributors to *High-Impact Practices in Online Education: Research and Best Practices* (Linder & Hayes, 2018) describe in impressive detail how they successfully implement and adjust high-impact practices for students studying online, chiseling away at assumptions that it is not possible to establish levels of student engagement comparable to those achieved in traditional classroom environments. Based on George Kuh's (2008) *High-Impact Educational Practices: What Are They? Who Has Access to Them? and Why They Matter*, contributors provide concrete strategies for first-year seminars, common intellectual experiences, learning communities, writing-intensive classes, collaborative assignments and projects, undergraduate research in the humanities and in the sciences, diversity and global learning, eservice-learning, internships, capstone courses, and library and information resources. The final chapter in Linder and Hayes's (2018) book identifies a variety of ways to embed librarians into an online course requiring research, based on the work of Edwards and Black (2012): chats, tutorials and webinars, announcements, blogs, and discussion boards where librarians can answer students' research questions.

Palloff and Pratt (2007) dedicate an entire book to describing strategies for creating online learning communities that engage students socially and with faculty to build and sustain "faculty and student presence and sense of community" (p. 32). Building on Gay's (2010) *Culturally Responsive Teaching: Theory, Research and Practice*, Woodley et al. (2017) share online strategies they use to acknowledge and draw on the range of contributions, perspectives, and experiences that students from different cultures bring to online classes. These practices, of course, are relevant to any class and successfully draw on LMS communication tools such as discussion boards and online posts to engage students continuously in debating issues, solving problems, or responding to individual students after each one facilitates a self-designed unit to teach to peers or lead an online discussion group. Being responsive to each student's needs and contributions to a course, often thought to be possible only in the face-to-face delivery mode, can indeed be actualized in online environments. This level of responsiveness is essential in a commitment to students' equitable progress toward and achievement of high-quality learning outcomes.

Open Educational Resources
Options for online teaching, learning, and assessment have also expanded in courseware, applications, and platforms now available across disciplines from third-party developers, as well as through open educational resources (OERs). OERs are repositories of ever-expanding resources for blended, online, and online components of face-to-face delivered courses. Examples include digital teaching, learning, and assessment materials; tutorials; online textbooks; instructional materials, such as online simulations; and faculty-developed open access online courses that are usually free to adopt or adapt based on Creative Commons licensing. OERCommons (n.d.) is a central OER site that uses search engines and filters to help refine an individual's search. For example, a search might be based on a subject, such as algebra; the level of the algebra course; and the conditions surrounding use of the source. Increasingly, OERs reflect the transformative capacities of emerging learning technologies discussed in the rest of this chapter; they continuously engage students in their learning and simultaneously provide faculty evidence of students' learning in real time. In contrast, consider PowerPoint. It is one of the most common current online teaching practices, representative of the first-generation of learning technologies. Until recently, it has not provided students with

opportunities to actively engage with content presented. Rather, it is a linear model of transmitting course content (see also "Narrative" technologies in Appendix 1A).

Seaman and Seaman's 2017–2018 survey of 4,000 faculty on teaching materials revealed that "Faculty awareness of OER has increased every year, with 46 percent of faculty now aware of OERs, up from 34 percent three years ago" (Seaman & Seaman, 2018, p. 2). High costs of textbooks, faculty practices of revising and remixing courses, and desires to access open content are some major reasons faculty cited for their use of OERs. Growing awareness, integration, and adaptation of OERs are contributing to faculty and other campus professionals' commitment to use a range of teaching, learning, and assessment materials to target the diverse academic needs of students across the demographic spread in a course. Chapter 3 describes an OER, a two-part hybrid MOOC, designed to empower faculty and others new to the digital teaching environment to effectively design technology-enriched courses that harness the potential of current and emerging technologies to develop students' communication, collaboration, critical thinking, creative thinking, and lifelong learning outcomes. Case studies illustrate how faculty have successfully located and integrated learning technologies in the processes of teaching and learning. A wiki component of the hybrid MOOC serves as a resource for locating specific types of current and emerging technologies.

Emerging Learning Technologies

Particularly from 2010 to 2020, new types of learning technologies or innovations in existing learning technologies have emerged in higher education. The capabilities of these technologies are based on new applications of AI-based tools, such as those in machine learning that aim "to support learning and to help understand learning" (Holmes et al. 2019, p. 83). Marc Benioff (2016), chief executive of Salesforce, a cloud computing company, referred to AI-based tools as "the defining technology of the 21st century" (para. 3). Fabian Westerheide (2019), an international expert on AI, defined *AI-based tools* as "the most important technology in the 21st century" (para. 2). AI is the technology that drives many of the conveniences individuals use on a daily basis such as Google Home, Alexa, or Cortana. Drawing on new applications of AI-based tools to realize research on teaching and learning, what are these new types of the emerging learning technologies in higher education? What distinguishes them from current learning technologies? They fall into the following three overarching categories:

1. Evidence-based learning technologies: LA-based technologies that have the capability to mine students' performance data to identify and report their performance patterns on tasks in real-time or near real-time and adaptive learning-based technologies that adjust course or module content based on continuous learner-generated performance data during use
2. Immersive learning environments and 3D technologies and tools: Technologies that draw on AI machine learning, image recognition, and natural language processing (Holmes et al., 2019), providing students new ways to experience and apply their learning
3. AI-driven tools and AI assistants: Technologies that have some human capacities (e.g., decision-making) and have the potential to support teachers and learners; still in early stages of experimentation

Evidence-Based Learning Technologies

Evidence-based learning technologies are structured with design principles grounded in research in the learning sciences and new applications of algorithmic models, techniques, and approaches developed in subfields of AI. The fact that evidence-based learning technologies generate evidence (as their name suggests) distinguishes them from current technologies. Specifically, LA- and adaptive learning-based technologies generate evidence of students' performance patterns to capture and document the dynamic nature of students' learning. Capturing these patterns represents the most recent definition of *learning* developed by the multidisciplinary contributors to *How People Learn II: Learners, Contexts, and Cultures*: "Learning is a dynamic, ongoing process that is simultaneously biological and cultural" (National Academies of Sciences, Engineering, and Mathematics, 2018, p. 9). Describing the systems within which individuals learn, the contributors further write: "Learners function within complex developmental, cognitive, physical, social, and cultural systems" (p. 2). Evidence-based technologies now position faculty and students on the frontline of each student's learning. They provide continuous evidence—technology-enabled real-time assessment—of each student's patterns of performance and underperformance while learning and applying that new knowledge along the trajectory of a course—new experiences for both faculty and students.

Several chapters in this book written are by designers of these evidence-based technologies and provide readers lenses through which to understand how research on learning and the use of algorithmic models, techniques, or approaches intersect in the design of these technologies. In chapter 2, authors DiCerbo and Belenky provide examples of how they think through their product designs, defining their driving purpose in each case as to not only use algorithms but also "to instantiate what we know from learning sciences research into the design of educational technology, as well as use technology to find new ways to promote good learning practice" (p. 85). Research on learning documents the importance of providing students with targeted and timely feedback (e.g, National Academies of Sciences, Engineering, and Medicine, 2018; Woolf, 2020). Research on the efficacy of timely and targeted student feedback is the driver behind Heit's Ecree platform described in chapter 7. Ecree was designed using an AI rules-based approach that provides students with automated human-quality feedback on their writing in real time. In chapter 8 Shea and Aytun describe the science of learning that underlies the design of an immersive environment professional scenario, the adaptive capabilities that position students to apply their learning, and the data-capturing technology that enables a particular platform to mine and report patterns of student performance and underperformance. Promoting "good learning practice," as DiCerbo and Belenky state in chapter 2, is the goal of this scenario, and AI tools are effective ways to promote good learning practice.

Learning Analytics.   Surveying the educational technology landscape in higher education over the last decade, Michael Feldstein (2019) offered his perspective in an opinion piece in *EdSurge*. He is an edtech blogger, consultant, and chief accountability officer at e-Literate. e-Literate (n.d.) was established in 2015 and is now an organization "dedicated to helping higher education and the education companies that serve them continuously improve in their efforts to enable more students to succeed in a 21st-Century world" (para. 1). Feldstein sees the last several years as ones during which there has been a shift from "a focus on adding new features" to technology products to "a focus on adding data-analytics tools" (para. 7).

In general, analytics is a scientific process that uses statistics, modeling, computer programming, and machine learning to mine data sets to discover and communicate meaningful patterns across those data. Based on new insights revealed by the resulting patterns, decision makers act to change unsuccessful behaviors, practices, procedures, or patterns. Depending on the type of data or information to be mined, there are different analytics approaches. A relative newcomer to the higher education learning technology landscape is LA. *LA* was first defined in 2011 by George Siemens (2011), the founding president of the Society for Learning Analytics Research (SoLAR), as "the measurement, collection, analysis and reporting of data about learners and their contexts, for purposes of understanding and optimizing learning and the environments in which it occurs" (para. 6). Note that this definition focuses on the educational purpose of these efforts: "optimizing learning and the environments in which it occurs" (para. 6). That same year Johnson et al. (2011) described the promise of LA: "to improve understandings of teaching and learning, and to tailor education to individual students more effectively" (p. 28). Their definition appeared in *EDUCAUSE's The 2011 Horizon Report*, a publication that identifies emerging technologies. In 2013, Clow, a senior lecturer at the Open University, declared LA to be the technology in higher education that "offers new routes for teachers to understand their students, and hence to make effective use of their limited resources" (p. 684).

The following year, Siemens and Baker (2012) also identified another kind of analytics-based learning technology that prompts faculty to take evidence-based actions based on student behaviors related to their learning: educational data mining (EDM). EDM software programs or applications comb through students' actions, behaviors, or decisions in a particular environment to document and represent degrees of students' engagement or performance in their coursework. An institution's LMS is one kind of environment that can be mined for student behaviors that may be indicators of difficulties students are having in a course. Students' keyboard strokes can reveal how frequently or even if a student reads resource materials; how long a student spends reading that resource; how often and with whom a student engages in an online discussion board; or when a student logs in or drops out of a course-based online activity. These kinds of data are often stored in an event log in an LMS. Low usage of course resources or lack of engagement in a discussion thread are sample indicators that might flag students who may be academically at risk or are underperforming in a specific context and thus may require interventions. Determining if interventions are necessary, however, is based on human judgment and discussion with an underperforming student; overreliance on data without human judgment can lead to incorrect conclusions.

Institutions are also using predictive analytics, another analytics-based learning technology, to mine large historical data sets related to previous students' behaviors, decisions, actions, or levels of engagement in their studies to identify historical patterns that identified students at risk. Those patterns of student behavior can be used to predict which currently enrolled students are academically at-risk within days or weeks of their first college course. As a real world example, Purdue University has received national attention for its home-grown course signals predictive model. The model mines student data from more than 20 student data points to identify students at risk within the first 2 weeks of taking their first course. Students receive a red, yellow, or green signal, viewed through the campus LMS, that indicates their likelihood of failing that early course. Students also receive an email with steps faculty recommend students take to improve academic performance (Purdue News

Service, 2009). In 2010, Purdue University made this technology available to other higher education institutions (Purdue News Service, 2010).

Georgia State University has taken predictive analytics to a grand scale. Each night, the institution's systems update 50,000 students' grades and records. Using 800 identified risk factors, the systems flag students who may be academically at risk (e.g., poor grades in introductory courses). An alert system triggers adviser meetings with students who have been identified as at-risk. The university's predictive analytics system has resulted in increased graduation rates for its high percentage of low-income and minority students, typically the first in their families to go to college (Dimeo, 2017). The EDUCAUSE Working Group (2015) at the Center for Analysis and Research stated:

> This ability [predictive analytics] to accurately predict future outcomes using learning data—called predictive LA—is of significant strategic value because it empowers stakeholders in the learning process (e.g., students, faculty, administrators, et al.) with intelligence on which they can act as means to achieve more desirable final outcomes. (p. 2)

In chapter 5 of this volume, Muljana, Placencia, and Luo describe how it is possible to use predictive, formative, and summative LA in an LMS to identify at-risk students early in a course (predictive); track students' performance along the trajectory of a course (formative); and evaluate the efficacy of faculty practices in that course based on students' performance levels on exit (summative). The third part of that chapter illustrates how faculty in one component of an engineering course used an LA approach, working together to identify the severity and probability of risks students face as they learn. With that shared knowledge, faculty then focused more course time on helping students address those risks and continued to monitor students' progress in sequential courses. In chapter 6, Qi describes a social network analysis (SNA) app she designed, with input from her faculty, that mines levels and types of student interaction in online discussion boards and represents those data visually. These visual data representations enabled faculty to develop a real-time understanding of which students and how well students engaged in an online course discussion board. These results prompted faculty to develop interventions for students who were disengaged or otherwise underperforming to invigorate their participation and improve their contributions.

LA software is also now being integrated into a range of digital options, such as interactive video presentations that enable faculty to identify the various challenges students face as they are learning. Students respond to questions embedded in the video, and the results are immediately reported to faculty, enabling faculty to address patterns of confusion or misunderstanding in real-time. Courseware that integrates LA software enables faculty and students to learn about often heretofore invisible and granular kinds of evidence that deepen insight into the specific causes of students' underperformance such as a discrete misstep in solving a complex mathematical problem or an incorrect action in performing an online experiment. Previously faculty simply did not always have the time to identify this evidence, particularly in large enrollment courses. Emerging digital courseware and other digital devices now capitalize on this capability, providing important new clues about the kinds of obstacles students face as they learn material before, during, and after a class session as they apply that knowledge in a related assignment or in their authentic work. The following examples illustrate some representative ways faculty might use LA-based technology in a course.

Individualized Real-Time Assessment of a Student's Performance. LA integrated into most LMSs enables faculty to monitor individual student performance continuously along the trajectory of a course. Specifically, LA has the capacity to identify student behaviors while a student is performing a task related to learning, such as the amount of time a student spends reading an online resource or engaging in an online discussion board, often an indicator of challenges a student faces (see chapter 5). LA also reports students' performance results on assessment methods used along the trajectory of a course, providing continuous evidence of the progress each student is making toward achieving high quality learning outcomes (see also chapter 5). The capability of LA to generate evidence of student learning in real time saves faculty time in scoring and in responding to students' performance. For example, automated, rather than manual, scoring can grade multiple choice, fill-in-the-blank, and some short answer tests or quizzes developed within the LMS. Results are then reported on faculty and student dashboards. Faculty, in turn, using a tool such as SpeedGrader, can insert either automated or individualized feedback to students into a comment section built into an LA-generated report. Similarly, LA documents individual and group performance levels on authentic tasks manually scored with rubrics that faculty or other educators build into the LMS with a rubric-builder tool. Faculty can provide feedback to each student by entering either automated or individualized comments into each rubric cell. Reducing typical time gaps between when students submit work and when they receive feedback, students benefit from timely feedback (see also chapter 5). LA also visually represents additional data on faculty dashboards, such as all students' overall performance on a task, individual performance levels, and student performance across sections of a course. Item analyses provide additional data about the assessment instrument used, such as the level of difficulty of a question or a list of the most challenging questions. In addition, LA can be taken to scale—an advantage for faculty who teach high enrollment courses.

Flipped classroom. In this approach to teaching, faculty might use assessment results generated by LA software based on questions students answer online about an assigned reading before a formal class session. Faculty can view patterns of performance and underperformance mined and reported by the LA software and (a) identify the range of real-time challenges students faced as they read and processed the reading and then (b) prepare materials as planned or develop alternative strategies to address those challenges during the next formal class meeting. In this use of LA, faculty benefit from a new opportunity to learn about individual and collective learning challenges that students faced in real time as they were learning new material, thus enabling them to address those challenges in the formal class before those challenges establish themselves as persistent student challenges.

Video platform. Designed to be integrated into an LMS, Echo 360's (n.d.) video platform enables teachers to create "active, engaged, and personalized video-based learning" (para. 1) made possible by LA software integrated into that platform. Specifically, faculty can continuously monitor how well each student in an online or hybrid course is learning course material presented in this delivery mode by embedding sets of questions in the video. LA mines students' patterns of responses to those questions and reports them on a faculty dashboard in real time, thus triggering faculty interventions or alternative teaching strategies to address those patterns in real time with individual students in a commitment to students' equitable progress.

Collaborative project. Interactive tabletops are a collaborative project tool, a type of software designed for small-group collaborative work in hybrid classes. Integrated LA software generates continuous real-time data to a teacher's dashboard. These data signal how well each student is performing in real time on individual steps of a small-group collaborative project, such as mapping a concept. Teachers use those data, including students' voice-reported, recorded data, to determine the kinds of interventions (and when and with whom) they should use to advance group work (Martinez-Maldonado, 2016).

Adaptive Learning-Based Technologies.   Adaptive learning-based platforms and tools have their roots in cognitive psychology and were used in the AI movement in the 1970s. More recently, they have emerged in the higher education landscape. Adaptive learning-based technologies individualize each student's learning. An individual generates data while learning (e.g., taking steps in a process, interpreting results, or selecting a formula to solve a problem). Adaptive learning-based technologies use these data to diagnose underperformance patterns, then identify and deliver customized materials, activities, or resources to meet each student's specific needs in real time, as that student is actively engaged in the learning process, rather than after the fact. Thus, adaptive learning technologies realize the importance of on-time, targeted feedback as an efficacious means of improving or advancing students' learning as it is unfolding. The processes of diagnosis and provision of targeted support continue until the student demonstrates achievement. Courseware that integrates adaptive learning technology or adaptive learning platforms circle back at other times to ascertain that a student continues to sustain improved performance of a previous underperformance pattern. If the underperformance pattern reoccurs, the cycle of diagnosis and assistance begins again. Adaptive learning-based technologies with integrated LA not only help students learn in real time but also report students' performance patterns to faculty in real time, alerting them to monitor students' sustained abilities to address patterns of underperformance in other contexts.

Emerging adaptive learning technologies are still largely considered to be in "experimental stages" (Pugliese, 2016, para. 4) on many campuses, but EDUCAUSE's *Horizon Report* estimated that broader adoption of adaptive-based learning technologies would happen between 2020 and 2021 (Alexander et al., 2019). An earlier projection of broader adoption was made in the *NMC Horizon Report: 2017 Higher Education Edition* (Adams Becker et al., 2017): They predicted 1 year or less. The following year, the projection was revised to 2 to 3 years (Adams Becker et al., 2018). Issues of time, resources, and cost to make further developments in adaptive platforms have held back broader adoption, together with the need for institutional cultures to accept this form of teaching and learning (Alexander et al., 2019). Shea and Aytun address some of these issues in chapter 8. However, recent developments in courseware, etextbooks, and intelligent tutoring programs powered by adaptive learning-based technologies that continuously engage students in their learning, as well as identify and address students' patterns of misunderstanding in real time, have encouraged increasing institutional use. Shea and Aytun describe the integration of adaptive technology into an immersive professional simulation on page 208.

Perhaps unfortunately, with increasing popularity *adaptive learning* has become a catchy buzzword. Some software developers use it to describe a genre of their products that may not actually be adaptive. The software packages are limited in their capacities to (a) provide multiple pathways for student learning, (b) collect and use real-time data about student performance, and (c) adapt and redirect content and support materials for individual learner's needs (using generic content and materials instead). As with any software product, it is always wise to request a complete demonstration in order to be fully aware of its capacities and features, the kinds of actionable data it provides, and how a specific digital option with adaptive capability aligns with course outcomes and design.

Similarly, the terms *differentiated, personalized*, and *adaptive learning technologies* are used interchangeably to describe courseware or other digital products that individualize students' learning, although they are distinct. In 2013, Phil Hill, educational technology consultant and analyst, distinguished how these terms differ based on the design of learning pathways. Differentiated learning technologies have preset learning pathways for students to take in a course or module. Personalized learning technologies feed students' performance results on an initial diagnostic instrument into a rules engine that determines an individual students' pathway and content. Data-driven adaptive learning technologies continuously take individual, student-generated data and adapt learning pathways and support materials to meet the specific needs of each learner (Hill, 2013).

Instead of selecting from existing adaptive learning-based courseware, etextbooks, or modules developed by educational technology companies, some faculty choose to design their own courses on customizable adaptive learning technology platforms such as the Smart Sparrow Adaptive eLearning platform (www.smartsparrow.com), which was acquired by Pearson in 2020. One real-world example is the development of an online adaptive eLearning introductory astrobiology science lab course for nonscience majors at ASU. The course is called Habitable Worlds. Students identify the possibility of habitable worlds beyond the Earth. This course was developed from a 3-year collaboration among the founding educational technology company, Smart Sparrow; ASU Online; and Professor Ariel Anbar of ASU's School of Earth and Space Exploration. For Anbar, the design of the course grew out of the challenge of engaging students in STEM:

> Historically, a major difficulty with engaging students in STEM is that science is too often taught as an encyclopedic collection of settled facts to be mastered. However, to Anbar, science is all about problem solving, motivated by big questions that cut across disciplines—something that cannot easily be taught through the lecture mode at scale. (Smart Sparrow, n.d., para. 2)

Horodyskyj et al. (2018) provide a detailed description of how Habitable Worlds, designed and built on the Smart Sparrow adaptive eLearning platform, engages students in an interactive and online inquiry-based science course. This is in contrast to current tools in the majority of LMSs that merely "provide limited templates for delivering content, favoring a passive, teacher-centered mode of instruction using video lectures and quizzes rather than enabling discovery and exploration" (Horodyskyj et al., 2018, p. 86). Instead, students in Habitable Worlds apply mathematical language and scientific concepts while engaging in online simulations and virtual field trips to identify possible other habitable worlds. Horodyskyj et al. reported that "we used adaptive design, whereby problem sets, initial experimental conditions, and simulator setups are randomly generated to create a unique version of an activity for each student, thereby minimizing cheating as well" (p. 88).

An integrated intelligent tutoring system fueled by adaptive learning-based technology provides students with real-time feedback to help them overcome learning challenges. Faculty also build in times to communicate with students in discussion forums and online chats, a particularly useful approach for addressing problems students face that cannot be addressed by automation. Faculty also build in times for community exchange among students. They further monitor students' course performance through assessment results generated by the integrated LA software and automated feedback provided to students based on specific mistakes they make. Thus faculty are able to see continuously how well students are performing, intervene when necessary, and adapt content for individual students. As of 2020, more than 3,000 students have taken this online course. Habitable Worlds is now also one among several online, open source, science-based, undergraduate courses available through Inspark (n.d.), a network that is "a global team of educators creating and sharing the next-generation courses to revolutionize science education" (para. 1). These courses were designed on Sparrow's adaptive eLearning platform and integrate various types of emerging learning technologies, such as intelligent tutoring systems, to support, develop, and continuously engage students in inquiry-based science learning. Habitable Worlds is now listed as HabWorlds within the Inspark Network (https://www.habworlds.org).

The Potential Impact of LA- and Adaptive Learning-Based Technologies

Many faculty may use analytic- and adaptive learning-based technologies solely for the time-saving benefits they offer in scoring or assessing student work—especially in high enrollment courses. But focusing only on those benefits may well limit them from realizing the full impact of these technologies. For example, technology-enabled real-time assessment minimizes traditional time gaps inbetween teaching, learning, and assessment. As a result, assessment is no longer layered onto student work as a separate process; it is integrated into the processes of teaching and learning in real-time or near real-time, positioning faculty and students on the frontline of students' learning as it unfolds. That integration is the catalyst for impacting or potentially transforming the teaching and learning processes and the traditional roles of teacher and student as is discussed in the next sections.

Developing Adaptive, Evidence-Based, and Research-Informed Faculty
Positioned on the frontline of student learning as a course progresses, faculty have the opportunity to identify and address individual students' patterns of underperformance along the progression of a course. They also have the built-in, real-time opportunity to gain valuable firsthand evidence about the efficacy of their longitudinal teaching practices based on students' performance patterns—across course demographics—captured in formative assessment results. Thus, faculty can become evidence-based teachers who examine students' performance results within the context of their specific teaching practices and approaches, such as pedagogy, means of delivery of content, strategies to present typically challenging material, and ways to position students to learn (see also chapter 5 for predictive, formative, and summative use of learning analytics).

Formative technology-enabled real-time assessment develops evidence-based teachers who nimbly adapt or adopt course material, teaching practices, strategies or alternative means for students to learn, tailoring approaches to address individual learning needs as the course progresses. Time saved marking routine coursework is time that can be dedicated to addressing individual students' needs in real time, helping students find the source of their patterns of underperformance and identify methods to overcome them. That time dedicated to individual students is a commitment to their equitable progress toward achieving high-quality student learning outcomes.

What if a teacher does not have a repertoire of practices or even resources to draw from to assist with the range of challenges students face? Certainly OERs provide options to consider, but there is considerable research on learning that documents efficacious practices that faculty should consult. Some of that research has existed for a long time. Some of it emerges through longer term research in the learning sciences. Some of it is now documented through long-term research on successful practices for teaching and learning online such as Carnegie Mellon's recently released research-based digital learning tools that are accompanied with longitudinal research results that support efficacious strategies promoting student learning. And some of it has been integrated into successful guides for designing online courses (Darby, 2019). Consulting research on learning as a means to advance one's practices, faculty have the potential to become not only evidence-based but also research-informed professionals.

How faculty teach in face-to-face or online delivered courses is often based on personal practices or preferences rather than on research on how students actually learn. With over 30 years of experience in the design of online learning, Donald Clark (2019) explained the importance of research on learning on the profession of teaching:

> It's not that all research is definitive, as science is always on the move, open to future falsification. But, as with research in medicine, physics in material science and engineering, chemistry in organic and inorganic production, maths in AI, we work with the best that is available. WE are duty bound to do our best on the best available evidence or we are not really a professional "profession." (para. 12)

Further, Clark identified how drawing on research on learning contributes to the profession of teaching. Specifically, research

- debunks myths or wrong-headed theories,
- informs teaching practices,
- provides objective data with which to make a case for using a specific practice or developing a proposal to advance a practice,
- helps explain to students why a specific approach is more effective, and
- helps faculty and campus teams identify learning technologies based on research. (paras. 7–11)

One useful online source for understanding how research on learning informs educational practices is MIT's Open Learning (n.d.) website. The site lists specific findings about successful ways students learn and then offers strategies, accompanied by examples, to help faculty develop those strategies within their own contexts. For example, in both face-to-face delivery and in online delivery, research documents that spaced learning is an effective alternative to focused practice drills as a means to recall or review a concept, principle, or process or even solve types of problems (see also chapter 2). In the spaced learning approach, students work with important material they need to review or recall over weeks or months rather than in a focused practice session (MIT Open Learning, n.d.).

Cultivating Self-Aware, Self-Regulated Learners

Faculty can use the time saved with real-time generation of assessment results to help individual students improve their levels of performance. In particular, they can develop students' potential to become actively engaged in identifying and surfacing the causes of or reasons for their own underperformance patterns. Acting as mentors, faculty guide students to reflect on those causes and reasons and identify resources (self and online) and strategies they will use to improve those patterns and continue to monitor themselves. That is, rather than students passively responding to a faculty directive about how to improve a weak performance pattern, faculty position students as agents for improving their work as part of the learning process. They self-reflect on causes and reasons for underperformance; self-identify strategies or resources that will enable their improvement; and self-monitor progress toward improvement. In taking agency for their improvement students develop their potential to become self-regulated learners.

According to Barry J. Zimmerman (1990), the foremost researcher on self-regulated learning, when developing agency for their learning, students become "decisive in their approach to learning" (p. 5). Contributors to *How People Learn II: Learners, Contexts, and Cultures* (National Academies of Sciences, Engineering, and Medicine, 2018) also focus on the importance of developing students' ability to become self-regulated learners: "Successful learning requires coordination of multiple cognitive processes that involve different networks in the brain. In order to coordinate these processes, an individual needs to be able to monitor and regulate his own learning" (p. 4). Self-regulation is a desirable attribute in 21st-century workplaces. In 2015, Fontana et al. identified the importance of this attribute: "In knowledge-intensive industries, the workplace has become a key focus of learning. To perform effectively, knowledge workers must be able to take responsibility for their own developmental needs, and, in particular, to regulate their own learning" (p. 320).

As illustrated in Figure 1.1, both faculty and students are the recipients of real-time assessment results. The teacher and learner circles overlap the central circle that represents technology-enabled real-time assessment generated by LA. Both are also learners. Faculty learn about, as well as from, assessment data. They become evidence-based teachers who nimbly adapt materials or practices to address individual student needs and research-informed professionals who draw on research on learning to identify and develop new practices or approaches or materials to meet the needs of students as they are learning. Students learn about their patterns of performance and, with faculty guidance, develop their potential to self-reflect on the causes of or

Figure 1.1. Potential impact of technology-enabled real-time assessment on teacher and learner roles.

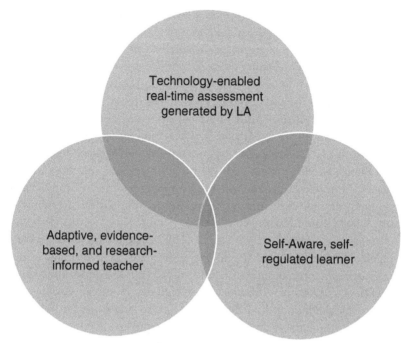

reasons for their underperformance challenges as a first step toward becoming self-regulated learners. Importantly, contributors to *How People Learn II: Learners, Contexts, and Culture* (2018) also point out that students' ability to self-regulate can be "improved through interventions" (p. 4).

Immersive Environments and 3D Technology and Tools

Virtual realities have dotted the landscape of higher education for quite some time, providing students opportunities to enter online environments and interact with others. One historic example is virtual educational gaming software. A variant of virtual realities is now possible using immersive environments and 3D technology that offer expanded opportunities for students to gain firsthand knowledge, practice skills in a safe environment, solve a complex problem drawing on multiple skill sets and knowledge within changing contexts, or demonstrate their creativity. AI has also contributed to developments in immersive digital learning environments and 3D technology and tools. These developments have been made possible by "AI machine learning, image recognition, and natural language processing" (Holmes et al., 2019, p. 147) that enhance students' learning experiences and enable students and faculty to produce new creations or translate ideas into 3D forms.

Placing learning directly in the hands of individual students addresses a major concern Diana Laurillard (2002) raised about the inefficiency of lecturing as a means of engaging students with academic knowledge, although it is a convenient method. Specifically, she said that "for the individual learner, the lecture is a grossly inefficient way of engaging with academic knowledge" (p. 94). Immersive learning environments and 3D technology have the potential to engage students, providing them opportunities to describe, narrate, explain, discover, practice or apply learning, and create. Contributors DiCerbo and Belenky, in chapter 2, point out the existence of these kinds of emerging learning technologies does not guarantee that students will learn. Instead, it is the responsibility of faculty to integrate these technologies effectively into course design and position students to engage in a particular task or assignment to ensure they benefit from their experience in an immersive environment. For example, rather than learning about the architectural characteristics of a specific culture from a teacher or even from pictures or video, students could first be asked to identify those characteristics in an immersive environment that represents that culture. Second, students could pool their observations and then present those observations during a full discussion with the faculty. Only after self-guided study might faculty then step in to identify features the group missed or ask students to elaborate on their observations. As with any selected technology, how faculty integrate it into a course and how students are oriented to engage with it are essential. Students teaching themselves is a powerful educational practice. David Gooblar (2018) is associate director of Temple University's Center for the Advancement of Teaching and writes a column on teaching for *The Chronicle of Higher Education*, "Pedagogy Unbound." He reiterates the importance of students teaching themselves:

> I sometimes worry that the word *teach* leads us astray in academe. The word suggests that our job as faculty members is to put new knowledge into our students' heads. But in my experience the best learning occurs when students teach themselves—when they discover something on their own. (para. 3)

Some immersive learning environments may also integrate LA and adaptive-based technology, reporting students' progress on faculty and student dashboards so that both groups take real-time steps to improve students' performance. Capabilities of these learning technologies enable students to interact with objects and other people or practice their learning in a range of environments, including those that are navigable or represent professional contexts similar to those students will work in after graduation. Among the immersive learning environments and 3D technology and tools that provide expanded and enhanced opportunities for students to learn are the following:

- *Virtual reality (VR) environments* completely immerse an individual into a 3D, computer-generated environment so that one becomes an observer or participant in it. Typically, VR requires the use of a case, such as Google Cardboard or Gear VE, into which an individual inserts a smartphone. VR may also require a headset, such as Oculus Go or the more recently released Oculus Quest. In the Reality Lab at Indiana University, students use VR to "walk through" buildings they have designed in an interior design course. According to the faculty member teaching that course, students "can experience proportion, space, and light. Does the space feel too big or too dark? That's an emotional insight you could never get from the CAD drawing" (Dorfman, 2017, para. 3)
- *Mixed reality (MR) environments* blend real-world and VR elements together, creating an interaction between the real-world and digital objects.
- *Augmented reality (AR) environments* add digital elements, such as computer-generated sounds, videos, or graphics, to a live environment.
- *3D technology* enables students to interact with and manipulate digital objects in immersive environments; perform tasks in online learning environments such as labs; and develop new understanding of structural or spatial relationships in, for example, a building.
- *3D tools* such as 3D printers and scanners enable student to translate concepts, ideas, and creations into dimensional representations. Besides students in art and design, students in other majors are using 3D tools. At St. John's University (2019), for example, pharmacy students explore 3D print medications.

The Impact of Immersive Learning Environments and 3D Technology and Tools

The emerging technologies discussed previously have the potential to provide opportunities for students to:

- Explore the nooks and crannies of often inaccessible environments, such as a museum, an ocean floor, or galaxies beyond the Milky Way.
- Apply some of the major desirable 21st-century workplace skills—critical thinking, collaboration, communication, creativity, and flexibility—to solve problems in a range of contexts. Contexts include authentic professional or workplace situations or issues, as well as social, political, economic, or environmental challenges humankind faces or may face. Immersive educational games, short simulations,

or fictional games also offer students opportunities to apply course outcomes, thus testing students' abilities to apply and transfer learning.

- Assume different identities or roles in immersive environments as navigators, explorers, narrators, creators, strategists, collaborators, communicators, critical thinkers, or flexible problem-solvers, thereby developing agency for their learning.
- Respond to changing scenarios built into an immersive environment, providing students with additional opportunities to demonstrate their abilities or transfer learning into a range of unexpected contexts or situations.
- Manipulate objects to deepen understanding (e.g., functional or spatial relationships).
- Bring to fruition new ideas or creations with 3D printers.
- Perform procedures virtually (e.g., lab work, clinics).
- Hone and receive feedback on execution of skills before a live performance of them is required (e.g., Virtual Speech, https:// virtualspeech.com/courses/). (See chapter 11 for the range of ways in which Still University's schools use a variety of digital scenarios to immerse students in professional situations.)
- Deepen understanding and even develop emotional responses to individuals or situations by assuming the characteristics or plights of others. For example, students studying to become healthcare providers can walk in the shoes of an Alzheimer's patient in VR in the "A Walk Through Dementia" series (Alzheimer's Research UK, n.d.).
- Boost creativity. Maya Georgieva has a background in digital literacy and storytelling and is cofounder and chief innovation officer of Digital Bodies, a global consulting group focusing on the impact of immersive VR/AR/MR and wearable technologies on education and society. She described the value of AR and VR in the creative classroom as follows:

Imagine students being able to really demonstrate their work in a 3D world. This leads to powerful new forms of storytelling. As VR and MR continue to evolve so will the stories we can create. Our mission is to push the boundaries of the medium to move beyond the known formats and deliver on the promise of truly transformative learning experiences. (DePaul, 2017, para. 22)

AI-Driven Tools and AI Assistants

The capabilities of AI to create intelligent tools and machines that have humanlike abilities based on algorithms for natural language processing, speech recognition, decision-making, and learning, among others, have the potential to contribute in new ways to teaching, learning, and assessment. Similar to voice-activated technologies in our homes, chatbots on some institutions already provide students with campus information or services. AI-driven tools that support student learning also already exist. An example of one intelligent tool is Edulai. It initially uses a skill checker to assess students' "critical thinking, problem solving, team work, communication, leadership, interculturism, and learning" (Smarthink, n.d., para. 3). If installed into an LMS, the tool continues to assess those outcomes when students demonstrate them in their work. Faculty are able to continuously monitor students' performance to determine when they need to intervene to help students improve their performance levels.

Some real-world AI collaborations are already underway. For example, IBM and Rensselaer Polytechnic Institute have partnered in a new approach to help students learn Mandarin. An AI assistant is paired with an immersive classroom environment. Students are immersed into different language learning contexts, such as a restaurant or public transit system, and practice speaking in those contexts with an AI chat agent (Neelakantan, 2020). Since 2016, Georgia Tech has been testing Jill Watson, a virtual teaching assistant who works alongside human teaching assistants (TAs) in an online course on AI. Results from the first round using Jill revealed students could not identify which TA she actually was among all the human TAs for that course (Maderer, 2017). Among their projections about the future of AI in education, Holmes et al. (2019) identified two distinct possibilities. First, students may one day have a lifelong learning AI companion—a personalized tutor "operating sometimes like a learning partner, other times as a guide through learning opportunities like a tutor and other times as an instructor helping a student determine what and how to learn" (pp. 157–158). Second, teachers may have an AI TA that would automatically "provide professional development resources to support teaching" (p. 160) and all relevant data about students' achievement from multiple sources to customize each student's learning experiences. In 2019, EDUCAUSE's *Horizon Report* projected that within 4 to 5 years there would be wider adoption of AI TAs on campuses (Alexander et al. 2019).

Part Three: A Taxonomy of Major Types of Current and Emerging Learning Technologies

Experts in learning technologies have taken different approaches to classifying learning technologies, leading others to periodically summarize them (e.g., Caladine, 2008; Sun Associates, 2001). For example, based on a four-part division suggested by Dewey (1943), Bruce and Levin (1997) classified learning technologies as media for learning through "inquiry, communication, construction, and expression" (p. 79). In 2002, Laurillard classified learning technologies based on forms of educational media she identified as "narrative, adaptive, interactive, communicative, and productive" (pp. 90–91). More recently, the College of Education at the University of Houston (n.d.) developed technology categories that align with 21st-century outcomes and lists of specific digital tools to enable students to attain those outcomes.

The taxonomy of current and emerging learning technologies, represented in Appendix 1A, values the work of those who have developed classification systems. It also incorporates and expands on their work within the context of the evolving 21st-century learning technology landscape. As a reference for faculty, campus leaders, and others who support and guide faculty and campus teams, the taxonomy contributes to initial discussions focused on identifying learning technologies that facilitate, contribute to, or support teaching, learning, and assessing student learning. Keep in mind the following developments as you refer to the taxonomy:

- Many emerging learning technology products, such as platforms, etextbooks, and courseware packages, now integrate several capabilities into their design. For example, etextbooks may allow students to interact with online materials or text, adapt material to address individual learning needs, and report student performance levels on both student and faculty dashboards.
- Learning technologies may be used for more than one purpose based on how they are integrated into the design of a course and how students are positioned to engage with them. For example, some communicative technologies may also foster collaboration and vice versa. Immersive learning environments may become the context within which students demonstrate their creativity or productivity. In addition, some assistive technologies may not only enable students with disabilities to learn and engage in course activities but also benefit all learners. (See also Box 1.1 on accessibility, and the category of "Assistive Technology" in the taxonomy in Appendix 1A.)
- Readers can further explore current and emerging learning technologies, learn firsthand how faculty have integrated them into courses, and even try some out by enrolling in the State University of New York's hybrid professional development massive open online course (MOOC). The MOOC is an OER, and participants can use

the associated wiki to search for specific types of learning technologies. This MOOC is described in more detail in chapter 3.

Will Thalheimer is a consultant and researcher specializing in learning fundamentals, instructional design, performance improvement, learning measurement, and workplace learning. He concisely summarizes the potential of emerging learning technologies identified in this chapter to engage individual students meaningfully in digital learning environments by comparing "typical elearning" with "Serious eLearning," represented in Figure 1.2.

Along the continuum of major learning technologies identified in the taxonomy and Figure 1.3 and expanded on in Appendix 1A, emerging technologies are distinguished by their potential to center teaching and learning on the criteria of "Serious eLearning." The shift toward "Serious eLearning" is evident in the capabilities of emerging learning technologies: learning analytics' generation of technology-enabled real-time assessment results for individual students along the trajectory of a course; adaptive learning platforms and other digital options that adjust content and support materials to meet the needs of individual students; and immersive learning environments and 3D technology and tools that offer relevant, engaging, and meaningful experiences that enable students to develop agency for their learning.

Targeted Major Resources to Assist in Identifying Learning Technologies That Meet Course-, Program-, or Institutional-Level Needs

The following major resources are especially useful in the process of narrowing down learning technology options based on relevant criteria for selecting technologies at the course, program, or institution levels:

Figure 1.2. Comparison between "typical elearning" and "Serious eLearning."

typical elearning	SERIOUS eLEARNING
content focused	Performance focused
efficient for authors	Meaningful to learners
attendance-driven	Engagement-driven
knowledge delivery	Authentic contexts
fact testing	Realistic decisions
one size fits all	Individualized challenges
one-time events	Spaced practice
didactic feedback	Real-world consequences

Note. Used with permission from Will Thalheimer (2020) on behalf of the eLearning Manifesto Organizers.

Figure 1.3. Representation of the evolving 21st-century learning technology landscape: From current to emerging learning technologies beginning with narrative technologies.

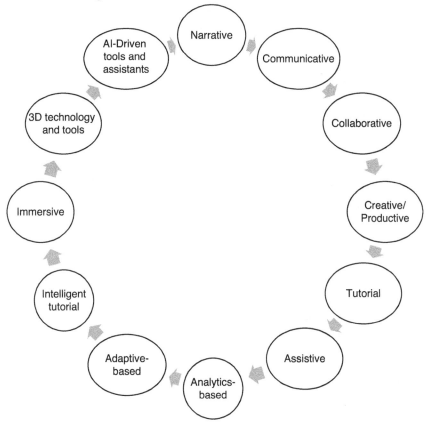

- Anstey and Watson's (2018) "Rubric for Evaluating E-Learning Tools in Higher Eduction" (Appendix 1B) represents a multidimensional evaluation of the functional, technical, and pedagogical aspects of eLearning tools.
- The Courseware in Context Framework (CWiC) (coursewarein context.org), developed in 2016 and revised in 2018, provides a vigorous framework for individual faculty, instructional designers, and administrators to explore, evaluate, or select available digital disciplinary courseware. The framework is the result of a collaboration among Tyton Partners, the Online Learning Consortium, and the Stanford Research Institute, with support from the Bill & Melinda Gates Foundation, and it is available online (cwic.learnplatform.com).

It begins with a faculty primer. "The CWiC Faculty Primer" consists of a product taxonomy to help faculty explore the functional capabilities of courseware to meet specified learner needs (e.g., collaboration or learner autonomy) as well as faculty needs (e.g., the desire to customize courseware).

○ The CWiC also includes a resource for instructional designers who are assisting faculty and campus teams with selecting courseware, "The CWiC Designer." This resource includes the product taxonomy as well as research on the learning science principles that underlie the capabilities of courseware and features of courseware used at the course or program level. With this additional information instructional designers are better able to help faculty and a campus team target the technologies that best meet their needs and those of their students.

○ The complete CWiC Framework also includes a resource for administrators, consisting of the product taxonomy, research on learning science principles, and guidance about institutional implementation of products.

Part Four: The Potential of Emerging Learning Technologies: Major Projects, Initiatives, and Digital Growth in Publishing Companies

Although the full impact of emerging technologies based on learning analytics, adaptive learning, and AI will be realized over a longer period of time still to come, major developments across the higher education landscape are contributing to realizing the potential of these emerging learning technologies.

Major Projects, Initiatives, and Digital Growth in Publishing

The following projects or initiatives in higher education, coupled with the growing commitment of publishing companies to design digital products that draw on the learning sciences and the capabilities of LA and adaptive learning-based technology, represent major current efforts to build awareness of and advance the use of emerging learning technologies in higher education.

The Every Learner Everywhere Network
In 2019, the Every Learner Everywhere (n.d.) network of 12 organizations (supported by the Bill & Melinda Gates Foundation) launched a pilot to work

with an initial set of higher education institutions to help them implement adaptive courseware in first-year foundational courses by:

- Comparing and selecting adaptive courseware products
- Using adaptive courseware to achieve broader institutional goals
- Redesigning courses to incorporate innovative, high-impact teaching practices
- Collecting and analyzing data
- Connecting practitioners and facilitating peer-to-peer learning (Every Learner Everywhere, n.d., pp. 1–2)

As a way to close persistent achievement gaps and improve completion rates for first-generation college students, low-income students, and students of color, professionals at Every Learner Everywhere worked initially with a small set of 2- and 4-year institutions, beginning in 2019. The organization has plans to expand nationwide to reach 200 institutions by 2022.

*Initiatives Informing Educational Practices Based
on Learning and Data Research*
The following initiatives will become major catalysts toward prioritizing a professional commitment to anchoring educational practices and selection of learning technologies in research on learning.

   The Empirical Educator Project (EEP) (http://empiricaleducators.net) is a network of people and organizations dedicated to transforming higher education using practices informed by research and data. EEP is an initiative of e-Literate (eliterate.us) and dedicated to the proposition

> that our institutions of higher education must and can transform themselves from the inside to meet the challenges of the 21st century. We can do this by drawing on the historic academic strength inquiry embedded in a community that provides peer review, by turning that strength to a core institutional task of enabling students to learn and thrive, and by evolving academic cultural institutions and processes to support these ends. (EEP, n.d., para. 1)

EEP's activities include an annual summit that promotes projects and content generated and endorsed by e-Literate. The summit aims to share the knowledge of the EEP network and make it more practically useful. EEP also includes vendors as partners whose products or services help students learn and who are "willing to be good-faith participants in the academic commons of empirical education" (EEP, n.d., para. 3). D2L has made a 3-year sponsorship commitment to EEP, which includes both educating their customers on the work and using their Brightspace platform as the home for experimentation with tools and techniques such as those donated by Carnegie Mellon University (M. Feldstein, personal communication, February 7, 2020). E-Literate's Standard of Proof webinars highlight evidence-based collaborations between EEP sponsors and universities. A listing of these webinars, as well as access to them, appears on eLiterate's website (https://eliterate.us/standard-of-proof-webinars/). One example of a standard-of-proof webinar is a webinar about Georgia State University's use of AdmitHub chatbots to decrease so-called summer melt (the time during which admitted or currently enrolled students choose not to enroll in the fall semester) and the randomized controlled trial the university conducted to prove that the chatbot was working (e-Literate TV, 2019).

Carnegie Mellon University announced in 2019 that it would gradually release digital learning software it has developed over more than a decade as a free, open source alternative to commercially developed options. Included among the releases are the university's underlying code so that faculty and others can customize the software. The release also includes the "university's pioneering adaptive learning platform, the Open Learning Initiative, as well as a learning analytics platform, LearnSphere" (Young, 2019, para. 1). Altogether the proposed software to be released represents more than $100 million in foundation grants and university-committed funds. The release of this digital software has the potential to advance research-based and data-driven teaching because these products have been developed based on the science of learning and longitudinal research on student achievement.

Carnegie Learning, Inc., a comprehensive learning technology company, announced in 2020

> its commitment to a new National Science Foundation (NSF)-funded project to build a Learner Data Institute that will harness the power of data to better understand how people learn, improve adaptive instructional systems, and make the learning technology ecosystem more effective and cost-efficient. (Business Wire, 2020, para. 1)

The project will be led by the director of advanced analytics at Carnegie Learning, Inc. and a professor of computer science at the University of Memphis, Tennessee. They will work with "researchers from universities, government agencies, and private companies to collaborate on improving educational outcomes everywhere" (Business Wire, 2020, para. 1). Carnegie Learning, Inc. has positioned itself to contribute substantially to this project. Its AI-driven software, built on an adaptive platform, was designed based on data from billions of students' actions gathered as hundreds of thousands of students solved complex real-world problems.

Digital Growth in Publishing Companies
Between 2018 and 2020 several publishers aimed for digital growth in acquiring adaptive learning technology and in developing etextbooks and other learning resource materials that integrate analytics and/or adaptive learning. Several high-profile acquisitions are worth mentioning. John Wiley & Sons (2018) acquired the assets of Knewton, a firm that specialized in adaptive learning technology and OER. After that, it acquired Learning House from Weld North to advance its digital learning tools for education. In 2020 Pearson acquired Smart Sparrow, a company that provides "course-authoring tools for faculty and instructional designers to build adaptive courseware" (Wan, 2020, para. 1). Pearson viewed this acquisition as an opportunity for faculty to design their own adaptive-based courses rather than predesigned adaptive courseware set by a developer (Wan, 2020). In 2019 McGraw-Hill and Cengage announced plans to merge to increase their already well-established digital presence. This merger met with resistance from consumer, faculty, and student groups concerned about—among other issues—how another textbook company merger, creating a smaller textbook market, could result in less competitive textbook pricing, a central issue for students (Busta, 2019). Eventually that merger was cancelled. Besides etextbooks, other digital tools publishers are likely to market are "assessment tools, adaptive content, lecture capture and homework assignments" (Paterson, 2019, para. 5).

Reflecting on the importance of anchoring digital tools in research on learning and drawing on the capabilities of emerging learning technologies, in 2018 MacMillan articulated a set of "Six Key Principles for Learning Experience Design" that underlie the development of their digital products:

> (1) develop learner motivation; (2) provide personalized and adaptive experiences; (3) target cognitive and memory elements; (4) build on well-constructed learning models; (5) create interactive and constructive opportunities; and (6) enable metacognition and self-regulation. (Slide 4)

A Projection

Online learning makes it possible for higher education to reach students across our demographics as well as across the globe. Of course, there are limitations and exceptions, such as those notable areas across the United States that lack broadband access, termed *education deserts* (Meyers, 2018). However, harnessing the potential of learning analytics and adaptive learning technologies enables higher education to teach and support students in increasingly more individualized ways, no matter when they enter or reenter our institutions, no matter the learning challenges they face. Ted Mitchell

(2019), president of the American Council on Education, best described the potential of these emerging technologies on society as well as the individual student when he said:

> We know that it is possible to deploy digital resources to serve social mobility, student success, and institutional progress. (para. 18)
>   These digital resources take many forms, such as learning modalities that offer instruction in more flexible and personalized ways, assessment tools that deliver meaningful information on student learning, and information systems that allow us not only to describe but to predict student progress and match students with resources when needed—or even before. What cuts to the heart of all of those innovations is one central innovation: the focus on and commitment to analytics and data-driven decision-making. (para. 19)

References

Adams Becker, S., Cummins, M., Davis, A., Freeman, A., Hall Gesinger, C., and Ananthanarayanan, V. (2017). *NMC horizon report: 2017 higher education edition.* The New Media Consortium. https://library.educause.edu/-/media/files/library/2017/2/2017horizonreporthe.pdf

Adams Becker, S., Brown, M., Dahlstrom, E., Davis, A., DePaul, K., Diaz, V., & Pomerantz, J. (2018). *NMC horizon report: 2018 higher education edition.* EDUCAUSE. https://library.educause.edu/~/media/files/library/2018/8/2018horizon report.pdf

Alexander, B., Ashford-Rowe, K., Barajas-Murphy, N., Dobbin, G., Knott, J., McCormack, M., Pomerantz, J., Ryan Seilhamer, R., & Weber, N. (Eds.). (2019). *Horizon report: 2019 higher education edition.* EDUCAUSE. https://library.educause.edu/resources/2019/4/2019-horizon-report

Alzheimer's Research UK. (n.d.). *A walk through dementia.* https://www.awalk throughdementia.org

Anstey, L., & Watson, G. (2018, September 10). A rubric for evaluating e-learning tools in higher education. *EDUCAUSE Review.* https://er.educause.edu/articles/2018/9/a-rubric-for-evaluating-e-learning-tools-in-higher-education

Beasley, W. (2012, May 2). Infiltrating the walled garden. *Hybrid Pedagogy.* https://hybridpedagogy.org/infiltrating-the-walled-garden/

Benioff, M. (2016, September 15). *Artificial intelligence will become the defining technology of the 21st-century.* Livemint. www.livemint.com/Science/LMgQKEAcoymrtpGz7JWSyJ/Artificial-intelligence-will-be-the-defining-tech-of-the-21s.html

Brown, M. (2015, June 3). The LMS of the future: Exploring the next generation digital learning environment. *EDUCAUSE Review.* https://er.educause

.edu/blogs/2015/6/the-lms-of-the-future-exploring-the-next-generation-digital-learning-environment

Brown, M., Millichap, N., & Dehoney, J. (2015, June 22). What's next for the LMS? *EDUCAUSE Review.* https://er.educause.edu/articles/2015/6/whats-next-for-the-lms

Bruce, B. C., & Levin, J. A. (1997). Educational technology: Media for inquiry, communication, construction, and expression. *Journal of Educational Computing Research, 17*(1), 79–102. https://doi.org/10.2190/7HPQ-4F3X-8M8Y-TVCA

Business Wire. (2020, February 4). Carnegie learning and the University of Memphis to create learner data institute to improve educational outcomes. https://www.businesswire.com/news/home/20200204005062/en/Carnegie-Learning-University-Memphis-Create-Learner-Data

Busta, H. (2019, August 1). *Pushback on Mcgraw-Hill, Cengage merger highlights materials access debate.* EducationDive. https://www.educationdive.com/news/pushback-on-mcgraw-hill-cengage-merger-highlights-materials-access-debate/560060/

Caladine, R. (2008). Taxonomies for technology. In L. A. Tomei (Ed.), *Encyclopedia of information technology curriculum integration* (pp. 833–838). IGI Global. https://doi.org/10.4018/978-1-59904-881-9.ch131

Chatti, M. A., Dyckhoff, A. L., Schroeder, U., & Thus, H. (2012). A reference model for learning analytics. *International Journal of Technology Enhanced Learning (IJTEL), 4*(5/6), 1–22. https://doi.org/10.1504/IJTEL.2012.051815

Clark, D. (2019, March 7). *Why learning professionals—managers, project managers, interactive designers, learning experience designers, whatever, should not ignore research.* Donald Clark Plan B. http://donaldclarkplanb.blogspot.com/2019/03/

Clow, D. (2013). An overview of learning analytics. *Teaching in Higher Education, 18*(6), 683–695. https://doi.org/10.1080/13562517.2013.827653

CWiC Interactive Framework. (2017). *The interactive courseware in context framework.* https://coursewareincontext.org/2017/01/27/learn-interactive-cwic-platform/

Darby, F. with Lang, J. M. (2019). *Small teaching online: Applying learning science in online classes.* Jossey-Bass.

DePaul, K. (2017, March 23). Outside the boundaries: Exploring virtual and augmented reality in learning. *EDUCAUSE Review.* https://er.educause.edu/blogs/2017/3/outside-the-boundaries-exploring-virtual-and-augmented-reality-in-learning

Dewey, J. (1943). *The child and the curriculum: The school and society.* University of Chicago Press.

Dimeo, J. (2017, July 19). Data dive. *Inside Higher Ed.* https://www.insidehighered.com/digital-learning/article/2017/07/19/georgia-state-improves-student-outcomes-data

Dorfman, P. (2017, June 13). IU's reality lab offers students an out-of-this-world experience. *Bloom Magazine.* http://www.magbloom.com/2017/06/ius-reality-lab-offers-students-an-out-of-this-world-experience/

Echo360. (n.d.). *The smarter video platform for education.* echo360.com

EDUCAUSE Learning Initiative. (2010, July). *7 things you should know about LMS alternatives*. EDUCAUSE. https://www.educause.edu/ir/library/pdf/ELI7062.pdf

EDUCAUSE Working Group. (2015). *The predictive analytics revolution: Leveraging learning data for student success*. EDUCAUSE Center for Analysis and Research. https://library.educause.edu/~/media/files/library/2015/10/ewg1510-pdf

Edwards, M. E., & Black, E. W. (2012.). Contemporary instructor-librarian collaboration: A case study of an online embedded librarian implementation. *Journal of Library & Information Services in Distance Learning, 6*(3–4), 284–311. https://doi.org/10.1080/1533290X.2012.705690

Eisner, E. W. (1993). Forms of understanding and the future of educational research. *Educational Researcher, 22*(7), 5–11. https://doi.org/10.3102/0013189X022007005

e-Literate TV. (2019). *Standard of proof: Summer melt, Georgia State University, and AdmitHub* [Video]. YouTube. https://www.youtube.com/watch?v=7NoYUa_VHfs

e-Literate. (n.d.) *About e-Literate*. https://eliterate.us/about-e-literate/

Empirical Educator Project. (n.d.) *About*. e-Literate. http://empiricaleducators.net/about/

Every Learner Everywhere. (n.d.). *Every Learner Everywhere: Helping institutions use new technology to innovate teaching and learning: An introduction*. http://www.everylearnereverywhere.org/wp-content/uploads/Every-Learner-Everywhere_An-Introduction.pdf

Every Learner Everywhere. (2018). *About us*. www.everylearnereverywhere.org/about

Feldstein, M. (2019, December 23). *Campus Edtech has shifted focus from tech to ed*. EdSurge. https://www.edsurge.com/news/2019-12-23-campus-edtech-has-shifted-focus-from-tech-to-ed

Fiock, H., & Garcia, H. (2019). How to give your students better feedback with technology: Advice guide. *The Chronicle of Higher Education*. https://www.chronicle.com/interactives/20191108-Advice-Feedback

Fontana, R. P., Milligan, C., Littlejohn, A., & Margaryan, A. (2015). Measuring self-regulated learning in the workplace. *International Journal of Training and Development, 19*(1), 32–52. https://doi.org/10.1111/ijtd.12046

Gay, G. (2010). *Culturally responsive teaching: Theory, research, and practice* (2nd ed). Teachers College Press.

Gooblar, D. (2018, May 1) Your students learn by doing, not by listening. *Chronicle of Higher Education*. https://www.chronicle.com/article/Your-Students-Learn-by-Doing/243277

Hill, P. (2013, October 15). *Differentiated, personalized & adaptive learning: Some clarity for EDUCAUSE*. e-Literate. https://eliterate.us/differentiated-personalized-adaptive-learning-clarity-educause/

Holmes, W., Bialik, M., & Fadel, C. (2019). *Artificial intelligence in education: Promises and implications for teaching and learning*. The Center for Curriculum Redesign.

Horodyskyj, L. B., Mead, C., Belinson, Z., Buxner, S., Semken, S., & Anbar, A.D. (2018). Habitable worlds: Delivering on the promises of online education. *Astrobiology, 18*(1), 86–99. https://doi:10.1089/ast.2016.1550

Inspark. (n.d.) *Transforming science education.* https://inspark.education/teach/about/

John Wiley & Sons, Inc. (2018, October 9). *Wiley signs definitive agreement to acquire learning house from Weld north* [Press release]. https://newsroom.wiley.com/press-release/all-corporate-news/wiley-signs-definitive-agreement-acquire-learning-house-weld-north

Johnson, L., Smith, R., Willis, H., Levine, A., & Haywood, K. (2011). *The 2011 horizon report.* The New Media Consortium. http://horizon.unc.edu/HR2011.pdf

Kuh, G. (2008). *High-impact educational practices: What are they? who has access to them? and why they matter.* American Association of Colleges & Universities.

Laurillard, D. (2002). *Rethinking university teaching: A conversational framework for the effective use of learning technologies* (2nd ed.) Routledge.

Linder, K. E., & Hayes, C. M. (Eds.). (2018). *High-impact practices in online education: Research and best practices.* Stylus.

Macmillan Learning. (2018). *Six key principles for learning experience design.* http://prod-catfiles.macmillan.cloud/MediaResources/instructorcatalog/legacy/BFWCatalog/uploadedFiles/Six_Key_Principles_Learning_Experience_Design.pdf

Maderer, J. (2017, January 9). *Jill Watson, round three.* News Center: Georgia Tech. https://www.news.gatech.edu/2017/01/09/jill-watson-round-three

Mallon, M., & Bernsten, S. (2015). Collaborative learning technologies. *Tips and Trends,* Winter, 1–6. https://acrl.ala.org/IS/wpcontent/uploads/2014/05/winter2015.pdf

Martinez-Maldonado, R. (2016, January 11). *Learning analytics and interactive surfaces: A dashboard for enhancing teachers' awareness in the classroom* [Video]. YouTube. https://youtu.be/gJz9Fxnm3lc

Meyer, A., Rose, D. H., & Gordon, D. (2014). *Universal design for learning: Theory and Practice.* CAST Professional Publishing.

Meyers. B. (2018, July 17). Who lives in education deserts? More people than you think. *The Chronicle of Higher Education.* https://www.chronicle.com/interactives/education-deserts

MIT Open Learning. (n.d.) *Research-based learning findings.* https://openlearning.mit.edu/mit-faculty/research-based-learning-findings

Mitchell, T. (2019, March 11). Changing demographics and digital transformation. *EDUCAUSE Review.* https://er.educause.edu/articles/2019/3/changing-demographics-and-digital-transformation

Muller, K., Gradel, K., Deane, S., Forte, M., McCabe, R., Pickett, A. M., Piorkowski, R., Scalzo, K., & Sullivan, R. (2019, October). *Assessing student learning in the online modality* (Occasional Paper No. 40). University of Illinois and Indiana University, National Institute for Learning Outcomes Assessment (NILOA).

National Academies of Sciences, Engineering, and Medicine. (2018). *How people learn II: Learners, contexts, and cultures.* The National Academies Press. https://doi10.17226/24783

Neelakantan, S. (2020, January 2). *Successful AI examples in higher education that can inspire our future. EdTech.* https://edtechmagazine.com/higher/article/2020/01/successful-ai-examples-higher-education-can-inspire-our-future

OERCommons. (n.d.). *Explore. Create. Collaborate.* https://www.oercommons.org

Pacansky-Brock, M. (2019, January 31). Untangling academic transformation through untethered equitable professional development. *EDUCAUSE Review.* https://er.educause.edu/blogs/2019/1/untangling-academic-transformation-through-untethered-equitable-professional-development

Palloff, R. M., & Pratt, K. (2007). *Building online learning communities: Effective strategies for the virtual classroom* (2nd ed.). John Wiley.

Paterson, J. (2019, May 7). *Publisher consolidation continues with Wiley, Cengage and McGraw-Hill Deals. EducationDive.* https://www.educationdive.com/news/publisher-consolidation-continues-with-wiley-cengage-and-mcgraw-hill-deals/554210/

Pugliese, L. (2016, October 17). Adaptive learning systems: Surviving the storm. *EDUCAUSE Review.* https://er.educause.edu/articles/2016/10/adaptive-learning-systems-surviving-the-storm

Purdue News Service. (2009, September 1). *Signals tells students how they are doing even before the test.* https://www.purdue.edu/newsroom/students/2009/090827ArnoldSignals.html

Purdue News Service. (2010, October 11). *Purdue-developed student intervention tech available nationally.* www.purdue.edu/newsroom/general/2010/101011CampbellCourseSigna.html

Quality Matters. (2020). www.qualitymatters.org

Schwartz, N. (2019, April 4).Will artificial intelligence make the college classroom more accessible? *EducationDive.* https://www.educationdive.com/news/will-artificial-intelligence-make-the-college-classroom-more-accessible/551988/

Seaman, J. E., & Seaman, J. (2018). *Freeing the textbook: Educational resources in U.S. higher education, 2018.* Babson Survey Research Group. https://www.onlinelearningsurvey.com/reports/freeingthetextbook2018.pdf

Shedd, K. (2017, September 25). The hero in the ancient near east. *Yale News.* https://news.yale.edu/2017/09/25/students-visit-lost-archaeological-treasure-virtual-reality

Siemens, G. (2011, February 27–March 1).1st International Conference on Learning Analytics and Knowledge (Lak '11), Banff, Alberta, Canada. https://tekri.athabascau.ca/analytics/

Siemens, G. and Baker, R. (2012, April). *Learning analytics: Envisioning a research discipline and a domain of practice.* Learning analytics and educational data mining: Towards communication and collaboration. Proceedings of the International Conference on Learning Analytics and Knowledge (LAK '12). Vancouver British Columbia, Canada. doi.org/10.1145/2330601.2330661

Smarthink.org. (n.d.) *Edulai.* https://smarthink.org/edulai

St. John's University. (2019, April 19). St. John's University students learn with the latest technology. *The Chronicle of Higher Education.* https://www.chronicle.com/paid-article/st-john-s-university-students/243?utm_source=pm&utm_medium=en&cid=pm

Sun Associates. (2001). *Finding the right tool for the task—four categories of technology use.* http://resources.sun-associates.com/categories.html

Thalheimer, W. (2020). *The eLearning manifesto.* https://elearningmanifesto.org

Tingen, J. (November 25, 2019). Kits: Building the NGDLE outside of the LMS. *EDUCAUSE Review.* https://er.educause.edu/blogs/2019/11/kits-building-the-ngdle-outside-the-lms

Tobin, T. (2019, August 12). Taking it way beyond accessibility: 5 + 4 = 1 approach. *EDUCAUSE Review.* https://er.educause.edu/articles/2019/8/taking-it-way-beyond-accessibility-5-4-1-approach

University of Houston, College of Education. (n.d.). *New technologies and 21st-century skills.* http://newtech.coe.uh.edu.

Virtual Learning Leadership Alliance. (2020). https://www.virtuallearningalliance.org

Wan, T. (2020, January 20). Pearson bets on adaptive learning (again) with $25 m acquisition of Smart Sparrow. *EdSurge.* https://www.edsurge.com/news/2020-01-22-pearson-bets-on-adaptive-learning-again-with-25m-acquisition-of-smart-sparrow

Westerheide, F. (2019, November 27). The artificial intelligence industry and global change. *Forbes.* https://www.forbes.com/sites/cognitiveworld/2019/11/27/the-artificial-intlligence-industry-and-global-challenges/#2cbb8b173deb

Woodley, X., Hernandez, C., Parra, J., & Negash, B. (2017). Celebrating difference: Best practices in culturally responsive online teaching. *Tech Trends.* 61, 470–478. https://doi.org/10.1007/s11528-017-0207-z

Woolf, N. (2020, February 10). What research says about giving effective feedback to students. *Inside SEL Research Brief.* https://insidesel.com/2020/02/10/researchbrief-feedback/

World Wide Web Consortium (W3C). (2020). *Making the web accessible.* Web Accessibility Initiative. https://www.w3.org/WAI/fundamentals/

Young, J. R. (2019, March 27). Hoping to spur "learning engineering," Carnegie Mellon will open source its digital learning software. *EdSurge.* https://www.edsurge.com/news/2019-03-27-hoping-to-spur-learning-engineering-carnegie-mellon-will-open-source-its-digital-learning-software

Zimmerman, B. J. (1990). Self-regulated learning and academic achievement: An overview. *Educational Psychologist, 25*(1), 3–17. https://doi.org/10.1207/s15326985ep2501_2

Appendix 1A: Taxonomy of Current and Emerging Learning Technologies

Current Learning Technologies	Definition
Narrative	This type represents the first generation of learning technologies—a linear model largely borrowed from printed texts. Identified by Laurillard (2002), "This describes learning technologies that solely transmit course content or materials, such as videos, lectures, or reading materials, but do not present new or additional information in response to learner actions" (p.126). Although many current learning technologies are designed to transmit course content and there is still room for this type of one-way technology, developments in emerging technologies now make it possible for students to interact with content delivered via narrative modes and for faculty to monitor and address students' patterns of understanding and misunderstanding in real time based on LA built into these modes. **Example: PowerPoint**
Communicative	This type builds community by translating the presence of teacher and students and the sense of community achieved in face-to-face courses into digital learning environments. It promotes lines of communication between faculty and a student or students, between a student and another student, or among a student and others (experts or students) outside a course. **Examples: Discussion Boards and Live Chats integrated into LMSs**
Collaborative	This category extends social interaction into collaboration as an effective means of learning and building knowledge. This is achievable through, for example, document collaboration, class discussions, group conferencing, and project management. **Example: Blackboard Collaborate** (www.blackboard.com/teaching-learning/collaboration-web-conferencing/blackboard-collaborate)

Current Learning Technologies	Definition
Creative/Productive	This type enables students to develop higher-order thinking skills, construct new meaning, or create and represent meaning in new ways, representing authentic performance-based evidence of student learning. This learning technology category was previously called *productive*, referring to a more utilitarian use of tools or resources that enabled students to perform course-based tasks. Examples included search engines; spreadsheets; online lab equipment; or specific software used in a discipline to observe, measure, or calculate. Typically faculty identify in their syllabi the specific online tools students will need to learn how to use to perform course-based tasks. However, when students use these tools on their own to analyze, access information, interpret, or represent their original ideas and produce their own work, they can demonstrate higher-order thinking and creativity. **Example: Tableau** (www.tableau.com)
Tutorial	This type supports learners' needs with preprogrammed lessons or pathways, but it does not have the capability to adapt to each student's individual needs. Commercially developed courseware may embed tutorials into content. Tutorials may also be stand-alone programs that serve as resources in a course to support students' learning, such as providing them additional practice. **Example: APA Style Tutorial, 7th Edition** (https://apastyle.apa.org/instructional-aids/tutorials-webinars)

Taxonomy of Emerging Learning Technologies

Emerging Learning Technologies	Definition
Assistive	This type enables students with disabilities to access course materials and fully participate in an online course or online component of a course, as well as engage with other students beginning on day one. It is largely based on federal accessibility requirements first established in section 508 under the U. S. Workforce Rehabilitation Act of 1973; the Americans with Disabilities Act of 1990; and, more, recently, web content accessibility guidelines developed by the World Wide Web Consortium that specify technical specifications to improve web content (www.w3.org/WAI/).
	Schwartz (2019), associate editor of *Education Dive*, stated that although not all accessibility software is 100% reliable, most are becoming more effective, such as "AI-powered speech-to-text tools" (para. 4). In addition, some existing accessibility software can actually benefit all students, as in the case of software packages that enable students to conduct keyword searches to review lesson transcripts (Schwartz, 2019). There is increased focus on meeting the learning needs of all students by preparing course materials based on principles of Universal Design for Learning and offering students alternative ways to represent their learning (Meyer et al., 2014).
	Example: JAWS Screen Reading Software (freedomscientific.com)

Emerging Learning Technologies	Definition
LA-Based	This type provides teachers and students with technology-enabled real-time assessment results based on software's capability to mine students' performance or behavioral patterns, prompting faculty to assist individual students with uncovering the causes of underperformance patterns, identifying strategies or ways to address those patterns, and self-monitoring progress toward continuous improvement. Digital options such as etextbooks, homework assignments, interactive video presentations, apps, and courseware are increasingly building in LA to engage students in their learning and to enable both faculty and students to monitor students' progress and address patterns of underperformance as they arise or persist. For predictive purposes, LA helps identify students who are likely to face learning challenges in that course, thus alerting faculty to the need to customize support materials and learning resources to enable those students to progress. For formative purposes, LA generates assessment results along the trajectory of a course based on embedded assignments, quizzes, activities, tasks or performances, alerting faculty to the need to continue to work with students to improve patterns. Formative and summative assessment results also become sources of evidence about the efficacy of faculty educational practices, interventions, or required course activities, leading adaptive faculty to make real-time course adjustments, such as in instructional methods or alternative opportunities for students to learn. **Example: HabWorlds** (www.habworlds.org)

(Continues)

Emerging Learning Technologies	Definition
Adaptive Learning-Based	This technology enables individual students to learn based on continuous real-time adjusting or scaffolding of content or feedback to meet each student's level of performance and learning needs. That is, content and support are specifically developed based on LA's diagnostic capability to continuously generate data for an individual student that automatically matches teaching material to the individual needs of the learner (i.e., adaptivity) or helps the learner decide what to do next by recommending different learning entities, "based on their preferences (i.e., adaptability)" (Chatti et al., 2012, p. 5). (Note the distinction among *differentiated, personalized,* and *adaptive* learning technologies discussed earlier in this chapter). Underperformance patterns reported to faculty prompt them to assists students to uncover the causes of these patterns and identify strategies or ways to address those problem areas in order to help individual students. Students should also be encouraged to self-monitor progress toward continuous improvement. Currently, adaptive based–learning technologies are available as platforms on which to build a course, are integrated into some commercial courseware packages, and are integrated into intelligent tutorial systems. **Example: HabWorlds** (www.habworlds.org)

Emerging Learning Technologies	Definition
Intelligent Tutorial	This technology, built on an adaptive learning platform, supports an individual student's learning needs by providing content and resources in response to a student's performance levels based on continuous data collected on each student, including, in some options, adapting to each students' level of engagement. Some systems may also integrate natural language processing algorithms to interact with a student. Some current tutorial platforms may consist only of a set system with preprogrammed lessons or exercises to which students respond; that is, they do not have an adaptive learning-based core that meets the specific needs of an individual student. Intelligent Tutoring represents a category where AI may have the potential to have the most impact.

Example: ALEKS (Assessment and Learning in Knowledge Spaces) (www.Aleks.com) |
| **Immersive Learning Environment** | This type of technology integrates many AI applications, such as those that enable individuals to perform a process or explore an environment, to provide experiential opportunities for students to assume independently or collaboratively a range of first-hand learner roles as narrators, explorers, investigators, problem solvers, critical thinkers, strategists, creators. Immersive learning environments can also provide opportunities for students to apply knowledge and practice a professional skill in a safe environment where feedback is also provided. (See, for example, the range of immersive learning experiences provided dental and medical students in chapter 11) The platforms upon which these environments are built may integrate LA and adaptive learning software that reports students' patterns of performance on faculty and student dashboards so that both parties can respond to patterns of underperformance in real-time within context (e.g., chapter 8).

Example: Yale Course: The Hero in the Ancient Near East (Shedd, 2017) |

(Continues)

Emerging Learning Technologies	Definition
3D Technology	This technology enables students to explore and manipulate items in fictitious or lifelike environments to deepen their understanding of the composition, design, or spatial and functional relationships among an object's components. It also enables them to perform tasks in online learning environments, as in the case of an online lab or in an online problem-solving scenario. To complement a lecture about the structural components of the heart, faculty could ask students to explore a 3D representation of it to develop their deeper understanding of the relationship among the components that might not be as evident in a 2D representation. **Examples: Classteacher** (www.classteacher/com/3Dlearning.php); **Virtual Labs** (www.labster.com)
3D Tools	These enable students to represent their concepts, designs, or creations dimensionally and reveal spatial and functional relationships. **Examples:** **3D Printers** (www.fusion3design.com); **3D Scanners** (www.ysoft.com)
AI-Driven Tools and AI Assistant	This technology simulates human capabilities, such as decision-making, that can be integrated as software tools into digital learning environments. AI assistants are capable of interacting with humans. AI assistants may serve as personalized learning companions in the role of teacher or tutor. AI TAs operate in the same way as a TA in a course; they "provide a teacher professional development resources to support teaching" (Holmes et al., 2019, p. 160). **Example: Edulai** (www.smartthink.org)

Appendix 1B: Rubric for eLearning Tool Evaluation

This rubric has been designed for instructors and staff as a formative tool to evaluate eLearning tools in higher education. *eLearning tools* are defined as any digital technology, mediated through the use of a computing device, deliberately selected to support student learning. The rubric supports a multi-dimensional evaluation of functional, technical, and pedagogical aspects of eLearning Tools.

Instructions

Not all rubric criteria are necessarily applicable to all eLearning tools and those using the rubric are encouraged to assess irrelevant criterion as "not applicable." The rubric does not identify a discrete threshold that an eLearning tool needs to cross before a tool should be used; the rubric is a formative tool intended to offer insight into the relative strengths and weaknesses of an eLearning Tool, as evaluated against a set of criteria.

Category	Criteria	Works Well	Minor Concerns	Serious Concerns	Not applicable
Functionality	Scale	The tool can be scaled to accommodate any size class with the flexibility to create smaller sub-groups or communities of practice	The tool can scaled to accommodate any size class but lacks flexibility to create smaller sub-groups or communities of practice	The tool is restrictive to a limited number of users and cannot be scaled	

(Continues)

Category	Criteria	Works Well	Minor Concerns	Serious Concerns	Not applicable
	Ease of Use	The tool has a user-friendly interface and it is easy for instructors and students to become skillful within a personalized and intuitive manner	The tool has an interface that may be confusing to either instructor or learner; there is limited opportunity for personalization	The interface is not user-friendly for either the instructor or learner; it is cumbersome, unintuitive, rigid, and inflexible	
	Tech Support/ Help Availability	Campus-based technical support and/or help documentation is readily available and aids users in troubleshooting tasks or solving problems experienced; or, the tool provider offers a robust support platform	Technical support and/ or help documentation is available but limited, incomplete, or not user-friendly	Technological support and/or help documentation is not available	
	Hypermediality	The tool allows users to communicate through different channels (audio, visual, textual) and allows for non-sequential, flexible/ adaptive engagement with material	The tool allows users to communicate through different channels (audio, visual, textual) but is limited in its ability to provide nonsequential, flexible/adaptive engagement with material	The tool is restrictive in terms of the communication channels employed (audio, visual, textual) and presents information sequentially in a rigid, inflexible format	

Category	Criteria	Works Well	Minor Concerns	Serious Concerns	Not applicable
Accessibility	Accessibility Standards	The tool meets accessibility guidelines (e.g., local accessibility legislation and/or W3C WCAG 2.0 standards)	The tool has some limited capacity to meet accessibility guidelines	The tool fails to meet accessibility guidelines or no information of compliance has been made available for the tool	
	User-Focused Participation	The tool is designed to address the needs of diverse users, their various literacies, and capabilities, thereby widening opportunities for participation in learning	The tool has some limited capacity to address the needs of diverse users, their various literacies, and capabilities	The tool is restrictive in meeting the diversity of needs reflective in the student body; the tool likely restricts some learners from fully participating	
	Required Equipment	Proper use of the tool does not require equipment beyond what is typically available to instructors and students (computer with built-in speakers and microphone, internet connection, etc.)	Proper use of the tool requires specialized equipment (e.g. unique device) that likely requires purchase at a low cost	Proper use of the tool requires specialized equipment requiring moderate to significant financial investment	

(Continues)

Category	Criteria	Works Well	Minor Concerns	Serious Concerns	Not applicable
	Cost of Use	All aspects of the tool can be used free of charge	Limited aspects of the tool can be used for free with other elements requiring payment of a fee, membership, or subscription	Use of the tool requires a fee, membership, or subscription; or use of the tool requires a purchase that is likely to pose a financial burden on students (exceeding $50 for a single half term course)	
Technical	Integration/ Embedding Within a Learning Management System (LMS)	The tool can be embedded (as an object via HTML code) or fully integrated (e.g., LTI-compliant tools) into an LMS while maintaining full functionality of the tool	The tool can be embedded within an LMS, perhaps with limited functionality, but cannot be fully integrated	The tool can be accessed only in an LMS through a hyperlink or static representations of the tool (e.g., file export), rather than a functional version of the tool itself	
	Desktop/Laptop Operating Systems	Users can effectively use the tool with any standard, up-to-date operating system	Users may encounter limited or altered functionality depending on the up-to-date operating system being used	Users are limited to using the tool with one specific, up-to-date operating system	

Category	Criteria	Works Well	Minor Concerns	Serious Concerns	Not applicable
	Browser	Users can effectively use the tool with any standard, up-to-date browser	Users may encounter limited or altered functionality depending on the up-to-date browser being used	Users are limited to using the tool through one specific browser	
	Additional Downloads	Users do not need to download additional software or browser extensions	The tool uses a browser extension or software that requires a download and/or user permission to run	The tool requires a past or version of a browser extension or software	
Mobile Design	Access	The tool can be accessed through either the download of an app or via a mobile browser, regardless of the mobile operating system and device; design of the mobile tool fully takes into consideration the constraints of a smaller-sized screen	The tool offers an app, but for only a limited set of mobile operating systems; tool is not accessible through a mobile browser; design of the mobile tool constrained by the limitations of the mobile device	Access to the tool is limited or absent on a mobile device	

(Continues)

Category	Criteria	Works Well	Minor Concerns	Serious Concerns	Not applicable
	Functionality	There is little to no functional difference between the mobile and the desktop version, regardless of the device used to access it; no difference in functionality between apps designed for different mobile operating systems	Core features of the main tool are functional on the mobile app but advanced features are limited; some difference in functionality between apps designed for different mobile operating systems, but has limited impact on learners' use of the tool	The mobile app functions poorly such that core features are not reliable or non-existent; significant difference in functionality depending on the mobile device's operating system used to access the tool	
	Offline Access	Offers an offline mode: Core features of the tool can be accessed and used even when offline, maintaining functionality and content	Offers a kind of offline mode, where the tool can be used offline but core functionality and content are affected	The mobile platform cannot be used in any capacity offline	

Category	Criteria	Works Well	Minor Concerns	Serious Concerns	Not applicable
Privacy, Data Protection, and Rights	Sign Up/Sign In	Use of the tool does not require the creation of an external account or additional login, such that no personal user information is collected and shared	Either instructors are the only users required to provide personal information to set up an account; or the tool has been vetted through appropriate channels to ensure strict adherence to local, institutional, or personal policies/ standards for protecting the collection and use of student personal data by a third party group	All users (instructors and learners) must provide personal information to a third party in creating an account, and there is some question or concern of the adherence to local, institutional, or personal policies/ standards for protecting the collection and use of such data by the third party group	
	Data Privacy and Ownership	Users maintain ownership and copyright of their intellectual property/data; the user can keep data private and decide if / how data is to be shared	Users maintain ownership and copyright of their intellectual property/data; data is shared publically and cannot be made private	Users forfeit ownership and copyright of data; data is shared publically and cannot be made private, or no details provided	

(Continues)

Category	Criteria	Works Well	Minor Concerns	Serious Concerns	Not applicable
Social Presence	Archiving, Saving, and Exporting Data	Users can archive, save, or import and export content or activity data in a variety of formats	There are limitations to archiving, saving, or importing/exporting content or activity data	Content and activity data cannot be archived, saved, or imported/exported	
	Collaboration	The tool has the capacity to support a community of learning through both asynchronous and synchronous opportunities for communication, interactivity, and transfer of meaning between users	The tool has the capacity to support a community of learning through asynchronous but not synchronous opportunities for communication, interactivity, and transfer of meaning between users	Communication, interactivity, and transfer of meaning between users is not supported or significantly limited	
	User Accountability	Instructors can control learner anonymity; the tool provides technical solutions for holding learners accountable for their actions	Instructors cannot control learner anonymity, but the tool provides some solution for holding learners accountable for their actions	Instructors cannot control learner anonymity, and there is no technical solution for holding users accountable to their actions	

Category	Criteria	Works Well	Minor Concerns	Serious Concerns	Not applicable
	Diffusion	The tool is widely known and popular; it's likely that most learners are familiar with the tool and have basic technical competence with it	Learners' familiarity with the tool is likely mixed; some will lack basic technical competence with its functions	The tool is not well known/foreign; it is likely that learners are not familiar with the tool and lack basic technical competence with its functions	
Teaching Presence	Facilitation	The tool has easy-to-use features that would significantly improve an instructor's ability to be present with learners via active management, monitoring, engagement, and feedback	The tool has limited functionality to effectively support an instructor's ability to be present with learners via active management, monitoring, engagement, and feedback	The tool has not been designed to support an instructor's ability to be present with learners via active management, monitoring, engagement, and feedback	
	Customization	Tool is adaptable to its environment: easily customized to suit the classroom context and targeted learning outcomes	Limited aspects of the tool can be customized to suit the classroom context and learning outcomes	The tool cannot be customized	

(Continues)

Category	Criteria	Works Well	Minor Concerns	Serious Concerns	Not applicable
	Learning Analytics	Instructor can monitor learners' performance on a variety of responsive measures; these measures can be accessed through a user-friendly dashboard	Instructor can monitor learners' performance on limited measures; or data is not presented in a format that is easily interpreted	The tool does not support the collection of learning analytics	
Cognitive Presence	Enhancement of Cognitive Task(s)	The tool enhances engagement in targeted cognitive task(s) that were once overly complex or inconceivable through other means	The tool enables functional improvement to engagement in the targeted cognitive task(s)	The tool acts as a direct tool substitute with no functional change to engagement in the targeted cognitive task(s)	
	Higher-Order Thinking	Use of the tool easily facilitates learners to exercise higher-order thinking skills (given consideration to design, facilitation, and direction from instructor)	The tool may engage learners in higher-order thinking skills (given significant consideration to design, facilitation, and direction from instructor)	The tool likely does not engage learners in higher-order thinking skills (despite significant consideration to design, facilitation, and direction from instructor)	

Category	*Criteria*	*Works Well*	*Minor Concerns*	*Serious Concerns*	*Not applicable*
	Metacognitive Engagement	Through the tool, learners can regularly receive formative feedback on learning (i.e., they can track their performance, monitor their improvement, test their knowledge)	Opportunities for receiving formative feedback on learning are available, but infrequent or limited (i.e., poor opportunities for tracking performance, monitoring, testing improvement, testing knowledge on a regular basis)	There are no opportunities for formative feedback on learning (i.e., lacking opportunities for tracking performance, monitoring improvement, testing knowledge on a regular basis)	

Appendix 1C: Additional Resources

Learning Technology Sites or Resources Referenced in Chapter 1

The following is a compilation of resources, tools, groups, and initiatives that are advancing the field of learning technology. Visit these sites for more information about some of the examples listed in this chapter and for deeper discussion of some topics discussed.

3D printer. www.fusion3design.com

3D scanner. www.ysoft.com

Adobe Connect. www.adobe.com/products/adobeconnect.html

ALEKS (Assessment and Learning in Knowledge Spaces). www.Aleks.com

APA Style Tutorial. 7th Edition. https://apastyle.apa.org/instructional-aids/tutorials-webinars

Blackboard Collaborate. www.blackboard.com/teaching-learning/collaboration-web-conferencing/blackboard-collaborate

Classteacher. www.classteacher/com/3Dlearning.php

The Courseware in Context Framework (CWiC). www.coursewareincontext.org

The Courseware in Context (CWiC). Learn Platform. www.cwic.learnplatform.com

Edulai. www.smartthink.org

Empirical Educator Project. (n.d.) http://empiricaleducators.net/about/

Every Learner Everywhere. (2018). *About us.* www.everylearnereverywhere.org/about

HabWorlds. www.habworlds.org

Inspark Network. www.inspark.education

JAWS. (n.d.). *JAWS.* freedomscientific.com

Kaptivo. https://kaptivo.com/kaptivo-overview/

MIT Openlearning. Research-based Learning Findings. https://openlearning.mit.edu/mit-faculty/research-based-learning-findings

OERCommons. https://www.oercommons.org

ProctorU. www.proctoru.com

Poll Everywhere. www.polleverywhere.com

Smart Sparrow. www.smartsparrow.com

Tableau. www.tableau.com

Upswing. www.upswing.io

Virtual Labs. www.labster.com

Virtual Speech. https://virtualspeech.com/courses/

World Wide Web Consortium: www.w3.org/WAI/

2

THE LEARNING SCIENCES AND EDUCATIONAL TECHNOLOGY

Kristen DiCerbo and Daniel Belenky

W̲e live in an era of remarkable change brought about by the pervasive use of new technologies. Our laptops, phones, and tablets help us extend and communicate with our social network through text, voice, and video; entertain ourselves and others; and manage our daily errands. For many of us, network-enabled digital devices are part of the fabric of our lives, and memories of life before the internet, mobile phones, and smart devices are either fading away or never existed.

Although this change has been slower to come to education, more recently it has been dramatically accelerated by the necessity of remote learning solutions in response to world events. In many places where technology has been implemented, it is a simple digital analogue of the paper-and-pencil experience, just replicating the print experience on the computer. For example, an online homework system might take a traditional problem set and transfer it, as-is, into the digital environment. This might allow for faster student feedback, but it otherwise ignores the new capabilities of technology that can change the experience of learners. Similarly, moving a lecture to video conferencing technology and delivering it in the same way as an in-person lecture does not take advantage of interactive and small group breakout features that the software may allow. On the other side of the spectrum, there are those, many of whom come from the technology industry, who have grand visions of how technology will change education but often little understanding of how it should be used to promote learning. This results in

The authors wish to acknowledge the input of Ross Metusalem in framing and developing some of the ideas in this chapter.

the proliferation of things like interactive whiteboards in classrooms without plans for what should be done on them. More recently, we frequently see advocacy of virtual reality solutions without explanation of what they can provide to foster learning that our current tools cannot.

This divide—between those who focus on learning with less optimism about technology and those who focus on technology with less understanding of learning—can be seen in conversations around *personalized learning.* One promise of technology is to "personalize" learning, or to create more individualized learning experiences. Attend educational technology start-up conferences and you will hear how artificial intelligence and machine learning will allow computers to present students with exactly the right content at the right time based on students' proficiencies, interests, goals, and study habits. Ask a group of teachers and school administrators at an online learning conference what *personalized learning* means and you will hear responses about student agency with no mention at all of technology.

In reality, personalized learning is not technology-driven learning, nor is it giving students unfettered choice. Personalized learning is developing more individual learning experiences for students within a system of multiple, interacting people and tools. To understand personalized learning, we must understand learning by the individual as the result of interactions with the interlocking and interdependent elements of the entire education system. We need to understand how interactions of students with teachers and technology create new rules and change roles and responsibilities in the system. In addition, these interactions will not be uniformly consistent but will vary based on the individuals actually in the system. The way students interact with technology tools will depend heavily on the teacher in the classroom. That sounds obvious, but too often the educational technology community appears to envision individual students working away at individual computers in isolation. Similarly, students interacting with technology will change the ways they interact with teachers, which is often summarily described (e.g., a move to being the "guide on the side") but seldom deeply explored. Finally, the ways that technology and people interact can change over time, as technology develops and people's values and beliefs about technology change.

Although technology is constantly evolving and systems are complex, there are decades of research studies confirming and refining what we know about learning, memory, and attention. For example, practice testing (i.e., attempts to retrieve information; such as, flash cards, quizzing oneself); spaced practice, where students review or recall content or concepts or practice solving problems across weeks or months in contrast to focused, one-off drill exercises; and elaboration have been shown to significantly improve the ability to store and retrieve new information (see Pashler et al., 2007). Researchers have identified effective methods by which to manage and regulate attention and moderate memory load (Mayer, 2014). The primary challenge for designers of digital learning experiences is not how to create complex algorithms or visually appealing environments, but how to instantiate what we know from learning sciences research into the design of educational technology, as well as use technology to find new ways to promote good learning practice. For example, knowing that learners will remember more if they frequently recall information from memory rather than simply reread material, how might we design a digital environment that encourages such recall opportunities?

This chapter will review three concepts from educational research and demonstrate how they can be used to design effective digital learning experiences. First, we will look at the use of principled assessment design to help ensure that engaging digital assessment tasks actually produce evidence of the knowledge and skills we want to assess. Second, we will review the research on effective feedback, delving into ways technology can help improve its delivery. Third, we will discuss the principles of metacognition known to improve learning outcomes and provide examples of how digital experiences can be designed to encourage students to plan, monitor, and reflect on their learning. In each case, we will begin with key learning principles and lead into the design of digital environments using these principles.

Principled Assessment Design

In a broad definition, *assessment* is the generation of evidence to make inferences about learners' knowledge, skills, and attributes. In traditional multiple choice assessment, this evidence is the correctness of the selected response. However, these activities (e.g., answering multiple choice questions) are relatively far from the real world tasks we want learners to be able to do. The alternative to traditional assessment items is to have learners engage in performance-based assessment, where they engage in more authentic activity. Although educators can create these performance-based assessments, they often take significant time to grade, and it can be difficult to grade them fairly across many students or across multiple graders (in the case of teaching assistants). In addition, it can take a long time to provide students with feedback when performance assessments must be hand scored. Technology provides us with opportunities to present more authentic tasks by simulating the real world and the possibility of more automated scoring of performance assessment. However, it is not the case that we can just collect every click a student makes in a digital environment and expect to make valid inferences about students' proficiency. It takes careful planning to create a technology-based assessment activity that assesses the intended knowledge and skills.

Principled assessment design refers to a broad family of frameworks or approaches to designing assessments with the goal of linking constructs of interest, to tasks, to evidence; common frameworks include evidence-centered design (ECD) (Riconscente et al., 2015), assessment engineering (Luecht, 2013), and construct modeling (Wilson, 2004). These approaches have been described in depth elsewhere, including what they share in common (Ferrara et al., 2017), and it is not the purpose of this chapter to explore these different approaches. However, at their core, they all seek to do the following:

- Define the knowledge, skills, and other attributes you want to measure in learners
- Identify the types of evidence you need to collect to make inferences about those things
- Create assessment activities that will elicit those kinds of evidence

ECD is probably the most widely used principled design approach and refers to these elements as the *student model, evidence model*, and *task model*, respectively. Using a principled design approach allows us to create more complex performance-based assessments by providing a framework with which to intentionally design the experience.

Principled approaches rely on the learning sciences in the definitions of models. To begin, the development of the student model often relies on research on learning progressions, or descriptions of how learners progress from novice to expert levels of understanding in a given domain. For example, students might learn the concept of geometric measurement of area first by counting unit squares and then by applying the formula as a short cut for counting. In addition, they learn area, a two-dimensional measure, before volume, a three-dimensional measure. These progressions help define what skills an assessment is meant to measure.

A simulation-based science assessment is an example of ECD in action. Educators teaching science aim to improve both learners' conceptual understanding of scientific principles and the practice of science. To create a simulation-based assessment, first, the knowledge and skills to be measured must be defined. In this case, the knowledge that needs to be measured is a student's ability to demonstrate understanding of Newton's first law of motion (science knowledge), and the skill that needs to be measured is a student's ability to use a control of variables strategy when designing experiments (only manipulating one variable between trials, a science practice). This is the student model. The next step is to determine what kinds of evidence would indicate a learners' proficiency with this knowledge and these skills. Newton's first law states that an object's velocity will not change unless it is acted upon by an outside force. So, evidence that students understand this principle might include making correct predictions about what will happen to an object's velocity under various conditions or explaining why a moving vehicle eventually stops if it isn't given more gas. Evidence of a student's control of variables would be observing whether that student varies one or more variables across trials in an experiment. Knowing what evidence we are looking for, we can design a digital activity that will elicit this evidence. For example, we might create a simulation with a truck that can be launched with varying degrees of force, with varying mass and friction. Learners can be asked to make predictions about what will happen with different levels of friction and then run an experiment to test their prediction. In a digital world, we can capture not only their prediction but also how they set up each trial of the experiment. The ability to capture this process data, or information about how the student set up the experiment, rather than just their final answer, allows us to make far more detailed inferences about learner knowledge and skill. In addition, we can assess multiple skills with the same activity. These are the advantages technology can bring if we also integrate careful research and design into it.

Rather than merely replicating our traditional notions of assessment and moving our pencil-and-paper tests directly online, we should consider the possibilities that technology creates for new thinking about assessment. The ability to capture data from learner activity allows us to gain more insight into how students solve problems, rather than just evaluate the correctness of their final answer. Evidence in the digital world might include not only correctness but also strategy employed, sequence of steps, and number of attempts made. However, without a planful approach to design, we often end up with interesting and engaging activities that do not actually elicit knowledge about the skills we are interested in assessing. Principled assessment design provides a framework to ensure assessment activities produce evidence that allows us to make inferences about the knowledge and skills we are interested in assessing.

Feedback

Educators and researchers have long acknowledged the benefits of providing formative feedback to learners. Even a small comment, correction, or hint delivered at the right time and in the right way has potential to change the course of learning fundamentally. This is commonly appreciated, as is the fact that providing feedback takes time—sometimes, a lot of time. Time constraints impose limits on the amount of feedback even the most devoted teacher can provide and on how quickly they can provide it. Digital technologies offer a promising solution. A well-designed digital learning tool, such as an online homework platform, can track learners' behaviors and responses and provide feedback in real time, with a granularity and immediacy that would not be possible otherwise. For example, when a learner makes a mistake or gets stuck on an individual step in a homework problem, a digital tool can immediately provide additional information such as a hint or a correction on that specific step, enabling the learner to identify the problem and take corrective action right then, while that student is still engaged with the problem. Of course, considering this a boon to learning assumes that the digital technology provides feedback *effectively*. Fortunately, the designs of feedback mechanisms in educational technology can and do draw on decades of learning sciences' research on effective feedback practices, both generally and in the context of digital technologies.

This section specifically focuses on *formative feedback*, which can be considered as information that is provided in response to a learner's performance on some task and is intended to guide further learning. In practice, formative feedback (henceforth "feedback") can take many forms, from an explicit correction on a homework assignment to a teacher's expression when a student makes a contribution to a class discussion. It can be provided by a teacher; a peer; an external resource (e.g., a book); or, as is the focus here, a piece of digital technology. Feedback can provide numerous learning benefits, depending on its specific content and delivery (more on this in a moment). A primary benefit of effective feedback is making clear to learners the gap between their current performance and desired performance. This can support learners' metacognitive reflection on their learning progress and ways of improving (Nicol & Macfarlane-Dick, 2006). Feedback also has the potential to reduce cognitive load—the amount of information a learner attempts to process cognitively at one time—by, for example, directing learners' attention to important information (Moreno, 2004). Certain feedback content also has potential to improve learners' motivation by, for example, fostering self-efficacy (Schunk, 1982; Schunk & Cox, 1986).

Decades of research on feedback have revealed many practices that make feedback more (or less) effective. Shute (2008) provided a helpful overview of this research, identifying over 30 evidence-based guidelines for effective feedback provision. These included the following:

- Provide elaborated feedback (i.e., feedback that provides explanation beyond response accuracy) that focuses on the learners' task performance and how it compares to desired performance.

- Avoid normative comparisons, praise, and discouragement.
- Promote positive orientations toward learning.
- Provide immediate feedback on tasks that are difficult for a learner, but delayed feedback for tasks that are simple for a learner.
- Provide low-achieving learners with more explicit correction and scaffolding than high-achieving learners, who may benefit more from facilitative feedback such as hints.

In particular, research has found that elaborated feedback helps learners have a better sense for what concrete next steps they can take to correct their mistakes and avoid them in the future (see Van der Kleij et al., 2015). One powerful approach that learning technologies have explored is wrong-answer specific feedback, so when students make particular errors indicative of a common misconception or difficulty, they can receive feedback that specifically addresses it. For example, Cybertutor, an intelligent tutoring system for physics (Morote & Pritchard, 2009), included specific hints about and responses to particular errors students made, something many current-generation educational systems provide, across a wide variety of topics.

When feedback is framed as part of a growth-oriented development process, focusing more on improvement than on performance, students are more likely to persist and achieve more (Paunesku, 2013). In addition, systems that take into account how far along a learning process the learner is can be more effective, withholding or providing only high-level feedback to students who have already developed some mastery of the material, but providing immediate and highly scaffolded feedback to learners who are just starting out and may feel lost otherwise (see Shute, 2008).

Most educational technology systems that provide feedback do so on discrete tasks that have a small set of expected responses, whether those are quantitative problems (e.g., chemistry, math), or multiple-choice or short-answer questions testing for recall of important information. Increasingly, however, systems are able to provide feedback on more complex behaviors, such as writing or using inquiry skills. By using ECD practices (like those described earlier), designers of these systems can offer students fine-grained feedback on the development of more complex skills. For example, Inq-ITS (see Gobert et al., 2013) is an intelligent tutoring system that monitors student actions in a variety of open-ended science tasks and subsequently generates a model of student proficiency on a number of subskills relating to scientific inquiry. In addition, the system can use this information to provide feedback during student engagement, resulting in a positive impact on outcomes (Li et al., 2018). For example, it can inform learners that an experiment they designed was correct in that it varied only one variable at a time, but that the variable examined did not address directly their stated hypothesis.

Metacognition and Self-Regulated Learning

Learners are not passive agents in academic environments. In particular, learners who succeed in their academic tasks are actively managing their own learning process by regulating their own behaviors, goals, motivations, strategies, and environment, among other factors. Research on this process of "self-regulated learning" (see Puustinen & Pulkkinen, 2001; Schunk & Greene, 2017) has documented a number of particular processes that contribute to student success. Although different theories and researchers posit slight variations in these processes, in general these models describe a cycle of planning one's activities, monitoring during the execution of the activity, and reflecting on one's learning and performance (Panadero, 2017). These kinds of behaviors are particularly critical when students are using learning technologies, as they are frequently using them by themselves and are fully responsible for managing their own progress (particularly in the case of online-only courses or massive open online courses [MOOCs]).

In particular, *planning* involves considering what the activity is asking the learner to do, using appropriate prior knowledge and experience to pick strategies and approaches that are likely to be effective, and creating a plan for how to go through the activity. *Monitoring* encompasses behaviors like thinking about which step one is on and how it relates to the others, asking self-check questions to ensure that one is on the right track, and changing strategies and approaches adaptively in light of one's judgements. Having completed the activity, a learner can then *reflect* on the alignment between one's expectations and the actual outcome, or on the effectiveness of particular strategies used, or compare approaches that worked for this activity to times when it wasn't as effective.

As noted previously, research on these processes tends to focus on the kinds of behaviors associated with student success. Said differently, self-regulated behaviors are generally the sorts of things that successful students engage in on their own. A significant body of research has examined how to help support all learners to engage in these behaviors, either through direct instruction on these processes or through careful design of learning environments that scaffold these behaviors. For example, Zepeda et al. (2015) taught students explicit strategies and prompts for planning, monitoring, and reflecting on their performance, and found that students could successfully adopt these approaches. In addition, they found that receiving this training led to improvements in motivation and performance on assessments of content knowledge and even better performance on a novel activity that assessed self-guided learning.

As students complete more of their learning activities in digital environments, these kinds of training can be integrated, on an as-needed basis, into the learning experience. One specific case involves using the data generated by student usage of learning platforms to reveal what strategies students use and how those are associated with different outcomes (as discussed earlier, this is most effective when created using ECD). A number of researchers, as well as educational technology companies, have developed so-called early alert systems that use large data sets from prior semesters to predict which students are at risk of dropping out or performing poorly in the course. Identifying that a student may be "at-risk" presents an opportunity to help that learner become more successful in regulating her own learning. For example, Bernacki et al. (2020) tested an approach where at-risk students received an email that provided a link to additional "Learning to Learn" resources, and found that those who used those resources performed better throughout the rest of the semester than those that did not.

A number of studies have specifically looked at how to support some or all of these self-regulated learning behaviors in digital learning environments. For example, MetaTutor (e.g., Azevedo, 2008; Azevedo et al., 2009) is a multimedia tool that helps teach complex science while also supporting the development of self-regulated learning (SRL) skills. Specifically, it models SRL processes, helps learners choose appropriate usage of SRL strategies, and then tracks student behaviors in a hypermedia learning environment for evidence of specific SRL behaviors (or their absence). As one example, if a learner is spending a long time analyzing a diagram that is not aligned to the current learning goal, an "agent" will pop up to ask the student if the student thinks it is relevant and then begin a dialogue about the student's response. Across more than a decade of research, the tool has been used to measure students' SRL behaviors (Bouchet et al., 2013) and scaffold improvements in SRL (Bouchet et al., 2016). Similarly, gStudy (Winne et al., 2005) and its updated version, nStudy (Winne & Hadwin, 2013), have a number of tools and ways of representing student behaviors back to the learner that can help learners overcome a number of challenges that might otherwise impede the use of SRL strategies. Another line of research has examined the Help Tutor (Roll et al., 2007, 2011), which was developed as an additional support in an existing intelligent tutoring system, with the goal of scaffolding not only student learning but also student help-seeking behaviors in the system, such as when to ask for a hint or how to proceed productively after using a hint.

In all of these cases, it is important to note that although using specially designed tools can support improved SRL strategies and behaviors in a given learning experience, the goals for all of these systems are to help learners develop generalizable skills that will transfer to other contexts. Roll et al. (2011), for example, tested how using the Help Tutor and receiving related training on SRL skills effectively prepared students to seek hints in other contexts when the Help Tutor was no longer in use, and also led to students' improved achievement of learning outcomes. As adoption of these kinds of tools increases, it will be important to consider ways of helping support that transition, from scaffolding and training in learning technologies to transferable skills that are used across learning contexts. As these technologies continue to evolve, they will continue to improve in how personalized they can make the supports an individual student receives. For example, students who are actively using productive learning strategies may actually be hampered when technologies intrude to provide a hint of what to focus on (Belenky & Nokes, 2009), and different students may benefit from particular sequences of activities to help build up their ability to self-regulate.

Adopting New Educational Technology

Despite the relatively long history of the research discussed previously, there are still many places where technology gets ahead of the learning sciences. One example of this can be found in the augmented reality (AR) and virtual reality (VR) space. There is a lack of clear, uniform understanding about the pedagogies that support virtual reality. Mikropoulos and Natsis (2011) surveyed over 50 papers between 1999 and 2009 that used virtual reality as a digital learning environment. Very few studies had a clear theoretical or pedagogical model in mind in their discussions of virtual learning environments.

Across implementations of AR and VR, it is not clear what learning need the technology is addressing that current learning environments do not. In the literature, it is difficult to identify indicators of improved student learning outcomes through a virtual reality environment. Three meta-analyses suggest that the instructional effectiveness of learning in a virtual reality environment is ambiguous (Lee, 1999; Sitzmann, 2011; Vogel et al., 2006). In addition, very few studies exist that discuss the effectiveness of virtual reality-based instruction on learning transfer from a virtual environment to the real world (Bossard et al., 2008). It may be that with more research and experimentation, uses that allow for active and collaborative learning beyond what exists now will be found. A recent paper suggested a more thoughtful approach to design and implementation of VR, including specification of the sequence of learning activities in a lesson, identification of the pedagogical practices to be employed, and an analysis of the strengths and constraints of VR that will determine its fit in the overall instruction (Cheng et al., 2018). It is these more thoughtful approaches that are more likely to lead to successful implementation of all kinds of new technology.

When deciding how to best approach adopting new technologies, it is important to consider what particular instructional challenges one is hoping the technology can improve and then identify ways in which particular technologies can potentially address those (see Belenky, 2019). Pedagogy should drive technology, rather than the opposite. We have decades of research that tell us what makes good learning, including assessments aligned to instruction that inform instruction, clear, actionable, immediate feedback, and opportunities to help learners become stewards of their own learning. Technology can help support each of these. In addition, it is important to make sure that the technology follows other baseline principles for effectively impacting learner outcomes, such as the following:

- Focus on clearly defined knowledge and skills (e.g., has learning objectives and minimizes distractions)
- Allow learners to construct meaning and demonstrate relevance (e.g., moves beyond passive learning)
- Provide timely, actionable feedback (e.g., descriptions of how to improve)
- Align with how memory works (e.g., avoids cognitive overload)

It is often instructive to keep the Gartner hype cycle (Figure 2.1) in mind when considering new educational technology. Although Gartner applies this cycle to all kinds of technology outside the sphere of education, those who have been in the education world will recognize the stages. New technology comes out and there are breathless reviews of how it will disrupt the classroom. Over a period of time, it becomes apparent that those promises will not be met, and the technology can be almost completely dismissed. However, with some technologies there is more careful research, study, and design that lead to implementation of technology in more thoughtful ways to support teaching and learning.

Concluding Thoughts

Technology can do more than duplicate existing print activities and practices, and we as educators should be looking at how it allows us to do things

Figure 2.1. Gartner hype cycle.

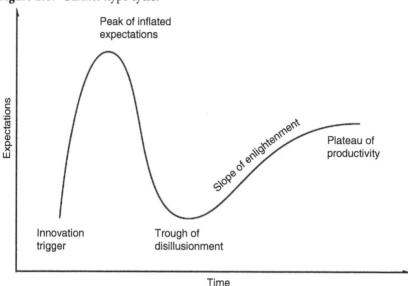

Note. Used with permission from Gartner (2020).

we could not do with print. In particular, digital learning activities should not look like paper-and-pencil activities on a computer screen. Rather, we should be looking at how technology can solve problems we have in our existing classrooms through new and different solutions. For example, many are concerned that our existing assessments do not allow students to demonstrate the skills they have learned as they would in the real world. If we look at what technology has to offer, we see that digital simulation–based assessments often allow learners to engage in more authentic activity, and gathering data from learner interactions might provide us a better understanding about how learners will use knowledge and skills in the real world. The conversation about this does not need to start with "Look at these cool simulations; what are they good for?" but with "We don't feel our current assessments accurately assesses the real world skills we want our students to learn. Can technology help us?"

In this chapter you have read examples of how the science of assessment design helps us build better, more authentic assessment with technology; how education research combined with technology helps us improve the ways students receive feedback; and how research on metacognition leads to technology solutions that help students become stewards of their own learning.

With these thoughtful approaches as guiding examples, the learning sciences can help build digital experiences that improve learner outcomes.

References

Azevedo, R. (2008). The role of self-regulation in learning about science with hyper-media. In D. Robinson & G. Schraw (Eds.), *Recent innovations in educational technology that facilitate student learning* (pp. 127–156). Information Age Publishing.

Azevedo, R., Witherspoon, A., Chauncey, A., Burkett, C., & Fike, A. (2009). MetaTutor: A metacognitive tool for enhancing self-regulated learning. In R. Pirrone, R. Azevedo, & G. Biswas (Eds.), *Proceedings of the AAAI fall symposium on cognitive and metacognitive educational systems* (pp. 14–19). Association for the Advancement of Artificial Intelligence (AAAI) Press.

Belenky, D. M. (2019). *Beyond the hype: Digital learning based on learning science.* Pearson. https://www.pearson.com/content/dam/one-dot-com/one-dot-com/global/Files/efficacy-and-research/reports/pearson-beyond-the-hype.pdf

Belenky, D. M., & Nokes, T. J. (2009). Examining the role of manipulatives and metacognition on engagement, learning, and transfer. *The Journal of Problem Solving, 2*(2), 102–129. https://doi.org/10.7771/1932-6246.1061

Bernacki, M. L., Vosicka, L. & Utz. J. (2020). Can brief, web-delivered training help STEM undergraduates "learn to learn"? *Journal of Educational Psychology 112*(4), 765–781. https://doi.org/10.1037/edu0000405

Bossard, C., Kermarrec, G., Buche, C., & Tisseau, J. (2008). Transfer of learning in virtual environments: A new challenge? *Virtual Reality, 12,* 151–161. https://doi.org/10.1007/s10055-008-0093-y

Bouchet, F., Harley, J. M., & Azevedo, R. (2016). Can adaptive pedagogical agents' prompting strategies improve students' learning and self-regulation? In A. Micarelli, J. Stamper, & K. Panourgia (Eds.), *International conference on intelligent tutoring systems* (pp. 368–374). Springer. https://doi.org/10.1007/978-3-319-39583-8_43

Bouchet, F., Harley, J. M., Trevors, G. J., & Azevedo, R. (2013). Clustering and profiling students according to their interactions with an intelligent tutoring system fostering self-regulated learning. *Journal of Educational Data Mining, 5*(1), 104–146. https://doi.org/10.5281/zenodo.3554613

Cheng, B. H., D'Angelo, C. M., Zaner, S., Kam, M., & Hamada, R. A. (2018). Teaching and learning using virtual reality: Identifying and examining two design principles of effective instruction. In J. Kay & R. Luckin (Eds.), *Proceedings of the 13th international conference of the learning sciences* (pp. 1687–1688). International Society of the Learning Sciences. https://doi.dx.org/10.22318/cscl2018.1687

Ferrara, S., Lai, E., Reilly, A., Nichols, P. D., Rupp, A. A., & Leighton, J. P. (2017). Principled approaches to assessment design, development, and implementation. In A. A. Rupp & J. P Leighton (Eds.) *The handbook of cognition and assessment* (pp. 41–74). Wiley. https://doi.org/10.1002/9781118956588.ch3

Gartner. (2020). *Gartner Hype Cycle.* https://www.gartner.com/en/research/methodologies/gartner-hype-cycle

Gobert, J. D., Sao Pedro, M., Raziuddin, J., & Baker, R. S. (2013). From log files to assessment metrics: Measuring students' science inquiry skills using educational data mining. *Journal of the Learning Sciences, 22*(4), 521–563. https://doi.org/10.1080/10508406.2013.837391

Lee, J. (1999). Effectiveness of computer-based instructional simulation: A meta-analysis. *International Journal of Instructional Media, 26*(1), 71–85. https://www.learntechlib.org/p/85364/

Li, H., Gobert, J., Dickler, R., & Moussavi, R. (2018). The impact of multiple real-time scaffolding experiences on science inquiry practices. In R. Nkambou, R. Azevedo, & J. Vassileva (Eds.), *International conference on intelligent tutoring systems* (pp. 99–109). Springer. https://doi.org/10.1007/978-3-319-91464-0_10

Luecht, R. M. (2013). An introduction to assessment engineering for automatic item generation. In M. J. Gierl & T. M. Haladyna (Eds.), *Automatic item generation: Theory and practice* (pp. 59–76). Routledge. https://doi.org/10.4324/9780203803912

Mayer, R.E. (Ed.). (2014). *The Cambridge handbook of multimedia learning.* Cambridge University Press. https://doi.org/10.1017/cbo9781139547369

Mikropoulos, T. A., & Natsis, A. (2011). Educational virtual environments: A ten-year review of empirical research (1999–2009). *Computers & Education, 56*(3), 769–780. https://doi.org/10.1016/j.compedu.2010.10.020

Moreno, R. (2004). Decreasing cognitive load for novice students: Effects of explanatory versus corrective feedback in discovery-based multimedia. *Instructional Science, 32*(1-2), 99–113. https://doi.org/10.1023/B:TRUC.0000021811.66966.1d

Morote, E. S., & Pritchard, D. E. (2009). What course elements correlate with improvement on tests in introductory Newtonian mechanics? *American Journal of Physics, 77*(8), 746–753. https://doi.org/10.1119/1.3139533

Nicol, D. J., & Macfarlane-Dick, D. (2006). Formative assessment and self-regulated learning: A model and seven principles of good feedback practice. *Studies in Higher Education, 31*(2), 199–218. https://doi.org/10.1080/03075070600572090

Panadero, E. (2017). A review of self-regulated learning: Six models and four directions for research. *Frontiers in Psychology, 8*(422). https://doi:10.3389/fpsyg.2017.00422

Pashler, H., Bain, P., Bottge, B., Graesser, A., Koedinger, K., McDaniel, M., & Metcalfe, J. (2007). *Organizing instruction and study to improve student learning* (NCER 2007-2004). National Center for Education Research, Institute of Education Sciences, U.S. Department of Education. http://ncer.ed.gov

Paunesku, D. (2013). *Scaled-up social psychology: Intervening wisely and broadly in education* (Doctoral dissertation, Stanford University). https://web.stanford.edu/~paunesku/paunesku_2013.pdf

Puustinen, M., & Pulkkinen, L. (2001). Models of self-regulated learning: A review. *Scandinavian Journal of Educational Research, 45*(3), 269–286. https://doi .org/10.1080/00313830120074206

Riconscente, M. M., Mislevy, R. J., & Corrigan, S. (2015). Evidence-centered design. In S. Lane, M. R. Raymond, & T. M. Haladyna (Eds.) *Handbook of test development* (pp. 56–79). Routledge.

Roll, I., Aleven, V., McLaren, B. M., & Koedinger, K. R. (2007). Designing for metacognition—applying cognitive tutor principles to the tutoring of help seeking. *Metacognition and Learning, 2*(2–3), 125–140. https://doi.org/10.1007/ s11409-007-9010-0

Roll, I., Aleven, V., McLaren, B. M., & Koedinger, K. R. (2011). Improving students' help-seeking skills using metacognitive feedback in an intelligent tutoring system. *Learning and Instruction, 21*(2), 267–280. https://doi.org/10.1016/ j.learninstruc.2010.07.004

Schunk, D. H. (1982). Effects of effort attributional feedback on children's perceived self-efficacy and achievement. *Journal of Educational Psychology, 74*(4), 548. https://doi.org/10.1016/j.learninstruc.2010.07.004

Schunk, D. H., & Cox, P. D. (1986). Strategy training and attributional feedback with learning disabled students. *Journal of Educational Psychology, 78*(3), 201. https://doi.org/10.1037/0022-0663.78.3.201

Schunk, D. H., & Greene, J. A. (2017). *Handbook of self-regulation of learning and performance.* Routledge. https://doi.org/10.4324/9781315697048

Shute, V. J. (2008). Focus on formative feedback. *Review of Educational Research, 78*(1), 153–189. https://doi.org/10.3102/0034654307313795

Sitzmann, T. (2011). A meta-analytic examination of the instructional effectiveness of computer-based simulation games. *Personnel Psychology, 64*, 489–528. https:// doi.org/10.1111/j.1744-6570.2011.01190.x

Van der Kleij, F. M., Feskens, R. C., & Eggen, T. J. (2015). Effects of feedback in a computer-based learning environment on students' learning outcomes: A meta-analysis. *Review of Educational Research, 85*(4), 475–511. https://doi .org/10.3102/0034654314564881

Vogel, J. J., Vogel, D. S., Cannon-Bowers, J., Bowers, C. A., Muse, K., Wright, M. (2006). Computer gaming and interactive simulations for learning: A meta-analysis. *Journal of Educational Computational Research, 34*(3), 229–243. https:// doi.org/10.2190/FLHV-K4WA-WPVQ-H0YM

Wilson, M. (2004). *Constructing measures: An item response modeling approach.* Routledge. https://doi.org/10.4324/9781410611697

Winne, P. H., & Hadwin, A. F. (2013). nStudy: Tracing and supporting self-regulated learning in the Internet. In R. Azevedo & V. Aleven (Eds.), *International handbook of metacognition and learning technologies* (pp. 293–308). Springer. https://doi.org/10.1007/978-1-4419-5546-3_20

Winne, P. H., Nesbit, J. C., Kumar, V., Hadwin, A. F., Lajoie, S. P., Azevedo, R., & Perry, N. E. (2006). Supporting self-regulated learning with gStudy software: The learning kit project. *Technology, Instruction, Cognition and Learning, 3*, 105–113.

Zepeda, C. D., Richey, J. E., Ronevich, P., & Nokes-Malach, T. J. (2015). Direct instruction of metacognition benefits adolescent science learning, transfer, and motivation: An in-vivo study. *Journal of Educational Psychology, 107*(4), 954–970. http://dx.doi.org/10.1037/edu0000022

3

EMPOWERING FACULTY TO DESIGN TECHNOLOGY-ENRICHED STUDENT LEARNING

A Constructivist and Connectivist Hybrid Massive Open Online Course

Roberta (Robin) Sullivan, Cherie van Putten, Emily Cole, Katrina Fulcher-Rood, Jessica Kruger, Gina Sipley, Rachel Rigolino, and Jennifer H. Herman

L earning technologies play a transformative role in teaching and learning in higher education. For almost every need, interest, or challenge that teachers and learners face, an educational technology tool seems to exist that is aimed at satisfying them, or at minimum, providing a way to bridge the distance. Although many teaching faculty understand the potential of technology to enhance teaching and learning on a conceptual level, in practice, instructors are often hesitant to use these resources in substantive ways. For a variety of reasons (e.g., limited time, resources, accessibility), learning new or staying current with existing as well as emerging technology tools presents a significant challenge to instructors.

This chapter focuses on one powerful way that teaching faculty can overcome this challenge: learning and exploring educational technologies through freely accessible massive open online courses (MOOCs), specifically hybrid MOOCs. This type of MOOC is dedicated to supporting those interested in learning about both popular and lesser-known educational tools and to provide a space to explore how to use them. This chapter highlights one such hybrid MOOC: Exploring Emerging Technologies for Lifelong Learning and Success (#EmTechMOOC), an open-access resource developed by the

State University of New York (SUNY). #EmTechMOOC (available at http://suny.edu/emtech) provides technology tools, information, and strategies to help users navigate an ever-changing and often volatile digital world. It is useful for people interested in enhancing teaching and learning in any setting or venue, but especially for those in higher education settings.

The goal of this chapter is for readers to become familiar with MOOCs as a viable and perhaps even more suitable alternative to traditional forms of professional learning about learning technologies. An additional goal is for readers to feel motivated to explore #EmTechMOOC in particular. It is one of the few hybrid MOOCs dedicated to exploring and learning about educational technologies.

This chapter is divided into three parts. Part One provides a brief review of the literature that informed our thinking about why learning technologies remain underused in higher education courses. This section also discusses online professional development as a means of addressing this problem, with specific emphasis on MOOCs. Part Two homes in on #EmTechMOOC as an example of a hybrid MOOC that well serves this task. Included in this section is the purpose of #EmTechMOOC and an overview of its components and design that are geared to enhancing teaching and learning as well as helping users learn how to integrate technology tools into their personal and professional lives. Part Three offers six scenarios drawn from our experiences of putting into practice what we learned from #EmTechMOOC in higher education courses. The focus on how particular technology tools were effectively used in higher education settings is intended to spark or further develop readers' ideas about how they might use technology tools in ways that can transform content and pedagogy in their own settings.

Part One: Understanding Faculty Reluctance to Learning Technologies and the Importance of Faculty Development

As the previous chapters of this book make clear, the transformative role that learning technologies can play in higher education is well established (Galanek et al., 2018; Garrison & Kanuka, 2004; Selwyn, 2007). Despite these conceptual understandings, the use of transformative technologies in everyday teaching practice remains far from ubiquitous (King & South, 2017; Selwyn, 2007). Although this disconnect is caused by many factors (Selwyn, 2007), this chapter focuses on addressing one that is frequently cited in the literature: faculty reluctance to use educational technologies in substantive ways (Johnson, 2013; King & South, 2017; Lillejord et al., 2018; Ludgate, 2013; Sibley & Whitaker, 2015).

It is important to note that our focus is understanding the factors that drive faculty reluctance as it pertains to using technology to transform pedagogy and student learning. We are not examining the issue of faculty resistance to using technology in any fashion, a dwindling problem (Lederman, 2018). Our more honed interest is guided by the notion that the relevant consideration is no longer *if* faculty are using technology but rather *how* they are using it (Lambert et al., 2014; Lillejord et al., 2018).

In the two sections that follow, we first discuss the scholarship that has informed our thinking about this obstacle and, second, a way to address it drawn from our experience—online learning in the form of hybrid MOOCs.

Faculty Reluctance to Use Educational Technologies to Achieve Their Transformative Potential

Some faculty have been hesitant to use educational technologies in their courses in substantive ways for many reasons, some rooted in individually held ways of thinking about teaching and learning and some more institutionally driven. Both sets of rationales are discussed here. For example, some faculty believe that technology will diminish the quality of instruction (Johnson, 2013; Marzilli et al., 2014; Sibley & Whitaker, 2015). In a study of faculty perceptions of technology (Johnson, 2013), several participants interviewed felt that the use of technology was distracting—so-called bells and whistles—and thereby took away from student learning. Additionally, some faculty hold nostalgic feelings for the more traditional models of teaching and learning they experienced themselves as students (Lillejord et al., 2018). Goodson et al. (2006) describe *nostalgia* as "idealized memories of the past" (p. 44), which can act as blinders in the face of different ideas, innovations, and/or changing situations. A further example of an individually held way of thinking that can be inhibiting is a lack of confidence in one's own technological abilities (Orlando, 2014). This is sometimes the case for teachers who, unlike most of their students, might not be digital natives and may feel too intimidated to use technology tools in anything more than superficial ways.

Faculty who choose to integrate educational technologies into their courses often use a narrow range of tools to digitally replicate tasks that could be done in a traditional classroom setting. A Gallup poll of community college presidents (Jaschik & Lederman, 2017) found that the most frequently used educational technology tools were linked to the campus's learning management system (LMS). Eighty-nine percent of professors polled were most likely to use an LMS such as Canvas, Blackboard, or Moodle to share syllabus information, and 71% used an LMS to share grades. Further, the survey revealed that more sophisticated tools embedded in an LMS for supporting students who need extra help or capturing lessons were less likely to be used.

Institutional obstacles are a second set of reasons some faculty have not taken up technology advances for teaching and learning. One main road-block is the limited opportunity for substantive professional development focused on technology in many higher education settings (Johnson, 2013; King & South, 2017; Marzilli et al., 2014). Another significant impediment is the lack of professional incentives for faculty to invest time in learning and experimenting with learning technologies (Johnson, 2013). At many research-focused institutions, faculty tenure and promotion continue to be largely based on research productivity. In these settings, faculty face a diffi-cult choice in spending precious and limited time to learn about and explore emerging learning technologies with the depth necessary to then use the tools in substantive ways in their courses (Johnson, 2013; King & South, 2017; Ludgate, 2013).

In conclusion, for personal and/or institutional reasons, many teaching faculty have been reluctant to use educational technologies in ways that could substantially impact teaching and learning. These factors do not operate in isolation and often interact to further entrench one's preference for more traditional instructional methods. In the next section, we highlight literature that focuses on online learning and more specifically, hybrid MOOCs, as a way of addressing the problem of faculty reluctance to engage with learning technologies in substantive ways.

An Online Professional Learning Platform for Faculty: Hybrid MOOCs

A promising solution to the problem of faculty reluctance in embracing learning technologies for teaching and learning is the growing popularity of online, on-demand, asynchronous learning opportunities, where learn-ing resources can be accessed anytime and anywhere. Online, on-demand professional development alleviates many obstacles (e.g., time, accessibility, learning pace) that faculty face when pursuing learning opportunities. This form of learning is also ideal for exploration and experimentation—the kind of engagement necessary for increasing confidence in making substantive changes to one's pedagogical practices (Sullivan et al., 2018).

Online learning opportunities can be accessed in many ways, such as vid-eos, stand-alone websites, professional learning communities, and MOOCs. Of these resources, MOOCs are less well known but growing in popularity. Here we briefly explain what MOOCs are, how they can be useful, and a type of MOOC well suited for faculty interested in learning about educa-tional technologies in explorative ways: hybrid MOOCs.

MOOCs are courses offered on the internet at no charge to large groups of people. MOOCs, a type of online learning platform launched in 2008, reflect "a continuation of the trend in innovation, experimentation, and the use of technology initiated by distance and online teaching, to offer learning opportunities in a massive way" (Siemens, 2013, p. 5). Figure 3.1 identifies

Figure 3.1. Definition of a *MOOC*.

Massive: The educational opportunity to extend to a wide audience regardless of their status or geographic location

Open: The ability for anyone to have access to the learning opportunity, thus democratizing knowledge

Online: Offered over the internet, which provides access anytime and from anywhere

Course: Structured content and learning activities

Note. MOOC is an acronym for massive open online course. Massive refers to the potential of extremely large enrollments; thousands of students register from all over the globe. Open can mean a few things, such as open enrollment to anyone who has internet access regardless of their prior learning. It can also mean that, at least initially, courses were free to anyone interested in registering. Some hold that open should refer to the concept of open access, meaning that the content not only is free and available to all but also holds at most a Creative Commons licensing status so that the content can be downloaded, saved, and even adapted for one's own purposes (with credit to the developer). Online is the means of content delivery. Course implies that there is some traditional convention of how a course operates, such as requiring enrollment, a start and end date, instructor-developed content delivered to the learner, and some means of assessment.

a MOOC's defining characteristics, which are loosely based on Decker's (2014) breakdown of the MOOC acronym.

MOOCs have evolved over their brief history into three main types; each carries important distinctions. The first iteration of MOOCs followed a format now referred to as *cMOOCs*. cMOOCs are based on a constructivist and connectivist model in which learners develop understanding through hands-on engagement and participation (Siemens, 2005). Constructionism is built on the educational theories of Piaget, Vygotsky, Dewey, and Montessori, among others, who affirmed that knowledge is cocreated among students and instructors. According to Siemens (2005), cocreator of cMOOCs, "Learning now occurs in a variety of ways—through communities of practice, personal networks, and through completion of work-related tasks" (para. 4). Early MOOC pioneers (Cormier & Siemens, 2010) wanted to tear down the walls of traditional classrooms and invite the community beyond the college campus into the pedagogical discoveries of courses. The idea motivating such a move was to enable knowledge to be coconstructed among not only university elite but also anyone seeking to learn (Haber, 2014). In describing the importance of connectivism in learning, Siemens (2005) noted, "Connections that enable us to learn more are more important than our current state of knowing" (para. 23). To date, these unlimited networks have created many opportunities to learn and share information.

The second iteration of MOOCs became known as extended MOOCs or xMOOCs. This type follows a more traditional classroom structure that relies on a teacher-centered approach with learners as knowledge consumers (Zawacki-Richter et al., 2018). Under this model, course delivery often includes video-recorded lectures and learning indicators are based on quizzes and tests. With the rise of platforms like Coursera, EdX, and Udacity in 2012, *New York Times* contributor Pappano (2012) dubbed this period as "The Year of the MOOC." This marked the beginning of a trend that shifted the emphasis of MOOCs from openness to massiveness of scale (Haber, 2014). Smithers (2012) well-captures the stark contrast between cMOOCs and xMOOCs: "In an xMOOC you watch videos, in a cMOOC you make videos."

We are now living in the time of third-generation hybrid MOOCs, with a dual emphasis on constructivism and connections to large groups of learners (Zawacki-Richter et al., 2018). This type of MOOC is based in a constructivist framework and an emphasis on active engagement. It stands in sharp contrast to the more lecture-based, passive learning format that characterizes xMOOCs. The emphasis of hybrid MOOCs on learning by doing is central to the connectivist roots of early cMOOCs (Zawacki-Richter et al., 2018), enabling rich learning opportunities for faculty. The massive enrollment numbers for MOOCs offer great potential to understand how a diverse range of students learn (Krause & Lowe, 2014).

In attempts to quantify the success of any type of MOOC, completion rates are not often the best indicators, as Wang and Baker (2015) explained. They noted that MOOCs draw a diverse mix of participants who have a variety of motivations that go beyond or do not even include course completion. For example, some individuals are seeking information available in part of a course and thereby need not complete the whole course to achieve their goals (Anderson, 2013; Shaw, 2019; Sullivan et al., 2019). In this way, MOOCs enable participants to customize their learning experience and to focus on areas most suitable to their needs and interests.

Some faculty view MOOCs with a degree of skepticism, a "fad" that will not become a central part of their pedagogical practice (Young, 2013). Nonetheless, to date, MOOCs continue to be the new frontier of online learning opportunities for faculty and others. Rather than resisting MOOCS, Fischer (2014) recommended that "the research community in the learning sciences should get seriously involved with MOOCs and influence their evolution" (p.157).

Some literature has focused on how MOOCs specifically can benefit faculty learning and use of educational technology (Blackmon, 2018; Krause & Lowe, 2014; Marzilli et al., 2014). However, more study is needed on several fronts: to better understand how MOOCs can be useful to faculty; which types are most effective and worthwhile; and, perhaps most importantly, to what extent (if any) faculty put their learning from this online learning platform into practice. Are faculty able to use what they learn to transform pedagogical practices and enhance student learning? This is the key question to be answered. This chapter, with its focus on one example of a hybrid MOOC, is a contribution to that end.

Part Two: #EmTechMOOC's Purpose and Overview

#EmTechMOOC has two main goals, one broad and the other focused. The wider goal is to help learners across the world explore technology tools through hands-on activities and reflective learning. Some of the tools available for experimentation include audio, blogs, wikis, collaborative spaces, ePortfolios, gamification, mobile apps, open educational resources (OERs), photos and images, presentations, productivity tools, resource libraries, simulations, social media platforms, and videos. #EmTechMOOC is open to anyone and is designed to foster a deeper comfort level with ever-changing technology. It accomplishes this by focusing on not only technology but also the concept of lifelong learning. A unique aspect of #EmTechMOOC is that it emphasizes active, hands-on exploration, discussion, and sharing among participants from around the world, many of whom are students and faculty. The connective nature of the learning community allows participants the opportunity to learn together and reflects a key part of #EmTechMOOC's innovative design.

The more focused aim of #EmTechMOOC is to help participants gain 21st-century technology skills. This goal rests on the premise that everyone needs 21st-century technology competencies to reach individual and collaborative goals (National Education Association, 2012). These competencies are wide-ranging and include abilities such as: effectively using technology (including mobile devices) to communicate across time zones and geographic locations; finding and sharing accurate information; and using information technologies as comfortably and seamlessly as most people are able to read and write. According to Jacobson and Mackey (2013), meta-literacy builds on information literacy competencies and emphasizes reflective practice as key to communicating, creating, and sharing information in today's participatory environments. As SUNY Chancellor Kristina M. Johnson (2018) noted in her inaugural address, "No matter what field a student goes into, you can bet that social networking, communications skills, and critical thinking will be required. So, we will emphasize these adaptive skills in all we do" (para. 48). This statement underscores the importance and relevance of integrating current and emerging technology tools into higher education teaching and learning, and by extension, makes clear the value of #EmTechMOOC for faculty and students.

The Origins of #EmTechMOOC

#EmTechMOOC grew out of SUNY's Tools for Engagement Project (TOEP), an on-demand self-directed professional development opportunity funded by a SUNY Innovative Instructional Technology Grant. In 2012, TOEP was collaboratively developed by a cross-campus interdisciplinary team of faculty and professional staff. The central aim of the project was to encourage SUNY faculty to apply tech-infused pedagogy to their teaching and research. #EmTechMOOC, which launched in 2018 as an OER, sought to expand the audience from primarily teaching faculty in the SUNY system to learners from around the world interested in personal and professional growth relative to learning technologies. OERs are teaching and learning materials that are freely available online for everyone to use (Downes, 2007). #EmTechMOOC is openly available on the internet and is delivered through the Coursera platform.

The Nuts and Bolts of #EmTechMOOC

The EmTech project consists of two associated parts: #EmTechMOOC and #EmTechWIKI, as illustrated in Figure 3.2. These parts, although offering stand-alone benefits, operate in complementary fashion, as we explain in the following sections.

MOOC

The learning activities in the MOOC provide accessible, curated information and application exercises pertaining to current and emerging technologies. The MOOC learning environment is structured around two main themes: lifelong learning and essential competencies—communication, collaboration, creativity, and critical thinking. Known as "the Four Cs of 21st-century skills" (National Education Association, 2012, p. 3), these overarching competencies have been identified as reflecting the skills, knowledge, and expertise students should master to succeed in work and life in the 21st century.

The themes of lifelong learning and the "Four Cs" are interwoven throughout the five course modules of #EmTechMOOC that participants are encouraged to explore, dabble in, or complete. The first module explicitly focuses on lifelong learning. The next three modules focus on the "Four Cs": communication, collaboration, creativity, and critical thinking. Modules include brief videos and discovery exercises that are designed to encourage participants to explore and interact with a selection of technology resources.

Figure 3.2. #EmTechMOOC and EmTechWIKI.

The discovery exercises direct participants to select objectives based on their needs and interests from #EmTechWIKI. We will describe the discovery exercises and the wiki search process in more detail in the following section.

The final module of the course is reserved for participants to finalize their ePortfolios, the content having been built through activities from earlier modules. In this final module, participants engage in a peer-review process to constructively evaluate ePortfolios of two fellow participants based on a rubric of criteria that should be included in a well-crafted ePortfolio. The peer-review evaluation process helps deepen participants' learning.

Wiki

The other main component of the course is the EmTechWIKI website. The wiki was built to complement #EmTechMOOC. It is a searchable collection of freely available tools, tutorials, and resources. Participants independently explore the wiki resources to complete the MOOC discovery exercises. Next, we briefly explain the learning process.

Participants select learning objectives targeted to the module they choose to work in that meets their needs and interests. The wiki then enables them to home in on emerging technology tools and resources that are well-suited to the desired learning objectives. For example, if a faculty member is interested in how to facilitate effective student collaboration, that individual might select the objective "Enhance Collaboration" under the Communication and Collaboration module as illustrated in Figure 3.3. A selection of the EmTechWIKI technologies that encourage collaboration will be shown, with links provided for further exploration and experimentation. This process helps faculty evaluate and select from a wide variety of freely available emerging technologies and also match appropriate technology tools to their particular needs.

Participants interested in building an ePortfolio will work directly with the resources that result from their #EmTechWIKI search to create an artifact as evidence of their learning through the hands-on discovery exercises within the #EmTechMOOC modules. The resulting artifact is then embedded within their personal ePortfolios. Participants also write a short reflection on their learning experience and how the tools with which they experimented might be useful in the future; this is added to their ePortfolios. Throughout their learning processes involving the wiki and the MOOC, participants are encouraged to engage in conversation on the MOOC discussion forums to share and receive support from peers and colleagues.

This hands-on, discovery-based learning process is central to #EmTechMOOC. The MOOC provides faculty with the tools and the space needed to explore instructional technologies and build their confidence before

Figure 3.3. A close-up of the wiki search process.

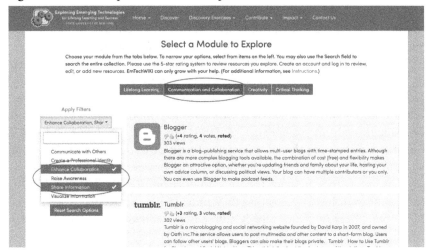

introducing a specific app or piece of software to students. The MOOC discussion forums offer a supportive learning community, another contrast to lecture-style xMOOCs.

EmTechWIKI is socially curated, which means that participants have the ability to add new tools and resources. They can also improve existing records by adding tutorials or other supporting information, or simply rate existing tools. This process helps future participants recognize items that are judged to be more helpful by the collective group of participants.

EmTechMOOC's Focus on Teaching and Learning

Although #EmTechMOOC is open to anyone interested in learning about and exploring technology tools, it is especially well-suited to instructors at all levels. This hybrid MOOC provides the structure and resources that faculty need to identify useful instructional tools and learn how to integrate them into their courses in ways that optimize student learning and engagement. It is designed to encourage a deliberate, gradual integration of new technologies, focused on addressing a specific pedagogical problem or learning objective. This incremental approach that involves time and space for exploration and experimentation is an effective process that can yield positive results.

In several ways, #EmTechMOOC has much to offer instructors in thinking through and taking actionable steps to integrate technology into their pedagogical practices. For example, to ensure that a technology tool adds substantive meaning to a particular course, the #EmTechMOOC purposefully builds in spaces for instructors to reflect on how a new app, software, or "cool tool" fits into the course aims and objectives. The clarity and intentionality that this reflective process affords also enables instructors to be transparent with students about why they are using a specific technology.

Additionally, #EmTechMOOC encourages instructors to survey students to gain an understanding of their perceptions about any newly adopted technology and their experiences with it. Surveying students is especially recommended at mid-semester, as it allows for any modifications or tweaks to be made in real-time to enhance students' experiences. Student feedback is essential for assessing the effectiveness of new educational technology tools and can help inform planning for future iterations of the course.

For instructors, perhaps the most important aspect of hybrid MOOCs such as #EmTechMOOC is that they provide supportive spaces for experimentation. Because #EmTechMOOC has the added feature of being self-paced, faculty are often able to incorporate what they learn into live courses. Additionally, MOOC participants can share their successes and challenges with others and together build a community that uses technology creatively and effectively to enhance student learning.

Early Outcomes of #EmTechMOOC

To date, in assessing #EmTechMOOC using ongoing, postparticipation surveys, we have found that this learning opportunity positively impacts participants' perception of technology and of themselves. Our internal survey results, collected in the first 2 years after the project launch, showed that more than 75% of survey responders reported that engagement enhanced their ability to use emerging technologies either very much or quite a bit. In addition, faculty reported feeling more confident when selecting and adopting learning technologies as well as more knowledgeable about how to use technology to improve student learning. In addition, participants also responded positively to the importance of developing lifelong learning habits, a central tenet of the course.

Part Three: Examples of Faculty Using Technology Tools to Solve Teaching and Learning Challenges

This section focuses on six examples drawn from our experiences as instructors in using the tools and resources found in #EmTechMOOC to enhance teaching and learning. These examples highlight a number of educational technologies available for exploration, experimentation, and application within the MOOC. Each example consists of three central features:

1. A teaching and learning challenge addressed with a technology tool
2. The action steps taken by the author/instructor in learning and experimenting with a tool on #EmTechMOOC or EmTechWIKI
3. The results of applying the technology tool, including the instructor's and students' perceptions of its usefulness and effectiveness

These examples are meant to illustrate how constructivist and connectivist learning opportunities such as #EmTechMOOC can be useful for faculty interested in integrating educational technologies into their pedagogical practices in ways that substantively elevate teaching and learning.

Example 1: Making Connections Through Reflection and Critical Thinking

This first example is drawn from Katrina Fulcher-Rood's experience teaching a course in communication disorders.

Challenge

In a class focused on understanding societal constructs and the impacts of disability, Fulcher-Rood wanted to create an activity in which students could curate and discuss information related to the personal narratives of individuals living with disabilities. Fulcher-Rood also wanted the students to share the information with the class and respond to others' contributions.

MOOC Experience

While enrolled in #EmTechMOOC, Fulcher-Rood learned that blogs lend themselves well to connectivist and constructivist learning paradigms. A blog is typically an individual website on which the owner posts information and ideas, usually focused on a particular topic or theme. Other invited group members can then comment on blog posts, pose questions, or add related materials. Particularly helpful for Fulcher-Rood was discovering that blogs can be framed to allow students to work with and learn from one another while curating and making new materials that relate to classroom knowledge.

After reviewing the purposes of blogs in the Communication and Collaboration module in #EmTechMOOC, Fulcher-Rood decided to create a learning activity in which blogs could be used to enhance student learning and engagement. Students would create blogs to curate and synthesize the information they gathered in class and from outside sources. To set up this activity, Fulcher-Rood reviewed different blogging platforms including the blogging feature on the LMS used on her campus that was easily available to students. In reviewing the various platforms, Fulcher-Rood rated them according to four features: ease of use, free student access, the ability to easily connect to other internet resources and people, and the capability to export and save student contributions. Based on these criteria, Fulcher-Rood was able to find a blogging platform that best fit the students' needs and learning outcomes.

Results

Fulcher-Rood discovered that the students' contributions to their own blog enabled them to construct new information related to what they were learning in the classroom. Each student was expected to contribute five new blog posts during the semester. In each post, students were expected to summarize a concept addressed in class, present a new artifact (e.g., website, blog, video, artwork, poem) related to the concept, and analyze the importance of the artifact. In addition to these blog posts, students were expected to post comments to the blogs of fellow classmates.

Overall, Fulcher-Rood was pleased with what the blogs had accomplished. End-of-semester course evaluations revealed that students enjoyed blogging, and all surpassed the minimum requirement of five blog posts. Many students even decided to create their own websites and blogs as a final project for the course. By providing spaces where students could learn from and encourage one another, the blogs fit with Fulcher-Rood's connectivist approach to learning. One area that needed improvement was in the length and quality of comments made in response to other classmates' posts. Students tended to post short and simple messages. As a remedy, the instructor now shares specific criteria for what to include in well-developed reflective comments.

Example 2: A Collaborative Process to Create New Knowledge

In this second example we review an example drawn from Fulcher-Rood's experience in teaching speech pathology.

Challenge

Graduate students in Fulcher-Rood's speech pathology course studying augmentative and alternative communication were involved in a semester-long project to create a clinically relevant deliverable for professionals or community members. During the semester, students were expected to provide ongoing feedback to group members and the instructor regarding their progress and next steps. The instructor did not want to use valuable class time to complete the updates and wanted students to have a permanent place to review past updates and project notes.

MOOC Experience

Learning about blogs and wikis through #EmTechMOOC enabled Fulcher-Rood to envision using these tools as a space for students to document experiences and progress with their community project. Fulcher-Rood chose a wiki tool for the project because her students would need to collaborate with one another as well as modify and add to information that was posted. In comparison to a blog, a wiki is a website that most often belongs to and serves the purpose of a group rather than an individual. It is more collaborative in nature than a blog because all contributors can add to, modify, and delete any content, even the original material. Fulcher-Rood decided to use the wiki feature available via the campus LMS, largely because her students were familiar with the platform. Additionally, the wiki did not need to be viewable by anyone outside the class.

Results

Each group created and maintained a wiki that demonstrated the group's progress with the project. Group members were expected to submit meeting notes, timelines, to-do lists, and final products. As students progressed and completed specific parts of the project, they updated the wiki to reflect their learning. Students knew that Fulcher-Rood was reading their wiki once a week to check on their progress and to ensure all group members were contributing. These wikis became collaborative spaces for students to plan activities and discuss their accomplishments and challenges outside of class.

As this example demonstrates, wikis offer collaborative spaces for students to share, learn, and reflect on classroom knowledge and apply that knowledge in new and novel ways. Wikis can foster student discussion and creativity while also allowing students to take ownership of their learning.

Example 3: Communicating Using Media

The third example is drawn from Jessica Kruger's experience teaching a course in public health.

Challenge

When confronted with converting a typical 15-week, face-to-face course into an accelerated 6-week fully online summer course, Kruger struggled with how to ensure that students enrolled in the summer session would be able to achieve the same learning outcomes as those in the traditional semester course. She needed to make thoughtful adjustments to the design of the course overall and, in particular, the structure of class assignments. Kruger also wanted to provide clear and concise information about the course content in ways that would foster student engagement and interest.

MOOC Experience

After searching EmTechWIKI under the objectives of "sharing information" and "increasing engagement and interest," Kruger discovered several options for adding relevant visuals into the course along with information about how to create audio, video, and other media. Already familiar with the benefits of using open educational resources (OERs), she explored the OER category in EmTechWIKI, which led her to OER catalogs and other resources. Here, Kruger identified relevant, preexisting videos through the video-hosting platforms listed in #EmTechMOOC.

Although the preexisting videos Kruger found would be useful in providing general information students needed, she still needed tools to help convey more detailed content. After continuing to explore additional tools and resources generated from her search of EmTechWIKI, Kruger discovered some promising options. For example, she found an article discussing tips for creating screencasts, which are videos that show what appears on a computer's screen. She also found several kinds of screencast creation software.

This information inspired her to try her hand at screencasting to provide her students with the detailed content that the OERs lacked. She created several 3-minute video lectures using narrated slide presentations that highlighted key points and summaries of complex course information. She interspersed video snippets of herself within the mini-lectures. To enhance the presentation, she explored the "photos and images" category on the EmTechWIKI and located several relevant images licensed under Creative Commons. Finally, to refine the video lectures and make them suitable to engage the interest of her students, Kruger turned to EmTechWIKI's video category and found a variety of freely available audio and video editing tools that were capable of completing simple and complex tasks.

The video category is one of the more actively searched areas in EmTechWIKI. Instructors who have participated in #EmTechMOOC often use video to create mini-video lectures, demonstrations, simulations, and to replicate course content that is inaccessible due to geographic location or dangerous conditions.

Results

Through the discovery exercises in the MOOC, Kruger realized that videos are capable of conveying a lot of information, and the best solution for her purposes was to locate existing videos as well as create new videos for her condensed summer course. She used audio and video in a variety of ways to supplement traditional course content. Many students were new to the online format, and the videos proved helpful in providing instructions about expectations throughout the course. In a post-course survey, students were asked how they felt about the short videos. One student wrote:

> I really appreciate the method of providing several, short videos that focus on one central idea rather than posting an hour-long video with many important ideas addressed. This method of listening to lectures allows for pausing and processing the idea of one video before proceeding to the next.

Including videos that also featured Kruger in this online learning environment brought a human element into the course and enabled the students to get a sense of her personality. Using this range of media formats helped convey information and allowed students to comprehend, appreciate, and remember the course materials.

With her growing confidence using technology tools, Kruger also encouraged her students to use media as an alternative to traditional text-based submission for some assignments. When alternatives of this type are provided, it is important to require the same level of rigor for all options. Kruger made clear to students that their work would be graded based on the same criteria that guided her assessment of traditional submissions. She stressed that students should concentrate fully on the desired objectives instead of inadvertently putting too much effort into the mechanics of creating the video.

The added option of allowing students to submit their assignments through the use of video allowed them to engage in constructivist pedagogy and to create videos to build new knowledge and personal meaning. Students could be creative in this venue, which fostered increased engagement and enjoyment. Additionally, Kruger found grading the video submissions to be very enjoyable. A further positive outcome was that one student reported using her project in a job interview that led to a job offer. The student's project enabled her to demonstrate her proficient use of new technologies to effectively communicate her message. Allowing students choice in the type of assessment proved to be a great opportunity for students to express creativity and master the content.

Example 4: Developing Online Communication Skills

The fourth example is drawn from Cherie van Putten's experience teaching a professional internship course.

Challenge

Van Putten's face-to-face internship course is designed to prepare students for the workplace environment by helping them develop professional work skills and acclimate them to current business practices. Students spend several hours working at an internship site each week but spend only an hour in class. With every class session pivotal, van Putten faced a dilemma upon discovering she would miss a class due to a conference she was scheduled to attend. It would be critical for students to work through the topics identified in the syllabus for that week's class, despite van Putten's absence.

MOOC Experience

Van Putten searched EmTechWIKI for tools that would help her achieve two goals: create meaningful content to cover the topics for that week's class and communicate the content from a distance. She reviewed resources within the Communication and Collaboration module and filtered the results to show items aligned with the objectives "communicate with others" and "share information."

Van Putten initially considered recreating the lecture portion of her course and providing students with a prerecorded video. She reviewed a number of resources about creating video and how to share videos with her students. However, as she explored the EmTechWIKI resources further, she concluded that a passive, one-way video was not the best solution. After evaluating the options, she decided on using web conferencing software.

Despite some trepidation, van Putten chose to structure that week's class as a web meeting. She referred to resources located in EmTechWiki related to how to run a successful web meeting, and then experimented with various web meeting functions in the application. After developing a plan for her class, van Putten practiced through a test meeting she arranged with a few colleagues.

Results

In the class session prior to the web meeting, van Putten logged on to the web meeting application and briefly showed her students what to expect and how to operate the necessary features. On the day of the class, van Putten was pleasantly surprised to find that her preparation had helped the meeting run smoothly. She had no problems logging in, using her camera and microphone, and sharing her slides.

As this was a career services internship course with a goal of acclimating students to real-world business processes, van Putten felt the time spent learning about web meeting applications was time well-spent. This included working through problems some students experienced with navigating the web meeting software. The web meeting provided the opportunity for students to experiment with many web conferencing functions, such as sending chats, annotating the screen, and sharing their screen content. An additional benefit was finding that the web meeting experience prompted students to work collaboratively to help each other troubleshoot video and audio difficulties.

Conducting a web conference allowed the students and van Putten to communicate, share information, and collaborate in a fashion that more closely resembled their regular face-to-face class meetings. The web conference fit well into the constructivist focus of the course, which centered on student-generated discussion and the instructor in a facilitator role. Additionally, students had an opportunity to practice a new and important skill, communicating via web conferencing. Virtual communication skills are becoming increasingly necessary during the job search process; many initial interviews are often conducted virtually.

Van Putten received positive feedback from students about the activity. Several commented that they were now less intimidated about participating in web conferences as part of their future careers. With the success of the activity, van Putten has continued to hold at least one web meeting for the course each semester. In facing her initial fears about how to select and implement web conferencing software, van Putten discovered that this technique added significant value to the course. Her students continue to benefit from the opportunity to build a skill that can be used both in the classroom and in the workplace.

Example 5: Cross-Cultural Interactions and Collaborations

The fifth example is drawn from Jessica Kruger's experience teaching a course in public health.

Challenge

Higher education institutions often seek out ways to create cross-cultural interactions among students. The SUNY Collaborative Online International Learning (COIL) initiative, for example, helps connect SUNY faculty with international partners. Faculty members, located in different parts of the world, work together to design and coteach course modules and even entire courses. Instead of only reading about another culture, students interact with their international peers to complete projects and construct meaning.

When designing a course in which students are expected to collaborate with individuals and groups around the world, faculty must be aware of potential obstacles. Some examples include: working collaboratively when participants communicate using different languages; working across time zones; and locating tools with directions in languages other than English that facilitate communication have directions written in only one language (usually English). In this scenario, we present a solution that Kruger, as a member of the COIL faculty, found to address the challenge of cross-cultural communication among students through her engagement in #EmTechMOOC.

MOOC Experience
One way to solve the time zone problem is to find applications and software that facilitate asynchronous communication. Kruger discovered a web-based virtual bulletin board on EmTechWIKI that would fulfill this function. The bulletin board enabled students to post photographs and pose questions at times that were convenient to their schedules, which led to meaningful discussion. Students had the time to reflect on the artifacts pinned to the board and then compose thoughtful responses.

Another option Kruger discovered was editing software that students used to create videos, which were then shared across classes. After creating introductory videos, the students produced follow-up videos in which they posed questions to their classmates. By using this technology, students could hear and see one another, with the added bonus that videos could be replayed to help those from different cultural backgrounds review and better understand the video stories.

Results
Learning how to collaborate effectively is an essential 21st-century skill. In the context of this COIL course, students were given technology tools that helped them work out effective ways to communicate with their global peers. Kruger used educational technology to help students build relationships with other students from around the world and provided spaces where students could establish global connections and refine their technology skills. These are two learning outcomes that students can readily apply in future courses as well as the workplace.

Example 6: A Creative Method to Provide Student Feedback

This final example is drawn from Jessica Kruger's teaching of another course in public health.

Challenge
One of Kruger's public courses consisted of a large undergraduate section with approximately 75 students. She wanted to think anew about providing feedback to her students on their writing submissions. In most courses of

this size, instructors rely on multiple-choice assessment activities that can be automatically scored. Although automated grading relieves the burden of grading separate essays, this method of assessment is usually less effective in determining whether a student has learned the course material. In addition, such tests do not give students the opportunity to improve their writing skills.

MOOC Experience

To provide students the opportunity to do more writing and receive meaningful feedback, Kruger explored the #EmTechMOOC for tools that offered an alternative to handwriting her comments. Under the section on Critical Thinking, Kruger focused her attention on the resources classified under the "gather and provide feedback" objective. Based on her exploration, she further narrowed her search, as shown in Figure 3.4, and focused on using video to provide students with feedback and to grade her students' work. Video would serve to replace the traditional method of providing feedback through written comments.

Results

Kruger found that giving video feedback took less time than traditional written feedback. By using video grading, she was able to give her students individualized feedback and help them achieve higher levels of learning. The process enhanced her efficiency and decreased the amount of time needed to grade large numbers of student submissions. Providing video feedback enabled students to see the instructor's facial expressions and hear Kruger's caring tone of voice. This more personal style of feedback seemed to help motivate students and to better understand the intention of Kruger's comments. Students' perceptions regarding receiving constructive feedback in this format were very positive and appreciative.

The interactive nature of video feedback has been widely reported by students as a more meaningful and engaging method of feedback (Denton, 2014; Kruger & Sage, 2020). Students reported that the video feedback increased the clarity of the comments and fostered a connection with the instructor (Kruger & Sage, 2020). Feedback is described in the literature as being most meaningful as a two-way communication process (Jones et al., 2012). Traditional class discussion between students and faculty is more challenging when feedback on papers, projects, or online/distance courses involves no synchronous interaction. Video feedback aligns with the constructivist nature by demonstrating what needs to be modified or added to students' papers or projects and connecting faculty and students.

Figure 3.4. Application of filters to narrow down a search.

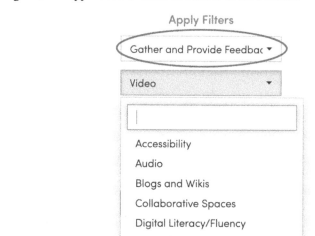

Final Thoughts

There is no shortage of learning technologies—many that are freely available—that can help faculty transform their pedagogy and practices in efforts to improve student learning and engagement. Yet, these technologies are often underused in higher education settings. One reason frequently cited for the discrepancy between the promise of technology and its minimal presence in higher education courses is faculty reluctance to integrate learning technologies into their practices. This chapter has focused on the potential that resides in hybrid MOOCs, an online learning opportunity available for faculty, as a way to overcome this reluctance. We have emphasized one hybrid MOOC that is well-suited for higher education teaching faculty interested in learning about, exploring, and experimenting with current and emerging technology tools: #EmTechMOOC. It is our hope that online spaces such as #EmTechMOOC encourage instructors to discover and experiment with technology tools they need and desire to support 21st-century teaching and learning.

References

Anderson, T. (2013). Promise and/or peril: MOOCs and open and distance education. *Commonwealth of Learning, 3*, 1–9. http://hdl.voced.edu.au/10707/327825

Blackmon, S. (2018). MOOC makers: Professors' experiences with developing and delivering MOOCs. *International Review of Research in Open and Distributed Learning, 19*(4). http://dx.doi.org/10.19173/irrodl.v19i4.3718

Cormier, D., & Siemens, G. (2010). Through the open door: Open courses as research, learning, and engagement. *EDUCAUSE Review, 45*(4), 30–39.

Decker, G. L. (2014). MOOCology 1.0. In S. Krause & C. Lowe (Eds), *Invasion of the MOOCs: The promise and perils of massive open online courses* (pp. 3–4). Parlor Press.

Denton, D. W. (2014). Using screen capture feedback to improve academic performance. *TechTrends, 58*(6), 51–56.

Downes, S. (2007). Models for sustainable open educational resources. *Interdisciplinary Journal of E-Learning and Learning Objects, 3*(1), 29–44. http://dx.doi.org/10.28945/384

Fischer, G. (2014). Beyond hype and underestimation: Identifying research challenges for the future of MOOCs. *Distance Education, 35*(2), 149–158. http://dx.doi.org/10.1080/01587919.2014.920752

Galanek, J. D., Gierdowski, D. C., & Brooks, D. C. (2018). *ECAR Study of Undergraduate Students and Information Technology* (Vol. 12, p. 12). https://www.educause.edu/ecar/research-publications/ecar-study-of-undergraduate-students-and-information-technology/2018/introduction-and-key-findings

Garrison, D. R., & Kanuka, H. (2004). Blended learning: Uncovering its transformative potential in higher education. *The Internet and Higher Education, 7*, 95–105. http://dx.doi.org/10.1016/j.iheduc.2004.02.001

Goodson, I., Moore, S. & Hargreaves, A. (2006). Teacher nostalgia and the sustainability of reform: The generation and degeneration of teachers' missions, memory, and meaning. *Educational Administration Quarterly, 42*(1), 42–61. http://dx.doi.org/10.1177/0013161X05278180

Haber, J. (2014). *MOOCs.* The MIT Press. http://dx.doi.org/10.7551/mitpress/10120.001.0001

Jacobson, T. E., & Mackey, T. P. (2013). Proposing a metaliteracy model to redefine information literacy. *Communications in Information Literacy, 7*(2), 84–91. https://doi.org/10.15760/comminfolit.2013.7.2.138

Jaschik, S., & Lederman, D. (2017). *Survey of faculty attitudes on technology: A study by Inside Higher Ed and Gallup.* Inside Higher and Gallup.

Johnson, K. (2018). *Chancellor Johnson's State University of New York (SUNY) state of the university system address.* State University of New York. https://www.suny.edu/about/leadership/chancellor/speeches/sotus-2018

Johnson, D. R. (2013). Technological change and professional control in the professoriate. *Science, Technology, & Human Values, 38*(1), 126–149. http://dx.doi.org/10.1177/0162243911430236

Jones, N., Georghiades, P., & Gunson, J. (2012). Student feedback via screen capture digital video: Stimulating student's modified action. *Higher Education, 64*(5), 593–607. http://dx.doi.org/10.1007/s10734-012-9514-7

King, J., & South, J. (2017). *Reimagining the role of technology in higher education: A supplement to the national education technology plan.* Office of Educational Technology EEUU. https://tech.ed.gov/files/2017/01/Higher-Ed-NETP.pdf

Krause, S. D., & Lowe, C. (2014). *Invasion of the MOOCs: The promise and perils of massive open online courses.* Parlor Press.

Kruger, J. S., & Sage, T. (2020). Video grading: Enhancing clarity and connection. *Journal of Educational Technology Systems, 48*(3), 407–415. https://doi.org/10.1177/00472395198673

Lambert, C., Erickson, L., Alhramelah, A., Rhoton, D., Lindbeck, R., & Sammons, D. (2014). Technology and adult students in higher education: A review of the literature. *Issues and Trends in Educational Technology, 2*(1). http://dx.doi.org/10.2458/azu_itet_v2i1_lambert

Lederman, D. (2018). Conflicted views of technology: A survey of faculty attitudes. *Inside Higher Ed.* https://www.insidehighered.com/news/survey/conflicted-views-technology-survey-faculty-attitudes

Lillejord, S., Børte, K., Nesje, K., & Ruud, E. (2018). *Learning and teaching with technology in higher education–a systematic review.* Knowledge Center for Education. https://www.researchgate.net/publication/327057633_Learning_and_Teaching_With_Technology_in_Higher_Education_-_a_systematic_review

Ludgate, H. (2013). *NMC Horizon Report: 2013 higher education edition.* The New Media Consortium.

Marzilli, C., Delello, J., Marmion, S., McWhorter, R., Roberts, P., & Marzilli, T. S. (2014). Faculty attitudes towards integrating technology and innovation. *International Journal on Integrating Technology in Innovation, 3*(1), *ArXiv Preprint ArXiv:1404.4334.* http://dx.doi.org/10.5121/ijite.2014.3101

National Education Association. (2012). *Preparing 21st-century students for a global society: An educator's guide to "the four Cs."* http://www.nea.org/assets/docs/A-Guide-to-Four-Cs.pdf

Orlando, J. (2014). Veteran teachers and technology: Change fatigue and knowledge insecurity influence practice. *Teachers and Teaching, 20*(4), 427–439. http://dx.doi.org/10.1080/13540602.2014.881644

Pappano, L. (2012, November 2). The year of the MOOC. *New York Times.* https://www.nytimes.com/2012/11/04/education/edlife/massive-open-online-courses-are-multiplying-at-a-rapid-pace.html

Selwyn, N. (2007). The use of computer technology in university teaching and learning: A critical perspective. *Journal of Computer Assisted Learning, 23*(2), 83–94. http://dx.doi.org/10.1111/j.1365-2729.2006.00204.x

Shaw, J. (2019, January 10). Can MOOCs predict the future of online education? *Harvard Magazine.* https://harvardmagazine.com/2019/01/mooc

Sibley, K., & Whitaker, R. (2015, March 16). Engaging faculty in online education. *EDUCAUSE Review.* https://er.educause.edu/articles/2015/3/engaging-faculty-in-online-education

Siemens, G. (2005). Connectivism: A learning theory for the digital age. *International Journal of Instructional Technology and Distance Learning (ITDL), 2*(1), 3–10. http://www.itdl.org/Journal/Jan_05/article01.htm

Siemens, G. (2013). Massive open online courses: Innovation in education? In R. McGreal, W. Kinuthua, & S. Marshall (Eds.), *Open educational resources: Innovation, research and practice* (pp. 5–16). Commonwealth of Learning and Athabasca University. https://oerknowledgecloud.org/sites/oerknowledgecloud.org/files/pub_PS_OER-IRP_web.pdf#page=31

Smithers, M. (2012, October 9). OH: In an xMOOC you watch videos, in a cMOOC you make videos [Twitter]. https://twitter.com/marksmithers/status/255562376659730434

Sullivan, R. R., Fulcher, K., Kruger, J., Sipley, G., & van Putten, C. (2019). Emerging technologies for lifelong learning and success: A MOOC for Everyone. *Journal of Educational Technology Systems, 47*(3), 318–336. http://dx.doi.org/10.1177/0047239518821065

Sullivan, R. R., Neu, V., & Yang, F. (2018). Faculty development to promote effective instructional technology integration: A qualitative examination of reflections in an online community. *Online Learning Journal (OLJ), 22*(4), 341–359. http://dx.doi.org/10.24059/olj.v22i4.1373

Wang, Y., & Baker, R. (2015). Content or platform: Why do students complete MOOCs? *Journal of Online Learning and Teaching, 11*(1), 17–30.

Young, J. R. (2013). *Beyond the MOOC hype: A guide to higher education's high-tech disruption.* The Chronicle of Higher Education.

Zawacki-Richter, O., Bozkurt, A., Alturki, U., & Aldraiweesh, A. (2018). What research says about MOOCs—An explorative content analysis. *International Review of Research in Open and Distributed Learning, 19*(1). http://dx.doi.org/10.19173/irrodl.v19i1.3356

4

A GUIDE FOR SUCCESSFUL INTEGRATION AND SUPPORT OF LEARNING TECHNOLOGIES

Danielle Leek, Matthew Olson, and Peter Shea

This chapter describes how to successfully integrate and support a learning technology adoption on a college campus. We believe that doing so is fundamentally a process of managing change, which, in the best of situations, poses many process-related and cultural challenges. When you factor in the significant financial and personnel investments often associated with learning technologies, you can see how important it is to get it right the first time with minimal wasted time and effort.

There are many different models of change and many process models for managing change. Any of these models may be helpful in understanding how to approach a learning technology project. Rather than rehash one of these models, we have chosen to describe a simple three-phases approach that offers a practical pathway through the complex, unexpected, and sometimes chaotic reality that college personnel are likely to experience when integrating and supporting a new learning technology on a college or university campus. As this chapter is intended to be a guide, it is purposefully directive. We make recommendations with the intent of sharing how decades of research and our own direct experiences inform an approach that does (often) work. It is our intent that all participants in developing an online course program (faculty, administrators, instructional designers, instructional technologists) will benefit from the recommendations we make here.

One caveat: book chapters on innovation adoption are often misleadingly linear, whereas the change process is not; change is recursive, uneven, and circuitous. The work of implementing learning technologies is much more human than any process diagram might imply. We like the concept of *agile messiness* to capture this idea. It is, and should be, complex, colorful, recursive, and engaging. Our term is derived from the Agile design project management methodology that originated in software development and requires practitioners to be "adaptable to the contingencies of the project environment" (p. 21) (Conforto et al., 2014). Two elements from the Agile design methodology that are of particular significance here are the importance of valuing "individuals and interactions over processes and tools" and prioritizing "responding to change over following a [strict] plan" ("Agile Software Development," n.d., para. 10). Throughout this chapter, we'll describe how embracing this design process approach—coupled with pedagogical theory and best practices—increases the likelihood of success.

In addition, by focusing on the process of integrating and supporting learning technologies, we have made a purposeful choice to exclude discussing some parts of the learning technology adoption cycle traditionally thought of as essential. For example, guidance on conducting needs assessments and evaluating learning tools can be found using the excellent resources curated and supported by organizations such as EDUCAUSE (see Anstey & Watson, 2018). Scholars and practitioners who make up these consortia have created a robust literature describing how to bring together key stakeholders, evaluate software for its compatibility with existing institutional systems, and review data privacy standards, which are all steps necessary to complete before choosing a learning technology for your campus. Not to be forgotten is the "end-of-life-cycle" phase that includes the important process of decommissioning an out-of-date learning technology. Information technology (IT) departments can provide key guidance in this area. Rather than walk on this well-tread ground, this chapter attends to what Scott Belsky (2018) calls the "messy middle," the difficult middle stretch of any innovation project where the initial enthusiasm for a new idea may be fading, stressed by the inevitable failures that come with integration and maintenance. Success in this phase requires strategies to optimize what's working in order to build momentum and keep key participants engaged.

We recognize that this is complex work, requiring skills across a number of domains. Change management, interpersonal relationships, project oversight, assessment, and quality control are only a few of the challenges that must be addressed during the learning technology adoption process. We have found that embracing the chaos is one way to make the process more engaging and more rewarding for all involved.

Therefore, we acknowledge that although there is no one path to follow, there are key steps that can be taken at critical decision points in order to best prepare for each phase of the middle-period. This chapter concludes with checklists for administrators, faculty, and instructional designers who are going to be involved in a learning technology project (see Appendices 4A, 4B, and 4C).

Phase One: Project Planning and Orientation

Successful integration of technology into the institution or a course initially involves the process of planning backward—envisioning initially what successful implementation of a specific technology will look like listed in the guiding planning questions identified in Phase One.

Strategic Planning

Let us assume your institution has selected a learning technology such as an adaptive learning tool, a mobile app, tablets, digital testing, smart boards, and so on. Just because you have selected a specific tool does not mean that your learning technology implementation will be successful. In fact, a great deal of work needs to happen prior to the launch of a learning technology pilot in order for innovation to avoid becoming yet another available software or hardware tool that no one actually uses. Using a backward design approach, we should first start by asking, "What are the final goals of the project?" Only by envisioning the end result of the learning technology being integrated and used successfully can we create a realistic project plan, decide who needs to be involved, acquire necessary resources, and create an assessment plan from the very start.

To plan successfully, you should ask the following 11 questions:

1. Where and for whom will the learning technology be used? (All students campus-wide? In specific departments and programs? Students at specific levels?)
2. How accessible is the technology as-is, and what accommodations might be necessary or possible? Is it 508 compliant? (This refers to the federal regulation for making IT accessible to people with disabilities.)
3. What pedagogical philosophy provides a rationale for the adoption of the new learning technology? (Is there a constructivist assumption associated with the new tool, or does it assume passive learning?)
4. What will be different about the learning environment on your campus once the technology is fully implemented?
5. What is the desired effect on student learning? How will this be measured?

6. How will teaching/program administration be changed following the implementation?
7. Apart from the initial cost of the technology, what will be the cost of sustaining it (the total cost of ownership)?
8. Whose participation is needed during the initial adoption?
9. What new skills will need to be developed? Will they require training for faculty and students?
10. How will the new learning technology be communicated to the larger college community?
11. Are there any existing college initiatives whose goals can be served by the new technology? How do they relate to the college's strategic plan?

Many of the answers to these questions may have emerged during the selection of the technology. Responses to these questions may be used to design a map from your starting point, or baseline, to your end vision. Beginning with the end in mind is not only a key strategy for moving learning technology project from start to finish but also an important way to avoid a key pitfall: making assumptions about who should be involved in your projects and the extent of the commitments needed. Too often campuses assume that any new learning innovation requires the participation of all students and all faculty in order to justify a return on investment. In truth, many successful projects may be focused on targeted programs and student cohorts. Also, it is important to understand how the technology initiative connects to your college or university strategic plan. Connecting to that plan can serve to guide your prioritization of activities, access funding sources, build executive support, and explain why this project was selected over other possibilities.

Functioning as a Team

Successful adoption of new learning technology is a team-based activity. Faculty, instructional designers, and administrators are all essential members of an effective learning technology adoption team. However, it should not be assumed that these three groups know automatically how to work together. They each approach learning technology from a different professional perspective. Students and vendors may also play important roles on the team. (See the appendices at the end of this chapter.)

Administrators, by their very role, must balance resource allocation across various projects and constituencies. If the driving force behind the new technology is faculty, there may be conflict when an administrator needs to limit funds and support for a new technology project. At the outset, administrators must make clear how proposals for new learning technology adoptions are assessed and how funding decisions will be made, because all suggested adoptions cannot likely be made within a fiscal cycle. Being transparent from the start will reduce unrealistic expectations for resources and underfunded initiatives.

Given their set of skills and competencies, instructional designers are uniquely situated to help at all levels of adoption of new learning technology (O'Neill, 2015). However, they are still relative newcomers to higher education institutions, and faculty members do not always understand the role of the instructional designer and the wealth of pedagogical knowledge that instructional designers bring to their work. Successful instructional designers possess emotional intelligence and are good at building relationships with faculty members, often applying Rogers's (2003) widely used taxonomy to determine whether their faculty partner is an innovator who embraces emerging technologies or is from the late majority and approaches new technologies cautiously and with anxiety. Another complexity in the relationship between faculty and instructional designers is the fact that instructional designers report to administrators. Faculty prize their independence and are often wary of taking too much direction from administrators in areas that are central to teaching and learning and intersect with academic freedom. If the instructional designer is seen as an agent of administration, this could hinder the level of trust and development of productive relationships with faculty. Therefore, instructional designers must carefully manage a triangulated relationship with administrators and faculty. For this reason, prior to any learning technology adoption project, it is a good idea for instructional designers to have already developed a relationship with their faculty partners.

Another good practice is to follow basic project management procedures and have all members of the team attend an orientation meeting where everyone discusses roles and responsibilities, project timeline, and deliverables. It is also important that one or two individuals take on the role of project manager. Another task for the orientation meeting is to examine carefully the assumptions that led to selecting the technology. It is very important to be mindful that evidence of successful adoption of this technology in other schools and colleges may not necessarily lead to successful adoption at your institution (Hollands & Escueta, 2017). Consider the institutional culture and be prepared to ask yourself whether it is a good fit. You may even assign someone the role of devil's advocate and have that person articulate all the reasons why you should *not* try to adopt the learning technology. (It is also prudent to offer some professional development around innovation adoption and the practices that lead to success.)

Returning to process matters, given the fast pace and multiple demands on college personnel, dates and times for follow-up meetings should be established immediately as well as a method or methods for communicating during the project. An email group list is the simplest approach for basic communication. However, you will want to consider capturing all your written communication in one place where it can be reviewed later to gather insights that might prove useful in future technology adoption projects as well as a method to track major implementations milestones. You could create a course site dedicated to the project in your school's learning management system (LMS) or use software tools like Slack.

Finally, it is wise to have a guiding project document that explains the rationale and scope of the project, something to which everyone can refer back when the project inevitably takes on a life of its own. This document will not only assist with the project management but also, along with the record of email communication, become part of the project archive, a repository of "lessons learned" to guide future learning technology adoption projects and to keep the current project on track ensuring the group does not "miss the forest for the trees."

One good example of a well-implemented Phase One was seen in the development of an online learning program at Middlesex Community College of Massachusetts in the 1990s (which was overseen by Matthew Olson). Although the impetus for online courses began with the administration wanting to reach students in new ways and save facilities costs, a cross-functional study group consisting of administrators, instructional designers, technology support staff, and faculty were tasked with identifying best practices. The group chose to build the college's nascent online learning program using a social constructivist model, emphasizing students' construction of knowledge through social interaction. Because the philosophical model and approach were determined in advance of technology selection, online learning tools could be selected based on their abilities to provide rich forums for interaction and collaboration. Further, administration was influenced to make policy decisions that would support the shared approach, such as limiting the maximum numbers of students in a class in order to promote more student-student and student-teacher interaction and increasing faculty stipends to allow more time to develop interactive lessons.

We have suggested ideas for structure and process, but, as we are guided by Agile messiness, we recommend continued flexibility, encouraging participants to act as problem solvers and idea generators in all stages of the technology integration process. Unexpected new ideas present opportunities to increase the relative advantage of the technology and increase the likelihood innovations will diffuse effectively throughout the campus. Sometimes users will find new inventive uses for new technology that would never have occurred to the "experts" on the implementation team.

Phase Two: Initial Implementation

Initial implementation is the phase in which the rubber hits the road. Implementation is an incredible learning opportunity and almost always leads to important revision before a project can move to scale.

It is widely recognized that enthusiastic learning technology early adopters among faculty and instructional designers can be the linchpins for bringing skeptical, resistant, or less-experienced faculty on-board (see Aldunate & Nussbaum, 2013). For example, in 2018 faculty in the nursing program at Bunker Hill Community College (BHCC) in Massachusetts chose to move from paper-based Scantron tests to a cloud-based, digital testing platform for all exams. Members from BHCC's Academic Innovation team provided support for faculty to learn and adopt the new platform. One might have thought the proper course of action would be to start with faculty and students in the first level course (Nursing I) so students could use the testing platform from the start of their experience. Instead, using knowledge from faculty self-assessments about their confidence with technology, the Academic Innovation team chose to begin the project with upper level (Nursing IV) faculty who expressed the most confidence with digital tools and a marked willingness to experiment. The early adopters not only embraced the new platform but also developed documentation materials to assist the next faculty cohort. In fact, one upper level faculty member came to serve as a "faculty champion" for the online testing initiative. Overall, faculty satisfaction with the new tool was high, student success improved, and late adopters reported that having a colleague as a mentor was a central part of their willingness to participate. (Note: This anecdote was drawn from the experience of one of our contributors, Danielle Leek.)

Introducing the Technology to Students

There is a common misconception that the students of today have a higher degree of fluency with a given new technology than previous generations. Although it is true that students born in the 21st century have grown up with a variety of digital technologies integrated into their everyday lives, it would be a mistake to assume that their learning curve of technology adoption is shorter than it is for older people. Also, access to many of these technologies has not been distributed evenly across socioeconomic groups and communities. Still, even though some tools may be new to some users, many of the technologies students use regularly (web browsers, tablets, smartphone apps) have been designed to be simple enough for small children to learn. Conversely, learning technology developed specifically for higher education (from an LMS to virtual reality headgear) often requires more effort and support to master than conventional learning technology.

Due to major economic changes, more people than ever before are coming to college, and many students enter college classrooms already anxious about their ability to succeed. Learning new technologies in addition to studying challenging subject matter adds to their cognitive load, which may exacerbate anxieties and even affect attitudes toward the subject matter and college in general. It is crucial for the technology adoption process to be as smooth and unobtrusive as possible. It is a good practice to identify students who adapt rapidly to the new technology and then engage them as peer tutors for their colleagues in the use of these tools. At Middlesex Community College in Massachusetts, student employees from the tutoring department were hired as "Blackboard LMS Ambassadors" to serve as peer support resources for students taking online classes. The student ambassadors were enrolled in online courses for the first month of class and helped other students to navigate both the technology of the online course and the support resources of the college. (This anecdote was drawn from the experience of one of our contributors, Matthew Olson.)

It also good practice to avoid assuming the value of adopting a new learning technology will be self-evident to students. It is important that the rationale for adding any tech is made clear to students, especially the ways in which the tech will help them achieve their learning goals. If you are in the pilot stage of adoption, make it clear that this adoption is an experiment intended to test the value of the technology in the classroom—and that the students' candid input is welcome in both the formative and summative phases of assessment. One interesting example of this reflexive nature of outcomes can be seen in a long-ago technology integration project in which one of the chapter contributors was bringing PowerPoint into grade school classrooms. Although the students and teachers could not immediately understand the need for a presentation tool, they found PowerPoint to be an excellent "book report maker" that allowed students to print out illustrated book reports.

Advice for Faculty

Faculty engaging in new learning technology adoption for the first time often underestimate how much extra effort will be needed to attend to both the learning technology adoption and their teaching responsibilities. Administrators also may not appreciate the time and effort faculty innovators make in these learning technology trial efforts. Lack of appreciation of faculty time and effort can result in the participating faculty feeling their efforts are unappreciated by the administration. This, along with the increased workload, can lead to eventual burnout. To avoid this scenario, other members of the team should be ready to support each other and put in place remedies when roadblocks and frustrations occur. If possible, it is prudent to assign the novice learning technology adopter a peer mentor—someone among the faculty who has prior experience with learning technology adoption and who can offer advice and emotional support. It is also advisable that the team in this project should have some of their meetings off campus—preferably during a lunch period—so they can get perspective and renew their personal connection by enjoying each other's company in an informal setting. Creating and maintaining team identity and morale is important for both the present technology adoption initiative as well as future ones. For example, at Middlesex Community College of Massachusetts, the Virtual Education Research Group (VERG) served as an incubator for cutting-edge experimentation with virtual worlds, also as a peer support for engaged faculty and staff (Cady et al., 2006).

Another issue when adopting new technology is that the technology may not fit neatly into the dominant instructional paradigm that still favors teacher-centered instruction. For example, virtual world technology that generated much excitement when first introduced failed to gain wide adoption in part because it did not fit easily into the learning model that both faculty and students expected. Accordingly, it is important to have ongoing conversations about how the learning technology being adopted may be integrated into the classroom learning experience. Faculty should seek out student insights for how the technology may be used. Student users can provide suggestions and ideas that may not have occurred to the instructor. Moreover, when student input is actively sought, the technology adoption process creates a space for dialogue between students and instructors.

Other Considerations

Despite the best of preparations, unforeseen occurrences and setbacks happen. Key members of the team may leave during the implementation phase, the IT person may discover issues that make continuing support of the learning technology adoption difficult or untenable, or a new administrator may question the value of the learning technology being adopted. This is where the Agile design approach comes in handy. Recognizing at the outset that achieving the project goal requires flexibility of strategy and the ability to revise plans based on changing circumstances is essential. Moreover, the instructional designer has a special opportunity to serve as a translator across faculty, IT, and administrative roles (Davidson & Olson, 2003). Although each of these stakeholders sees learning technologies from their own vantage points—as technology to deploy and maintain by IT, as strategic expenses to achieve outcomes by administration, and as a means of promoting deep learning by faculty—the instructional designer's unique vantage point brings all these perspectives together. Therefore, when problems do occur, the instructional designer is best suited to get to the heart of the matter and negotiate common understandings and viable solutions.

By way of example, one school in our experience was seeking to bring an iPad initiative to scale but neglected to consider how the influx of iPads would increase the use of the LMS on mobile devices. Suddenly, the LMS, which had proven so reliable in a mostly PC environment, was problematic when used on an iPad. From a faculty perspective, the new learning technology wasn't working. From administration, there was concern that a poor investment had been made, and from IT there was an unanticipated surge in support calls related to LMS use on a mobile platform. It was the instructional designer with her broad perspective who took the lead, working with IT staff and faculty to identify necessary work-arounds (browser upgrades, faculty training, and feedback to the LMS provider), keeping the project on the desired trajectory.

When in the weeds of a project it is also easy to overlook or forget about the need to communicate with external stakeholders, including administrators and faculty, who are not directly involved in the project. Each member of the adoption team should take responsibility to communicate with others about the project, its potential value to the institution, and ways it will help serve students and the school's strategic goals. A successful project done in isolation will be far less impactful in regard to cultural change than one that is well understood by the entire community. Successful learning technology integrations can be both points of pride and marketing strategies for institutions.

Accessibility Issues

An extremely important issue that needs to be addressed early on is accessibility. In the United States, federally funded schools are required to adhere to Section 508 of the United States Workforce Rehabilitation Act of 1973, which requires technology to be accessible to people with disabilities (Seifel, 2015). In addition to government regulations, universal design for learning best practices inherently address principles of equity and inclusion and should be used. If universal accessibility is not possible, strategies should be in place to accommodate students who may not otherwise get the full benefit of a learning technology adoption. These issues serve as a useful reminder that we do not adopt learning technology simply for the sake of adoption but to promote specific learning outcomes. If the technology you wish to adopt has accessibility issues, return to the learning outcome that it is intended to serve and research potential supplementary technology tools that might address the gap. It is also incumbent on the instructional designer to provide feedback to vendors about potential solutions to accessibility issues and to drive product development toward universal design principles.

Phase Three: Assessment

Two critical decisions guide this phase of an innovative leader's work: "Where did we fail?" and "How do we move forward?" We have purposefully left out the question, "Where did we succeed?" Embrace your successes. As education technology innovators and leaders, your failures are much more interesting and important. Failures produce teachable moments and are the source of all our innovation. By understanding where failure has occurred, leaders can effectively help navigate a campus forward to success, even if that means making the difficult decision to end a project or leave a technology behind.

At the outset, your team should develop a series of metrics that will help establish whether the adoption was a success. Table 4.1 is a (very simple) sample rubric that could help with such an evaluation.

A successful assessment plan requires collecting data from all stakeholders including students, instructors, IT support, and administrators involved in the project. Ideally, at the end of a project, a report should be generated that includes everything learned as well as the final judgment as to whether the adoption was successful. The ratings in Table 4.2 may be applied.

The project team should not fear failure. Adoption of any innovation involves multiple risks, and every attempted innovation yields insights that may guide future projects as well as build experience that increases expertise

TABLE 4.1
Sample Rubric to Assess Success of Adoption

Project Element	Rating (0–10)	Notes
Ease of student adoption of technology		
Ease of faculty adoption of technology		
Ability of IT to support technology and overcome issues		
Impact on student performance and achievement of learning outcomes		
Unanticipated outcomes		

Note. On this scale, 0 is very unsuccessful and 10 is very successful.

TABLE 4.2
Overall Project Ratings

Rating	Description
Completely Successful	The project succeeded in all goals, and the next step is to create a plan for scalability and sustainability.
Partially Successful	Although some goals were met, there were issues that suggest the need to retool the process and try again with the pilot stage.
Unsuccessful	The technology did not achieve the goals and proved a poor fit for the institution or program culture.

in bringing new ideas and tools, which in turn helps promote student learning and success.

Conclusion

The contributors of this chapter hope this attempt to describe and address the "messy middle" of the learning technology implementation process provides a modicum of utility for faculty, as well as instructional designers and administrators engaged in learning technology change efforts. By considering challenges associated with each of the three phases in advance—project planning and orientation, initial implementation, and assessment—instructors may head off some of the traditional problems associated with learning technology integration. We live in the age of Moore's Law ("Moore's Law," n.d.) with a continual flow of new technologies and tools coming to us on a daily basis, each promising to make a fundamental change to teaching and learning. But the reality is, and has always been, that although many new technologies may indeed be "game changers," it is only with effective processes, communication, support, and laser-focused attention to student learning outcomes that meaningful change is possible.

Contributors' Note

As we closed on this chapter, we found ourselves in the midst of an unprecedented time in higher education. The global pandemic of the COVID-19 virus, among its many impacts, created an instantaneous and dire need for quickly putting teaching and learning online. The many colleges closing their physical campuses and announcing their quick conversion to virtual instruction, with little or no plan to do so, made obvious how rarely new digital learning is actually infused into business as usual in higher education.

In this chaotic time, there has been a heroic amount of cooperation among instructional designers from around the world who used social media to share idea and resources, as well as kept their colleagues' spirits uplifted. In one of these social media communities, Amanda Daniels (2020), a member of Facebook's Instructional Designers in Education group, articulated what may be the core piece of wisdom for higher education professionals moving instructors into an online environment: "Keep it simple and make it personal."

References

Aldunate, R. & Nussbaum, M. (2013). Teacher adoption of technology. *Computers in Human Behavior, 29*, 519–524. https://doi.org/10.1016/j.chb.2012.10.017

Agile software development. (n.d). In *Wikipedia*. Retrieved June 21, 2020. https://en.wikipedia.org/wiki/Agile_software_development

Anstey, L., & Watson, G. (2018, September 10). A rubric for evaluating e-learning tools in higher education. *EDUCAUSE Review*. https://er.educause.edu/articles/2018/9/a-rubric-for-evaluating-e-learning-tools-in-higher-education

Belsky, S. (2018). *The messy middle: Finding your way through the hardest and most crucial part of any bold venture*. Portfolio Penguin.

Cady, D., Kalivas, D., Margulis, D., & Olson, M. (2006). Creating a community of practice to support technological innovation in the community college. *Community College Journal, 77*(2), 17–19.

Conforto, E. C., Salum, F., Amaral, D. C., Silva, S. L., & Almeida, L. F. M. (2014). Can agile project management be adopted by industries other than software development? *Project Management Journal, 45*(3), 21–34. https://doi.org/10.1002/pmj.21410

Daniels, A. (2020, March). Instructional Designers in Education [Facebook Group] https://www.facebook.com/groups/1526889350715555/

Davidson, J., & Olson, M. (2003). School leadership in networked schools: Deciphering the impact of large technical systems on education. *International Journal of Leadership in Education, 6*(3), 261–281. https://doi.org/10.1080/1360312032000138692

Hollands, F., & Escueta, M. (2017). *EdTech decision-making in higher education* [White Paper]. Center for Benefit-Cost Studies of Education Teachers College, Columbia University. http://symposium.curry.virginia.edu/wp-content/uploads/2017/06/WG-B-Edtech-Decision-Making-in-Higher-Education_FINAL.pdf

Moore's law. (2020). In *Wikipedia*. Retrieved June 21, 2020. https://en.wikipedia.org/wiki/Moore%27s_law

O'Neill, E. (2015, May 12). 7 things you should know about developments in instructional design. *EDUCAUSE Review*. https://library.educause.edu/resources/2015/5/7-things-you-should-know-about-developments-in-instructional-design

Rogers, E. M. (2003). *Diffusion of Innovations*. (5th ed.). Free Press.

Seifel, T. (2015, September 9). Accessibility for e-learning: Section 508 and WCAG. *Association for Talent Development*. https://www.td.org/insights/accessibility-for-e-learning-section-508-and-wcag

Appendix 4A: Checklist for Administrators

Responsible Party	Task	Complete (Date)
Whole Project Team	Meets to discuss rationale for technology adoption	
Whole Project Team	Creates project plan document that describes the goals of the pilot, responsibilities of each member, project timeline, and final evaluation of the project	
Administrator	Assesses cost and information technology (IT) support elements of adoption	
Administrator	Assesses sustainability cost if adoption is successful	
Whole Project Team	Creates a timeline for piloting the technology and sets project review meeting dates	
Whole Project Team	Creates a plan for communicating this project to the larger college community (while making it clear how the project fits into the college's larger strategic goals)	
Administrator	Periodically checks in with faculty and instructional designer to see if there are any unexpected issues with which the instructor or instructional designer needs assistance	
Whole Project Team	Reviews and reports on final project outcomes	

Appendix 4B: Checklist for Faculty

Responsible Party	Task	Complete (Date)
Whole Project Team	Meets to discuss rationale for technology adoption	
Whole Project Team	Creates project plan document that describes the goals of the pilot, responsibilities of each member, project timeline, and final evaluation of the project	
Whole Project Team	Creates a timeline for piloting the technology and sets project review meeting dates	
Whole Project Team	Creates a plan for communicating this project to the larger college community (making it clear how the project fits into the college's larger strategic goals)	
Faculty	Plans the integration of the new technology into course	
Faculty	Meets with instructional designer to discuss issues around implementation	
Faculty	Confers with faculty colleagues who have experience testing new technology	
Faculty and Instructional Designer	Test drives the technology before classroom adoption to identify unforeseen issues and discusses strategies for addressing unanticipated problems that arise during piloting stage	
Faculty	Adds tutorials on using the new technology available in the course learning management system (LMS)	
Faculty	Creates methods for formative and summative assessment of technology's impact	
Whole Project Team	Reviews and reports on final project outcomes	

Appendix 4C: Checklist for Instructional Designer

Responsible Party	Task	Complete (Date)
Whole Project Team	Meets to discuss rationale for technology adoption	
Whole Project Team	Creates project plan document that describes the goals of the pilot, responsibilities of each member, project timeline, and final evaluation of the project	
Whole Project Team	Creates a timeline for piloting the technology and sets project review meeting dates	
Whole Project Team	Creates a plan for communicating this project to the larger college community (making it clear how the project fits into the college's larger strategic goals)	
Instructional Designer	Meets with faculty to discuss issues around implementation	
Faculty and Instructional Designer	Test drives the technology before classroom adoption to identify unforeseen issues and discusses strategies for addressing unanticipated problems that arise during piloting stage.	
Instructional Designer	Meets with IT to discuss implementation and support strategies for technology	
Instructional Designer	Creates or curates tutorials that explain how the technology is used	
Instructional Designer	Communicates regularly with faculty to see if assistance is required	
Instructional Designer	Shares with vendor any issues that arise with technology and devises solutions.	
Whole Project Team	Reviews and reports on final project outcomes	

PART TWO

SOME REPRESENTATIVE EXAMPLES OF COURSE-BASED USE OF EMERGING LEARNING TECHNOLOGIES

5

APPLYING A LEARNING ANALYTICS APPROACH TO IMPROVE COURSE ACHIEVEMENT

Using Data Stored in Learning Management Systems

Pauline Salim Muljana, Greg V. Placencia, and Tian Luo

Amazon recommends items we want to purchase and Netflix suggests movies that match our interests (Dietz et al., 2018), curated approaches that seem like magic—in reality, both businesses strategically use data analytics to meet their consumers' needs better. It is no surprise then that some colleges and universities have turned to data analytics, long used in business and marketing, to find ways to support students' needs successfully. Specifically, campuses are using learning analytics (LA), a subtype of data analytics. For example, Stanford University has developed the Open Analytics Research Service (OARS), a system that uses data visualization to help faculty monitor an individual student's learning progress across courses and adjust instruction dynamically in real time to improve each student's progress toward achieving mastery-level learning outcomes (Thille & Zimmaro, 2017).

DEFINING *LA*

LA is popularly defined as "the measurement, collection, analysis, and reporting of data about learners and their contexts, for the purpose of understanding and optimizing learning and the environment in which it occurs" (Siemens & Long, 2011, p. 34). This definition highlights a few key points underlying the LA concept. The emphasis rests on measuring learners and learning outcomes within a specific context through data analysis with the aim of recommending improvements in students' learning and the environment in which that learning occurs. LA mines and reports data related to patterns of students' performance so that faculty can monitor students' current learning progress to identify patterns of underperformance that they need to help students improve. Faculty can implement this approach either outside of or within an institution's learning management system (LMS). In the Stanford University example mentioned previously, OARS provides faculty with an Instructor Dashboard to help them (a) monitor individual student's learning behaviors and progress according to each learning objective in a course and (b) predict the likelihood that "a student would be able to respond correctly to previously unseen problems or questions related to a specific learning objective" (Thille & Zimmaro, 2017, p. 21). OARS itself is external to LMS, which is not a native or built-in analytics tool within an LMS; however, it can be integrated into various LMS platforms.

Not all institutions have the resources to purchase an online LA program or to develop one in-house; however, native, built-in analytics tools bundled into an LMS can be used to harvest course usage data that capture students' learning behaviors. Examples include: the number of times and types of course resources a student accesses, number and content of discussion posts a student generates, assessment submission timestamps, and grades (Dietz et al., 2018; Dietz-Uhler & Hurn, 2013). Faculty can gain an evidence-based understanding of student performance patterns based on these kinds of data, thus enabling them to identify and implement actions to improve underperformance patterns. With either externally developed analytics tools or those integrated within a LMS, LA overall highlights the role of data-driven evidence as a means for faculty to identify students at risk early on in a course or along their progression and then implement the most expedient interventions. Although often instinct may also prompt us to act, LA corroborates instinct via data (Dietz-Uhler & Hurn, 2013; Lu et al., 2017).

To support faculty at institutions without external analytics systems that have to be purchased separately or developed in-house, this chapter focuses on the effective use of LA to support students' successful attainment of course outcomes, based on data already available to faculty in their institutions' LMS. Specifically, we intend to motivate faculty to practice using predictive, formative, and summative LA at the course level. Faculty consulting these kinds of real-time learning data are able to implement just-in-time support and interventions to improve students' learning outcomes, as well as use these data to improve the next iteration of a course. Faculty working in an institution that already has an analytics system can also benefit from this chapter based on examples of how faculty draw on analytics data to develop or identify interventions that improve students' learning outcomes.

This chapter consists of three parts:

- Part One: Three Uses of Course-Based Learning Analytics describes how LA reports predictive, formative, and summative data about student performance in a course and how these data benefit both faculty and students.
- Part Two: Integration of Learning Analytics Approaches Into Your Course Design and Structure describes and illustrates principles of integrating LA into the design and structure of your online or hybrid course to continuously improve your students' learning
- Part Three: Integration of Learning Analytics Into an Engineering Course provides an example of how LA approaches have been integrated into an industrial engineering course designed to identify and then address risks students face as they learn.

Part One: Three Uses of Course-Based Learning Analytics

We use scholars Ifenthaler and Widanapathirana's (2014) LA benefit matrix as a framework for the three uses of LA, as it appeared in "Development and Validation of a Learning Analytics Framework: Two Case Studies Using Support Vector Machines," and expand Muljana and Placencia's (2018) framework for using built-in analytics tools within LMS platforms throughout the semester. The following uses of LA provide faculty course-based data about student learning: (a) predictive, to identify students early on in a course or in their academic careers who appear to be at risk and, therefore, need additional support to succeed; (b) formative, to track students' real-time progress in a course; and (c) summative, conducted at the end of a course, to identify the specific interventions and practices that promote student learning so that faculty can then integrate those effective practices into the next iteration of that course (Ifenthaler, 2017; Ifenthaler & Widanapathirana, 2014; Muljana & Luo, 2020).

Predictive Analytics Approach

A predictive analytics approach provides early evidence about the likelihood of each student's academic success based on, for example, potential learning issues or challenges students face early on in a course (You, 2016). Researcher You from South Korea examined the impact of students' early course behaviors in an online synchronous course that employed online instructional materials and offline exams, based on student behavioral data stored in the LMS. According to researcher You, results of the behavioral data mined in the LMS revealed that students' early patterns of (a) virtual class attendance, (b) assignment submission timestamps, (c) frequency of access of the course materials, and (d) number of downloads for the course materials were strong predictors of course achievement (as cited in Muljana & Luo, 2020). Access to these kinds of student data early in a semester prepares faculty to identify and implement just-in-time interventions for the range of learners in their course. Examples of interventions that help students early on in a semester—conducted before the first major test or exam—include the following: providing students learning tips; scaffolding content with which students struggle; making the case for regular attendance and regular study times to review course instructional materials, both of which contribute to students' overall progress in the course and final performance; and encouraging students to submit assignments for feedback before official deadlines.

Formative Analytics Approach

Formative analytics provides real-time data about students' actual performance along the trajectory of a course, prompting faculty to make on-time adjustments in teaching and learning strategies and course materials for those who are having difficulty as well as for those who are successful and need more challenges. In 2015, Yen et al. provided an excellent example of using formative analytics in an online course that enrolled 869 undergraduate students in their article, "An Analytics-Based Approach to Managing Cognitive Load by Using Log Data of Learning Management Systems and Footprints of Social Media," published in the *Journal of Educational Technology & Society* (as cited in Muljana & Luo, 2020). According to Mayer, human cognitive processing capacity is limited (as cited in Yen et al., 2015). Specifically, it is known that our working memory is limited (Miller, 1956). When students process information during a learning event, they also consume part of working memory capacity and may possibly maximize the capacity depending on the subject difficulty, prior knowledge, and how their information is presented. This type of information load in the working memory is called cognitive load (Sweller et al., 1998).

Although overloading working memory can hinder learning (Abeysekera & Dawson, 2015), there are strategies that educators can use, such as through instructional methods. In their study, Yen et al. (2015) mined and analyzed LMS data such as students' browsing time and interaction in discussion forums to reveal whether students were experiencing cognitive load during online discussion participation. They identified the browsing time indicator by dividing the total browsing time by the module duration. For instance, if a student spent 3 hours (180 minutes) on a 10-minute module, the browsing time indicator would be 18. Yen et al. (2015) identified the density of discussion posts by calculating an average of the total number of posts generated in 3 consecutive days. For example, if a student generated three posts, five posts, and four posts in 3 successive days, the density of posts for this student would be four. Yen et al.

(2015) additionally identified the increased number of views in the discussion forum by calculating the total number of views for the post on a particular day. These researchers also assigned a subject matter expert to review the modules to identify which ones were categorized as easy and difficult. Increased browsing time in the difficult modules may represent a high cognitive load. Low post density and number of views may imply no or low cognitive load; however, it may also imply a high cognitive load if the subject is complicated and students do not know what to post in the forum. High post density and number of views may imply a possibility of high cognitive load.

As a result of their findings, researchers reported that they simultaneously adjusted instructions and online discussion prompts while analyzing the LMS log data to direct students experiencing high cognitive load to focus continuously on the main discussion topic (Yen et al., 2015). Additionally, they offered actionable interventions in line with the LMS data analytics that show browsing time, density of discussion posts, and the number of views in discussion forums. These researchers discovered that continuously consulting students' course usage data helped them identify and then develop interventions to support students' learning, such as providing students proper directions, feedback, and reinforcement.

Summative Analytics Approach

Summative analytics provides end-of-course data about the impact of student behaviors or strategies employed in a course to identify those that supported or improved student learning. For example, in 2016 researcher Firat reported the correlation between the time students spent on accessing course materials stored in an LMS to support a traditional face-to-face course and their final course grades (as cited in Muljana & Luo, 2020). Specifically, students who spent an average of 207 minutes or more each week reviewing course-related materials on the LMS achieved higher final grades than those students who spent less than that average time. This correlation offers an important implication about providing time management strategies to students in the next course iteration to promote their interaction with instructional materials and, thereby, optimize their course performance. For example, faculty may consider employing the following strategy in the next cohort: If the LMS usage data displays a low frequency of course accesses, a reminder to participate can be included in a course announcement or learning tips can be included in a module. Such reminders convey to students the importance of regularly setting aside a specific time to review course materials. It is important to note that research indicates those who regularly access course materials more often achieve better grades than those who spend less time accessing the course materials (Zimmerman, 2012). Figure 5.1 shows such a report retrieved from Blackboard (a common LMS) depicting the number of accesses and time spent on the platform. Other LMSs such as Canvas, Moodle, and Brightspace, have similar tools to obtain this kind of report. For further detail and resources about built-in analytics tools in other LMSs, see Muljana and Placencia's (2018) "Learning Analytics: Translating Data Into 'Just-in-Time' Interventions." Muljana and Placencia (2018) also provide ideas regarding the actions that instructors can perform by using the analytics tools within LMSs.

Part Two: Integration of Learning Analytics Approaches Into Your Course Design and Structure

Implementing predictive, formative, and summative LA into an online course is most effective when course tasks or activities and assessment

Figure 5.1. A Blackboard Course Access Report classified by hours and days.

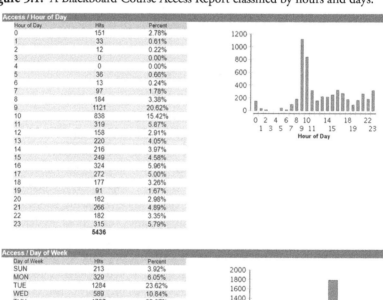

Note. In this figure, most course accesses occur on Thursdays and Tuesdays. Based on student access times, students mostly access the course site at 9:00 a.m. and 10:00 a.m. These data were retrieved at the end of the course; therefore, the number of hits looks high. Used with permission from Blackboard Inc.

methods align with expected learning outcomes and when effective pedagogical approaches enable students to achieve those outcomes. Additionally,
alignment of these core course components within a hierarchical and logical course structure (illustrated in the top left-hand quadrant of Figure 5.2)
helps students purposefully navigate and access course materials.

To prepare your online or hybrid course, instead of simply uploading
course content to the LMS, using Wiggins and McTighe's (2005) principles
of backward design model provides useful guidance. The design step starts
with formulating the learning outcomes by stating what students should be
able to achieve from the course. These learning outcomes drive the aligned
learning activities included in the course content and the types of assessment that enables students to demonstrate or represent their attainment of
specific outcomes. Learning activities, as well as the instructions that accom-
pany them, should be purposely aligned with the learning outcomes so that
the teaching and learning processes will help students learn and achieve the
specified learning outcomes.

These three core components—learning outcomes, learning activities/
tasks, and assessment—are segmented in meaningful units so that students
can incrementally achieve the outcomes. Especially for online courses,

Figure 5.2. Implementation of learning analytics approach to promote successful
course achievement.

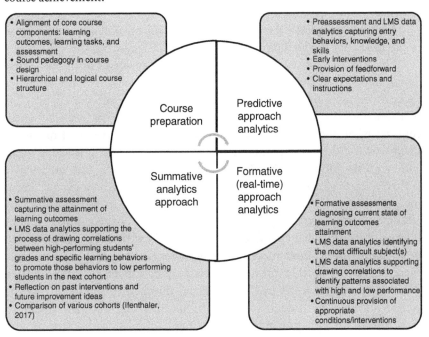

presenting course content by weekly modules, lesson units, or topic organizes content and units of instruction into meaningful components that should align with course learning outcomes. Each unit should have learning outcomes with tasks designed to align with them and ordered by level of complexity. For example, initial learning outcomes and aligned tasks in a course might address lower levels of knowledge (e.g., memorization of facts); subsequent outcomes and aligned tasks might address higher-order outcomes, such as the application of knowledge or the analysis of information, mirroring Bloom's taxonomy (Anderson & Krathwohl, 2001).

In addition, based on the principles of course design recommended by Swan et al. (2000) and Simunich et al. (2015), course materials or resources that support student learning should be accompanied by explicit instructions about how each contributes to student learning and should be easy to locate on students' online course dashboard. Difficulty in navigating course materials or resources can undermine students' curiosity or willingness to explore course materials or resources, resulting in missed opportunities to improve or advance their learning.

Working with faculty in designing their online courses, instructional designers (IDs) often use the elements listed in Table 5.1 to assist faculty who are building an online or hybrid course. That table illustrates how two modules of an Applied Instructional Design Tools course, designed to have students apply their instructional knowledge to real-world instructional technology problems, used that format.

Table 5.1 served as a "blueprint" for all remaining modules of that course in the LMS; one of the modules is represented in Figure 5.3.

The alignment of core course components—ensured during the course design and driven by the learning outcomes—sets a firm foundation for the employment of predictive, formative, and summative analytics further described in the next sections. Once your course has been designed, consider what and when you want to learn or can learn (based on stored LMS data) at the three points in time: predictive (when a learning event commences), formative (while learning is occurring), and summative (when wrapping up the semester). Throughout the teaching and learning process, faculty can monitor students' learning progress by continually asking questions pertaining to what students are or are not learning, how they are learning, what "roadblocks" they face, how those "roadblocks" can be overcome, what their successful achievements are so far, and how their successes can be further promoted (Muljana & Placencia, 2018; Sclater, 2017). Data stored in an LMS, such as (a) number of times and types of course resources a student accesses, (b) number and content of discussion posts a student generates, (c) assessment submission timestamps, and

TABLE 5.1

Alignment of Learning Outcomes, Learning Activities, and Assignments/Assessments in an Applied Instructional Design Course

Module	Learning Outcomes	Learning Activities	Assignments/Assessments
Module 1—Static Graphic	• Develop a working knowledge of features and functionality of static graphics tools. • Use Adobe Photoshop or its alternative to create and modify static images and graphics.	• Complete a short course *Up and Running With Adobe Photoshop Elements*. • Watch Lynda.com video tutorial *Photoshop Elements 14 Essential Training*. • Watch video tutorials of a Photoshop alternative called Pixlr.	• Complete Mini Tools Project 1: Select a topic and use the editing features in Adobe Photoshop Elements or its alternative to construct an image demonstrating the topic. • Start planning for the module development final project: Write a proposal and design document.
	• Discuss the application of universal design principles.	• Watch a video on *Universal Principles of Design*.	• Post reflections and respond to others' reflections on *Universal Principles of Design*.

(Continues)

TABLE 5.1 *(Continued)*

Module	Learning Outcomes	Learning Activities	Assignments/Assessments
Module 2—Audio and Sound	• Develop a working knowledge of features and functionality of audio and sound tools. • Use Audacity or its alternative to create and edit audio and sound files.	• Watch Lynda.com video tutorials: *Learning Audacity and Cleaning and Repairing Audio*. • Read *Audacity Installation Guide*. • Watch a video on *How to Install and Use Audacity in 20 Minutes*. • Install Audacity. • Watch a video tutorial: *Use Audacity Sound Editor to Cut and Fade In/Out Audio Files*.	• Complete Mini Tools Project 2: Create a podcast or audio sound file regarding a topic relevant to a selected grade level. • Complete Peer Review: Provide a review for a classmate's Mini Tools project.
	• Discuss the application of universal design principles.	• Watch a video on *Universal Principles of Design*.	• Post reflections and respond to others' reflections on Universal Principles of Design.

Figure 5.3. The first module of the Applied Instructional Design Tools course.

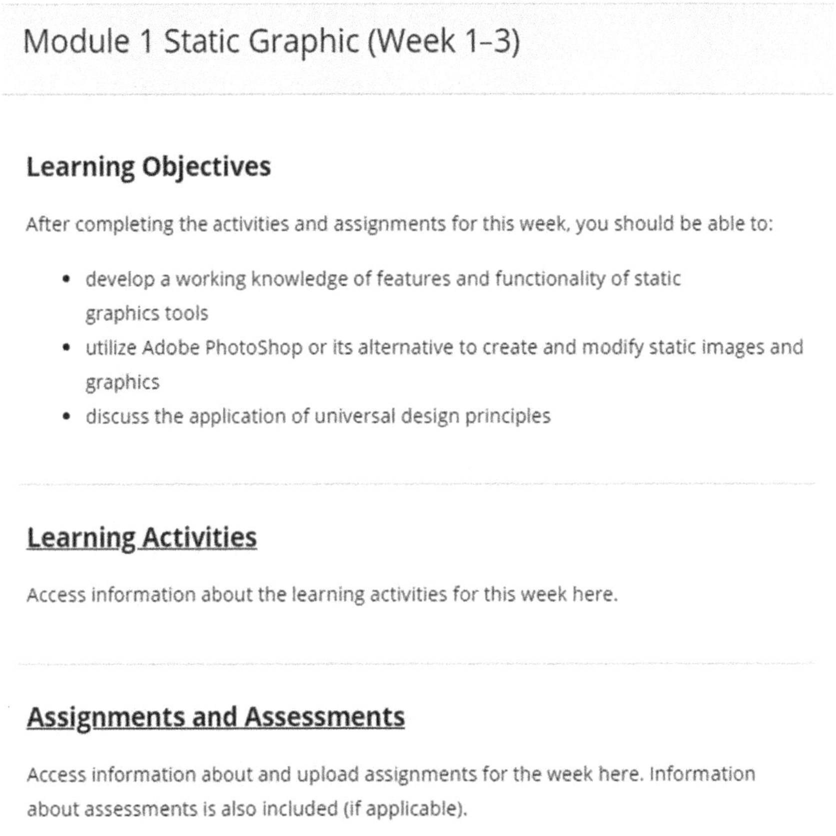

Module 1 Static Graphic (Week 1–3)

Learning Objectives

After completing the activities and assignments for this week, you should be able to:

- develop a working knowledge of features and functionality of static graphics tools
- utilize Adobe PhotoShop or its alternative to create and modify static images and graphics
- discuss the application of universal design principles

Learning Activities

Access information about the learning activities for this week here.

Assignments and Assessments

Access information about and upload assignments for the week here. Information about assessments is also included (if applicable).

(d) grades (Dietz et al., 2018; Dietz-Uhler & Hurn, 2013), are useful to assist faculty in addressing these roadblock questions at the three points in time.

Uses of Predictive Analytics in a Course

A predictive analytics approach used in a course reveals patterns of student behaviors in relation to expected outcomes for that course. As Bloom (1976) postulated, entry cognitive and affective behaviors are among several variables predicting whether students can potentially master a learning objective. If students possess the required preknowledge, interests, motivation to learn, and self-confidence about their learning abilities, they will be more likely to achieve a learning outcome at a faster pace than students who lack those characteristics (Bloom, 1976). According to Richey et al. (2011), authors of *The Instructional Design Knowledge Base*, entry behaviors, knowledge, and skills assist students in processing new information. Yet, as Miller-First and

Ballard (2017) explained in "Constructivist Teaching Patterns and Student Interactions," students' prior knowledge and experiences also influence how students relate to and make sense of new information, contributing either positively or negatively to their academic progress in a course. All of these behaviors are in line with the findings of LA-related studies, in which these behaviors are predicting factors influencing academic achievement.

Thus, using LA tools built into an LMS can assist faculty learn about students' preknowledge, interests, motivation to learn, and self-confidence about their learning abilities. Specifically, early data obtainable through an LMS can be analyzed to gain an understanding of students' prior experiences, motivations, and learning strategies and to inform faculty regarding interventions needed to alleviate students' potential struggles. These data can be obtained through a variety of means, discussed in the following sections.

An Entry Survey

An entry survey can inquire about students' prior experience(s) related to the course subject. Such a survey may also include questions about students' motivation and strategies for learning in general. Students' responses to the survey about motivation and learning strategies help faculty develop early course interventions. If, for example, results indicate that certain students lack effective learning strategies, faculty can plan to embed tips regarding learning strategies in weekly announcements or in instructions within each module or task. Optionally, a brief module discussing effective learning strategies can be developed and placed in the course LMS site before students move on to the next course module.

A Pretest

Administering a pretest is another way to gain an understanding of students' entry cognitive abilities. The scores or grades on a pretest can help faculty build interventions into a course. For example, students with low knowledge pretest scores might receive alternative materials briefing them on prerequisite topics along with concrete examples or additional time to complete assigned learning tasks. Students who possess advanced knowledge on a pretest may immediately begin the assigned learning tasks and use the extra time to review other enriching materials.

A Discussion Forum on Student Motivations and Goals

Faculty may also pose questions in an LMS discussion board, asking students why they are taking a course and what they wish to accomplish by the end of it. Students' responses to these kinds of discussion board questions help faculty identify students' entry-level knowledge or skills, as well as serve as an icebreaker to promote active engagement among students and with faculty. For instance, the faculty teaching the aforementioned Applied Instructional Design Tools course used the following ice-breaker discussion prompt:

> Please use this forum to provide a brief introduction to the class. Since much of our work in this class revolves around our asynchronous class discussions and peer learning, please describe your work experience and academic background, as well as your familiarity with design and development tools. You may also tell us what you are expecting to learn and what makes you excited about this class.

Students' responses to this first discussion board helped the faculty member gain an understanding of students' backgrounds, such as prior knowledge and familiarity with tools in the field. The qualitative data analyzed from discussion posts such as the preceding one, help faculty understand how many students have relevant prior knowledge regarding instructional design; how many students have prior experience designing a learning product using an instructional design model; or what kinds of goals motivate them to take a course. For example, do they simply take the course to fulfill the program requirement? Do they perceive a need to learn about applied instructional design techniques due to the job demands?

Additionally, many built-in predictive analytics programs in LMSs enable faculty to learn early on how many students have participated in a discussion board and which students are active or passive in the discussion, providing a quick prediction of which students may stay active or passive in the subsequent discussion forums. In turn, the faculty may start thinking of types of actionable interventions to foster student engagement in upcoming discussion boards.

Individual Students' LMS Usage Data

LA-related software built into an LMS can also mine and report individual student's LMS usage data early in the semester based on LMS logs. Examples of usage data stored in LMS logs are the number of times each student accesses course materials and the amount of time each student spends working with those materials. Levels of activity based on these kinds of behavioral data help faculty identify students who may be at risk early in a semester and prompt them to investigate the causes of low levels of activity, often leading to developing early interventions.

Table 5.2 identifies some representative kinds of data that can be reported along with a list of interventions faculty might take.

TABLE 5.2
A Predictive Analytics Approach Using LMS Data to Develop Early Interventions

LMS Data	LMS Tools	What and How to Analyze	Early Interventions
Results of presurvey on students' motivations, goals, and prior experiences	Blackboard: Survey Canvas: Survey Moodle: Choice, Feedback	Analyze survey results to discover the most frequently mentioned motivations or goals Discover whether students have prior experience related to the topics discussed in the course	Provide tips on learning strategies, metacognitive perspective (e.g., differences between learning and studying) in weekly announcements, and instructions for learning tasks and assignments Optionally, discuss learning strategies through a special brief "workshop" in a class session during the second week of the semester
Results of pretest assessing students' prior knowledge	Blackboard: Test, Item Analysis Canvas: Quiz, Quiz Statistics, Item Analysis Moodle: Quiz, Quiz Reports, Quiz Reponses, Quiz Statistics	Analyze scores Discover the most difficult items	Provide alternative, quick overview materials briefing the students on prerequisite topics

Responses to ice-breaker discussion forum	Blackboard: Discussion Board, Performance Dashboard Canvas: Discussions, Analytics, Discussions, Speedgrader Moodle: Forum, Logs, Activity Reports	Categorize responses according to terms most frequently mentioned regarding students' goals, motivation, prior knowledge, and experiences	Implement previous interventions
Total hits occurring in the LMS course site during the first week	Blackboard: Course Reports Canvas: Course Statistics, Analytics Moodle: Logs (within Reports), Statistics	Establish the day or time when students most frequently access the LMS	Update and adjust instructions and course content before the peak day/time to reduce the likelihood of students missing updates
Total time accessing the LMS course site during the first week	Blackboard: Course Reports Canvas: Course Statistics, Analytics Moodle: Logs (within Reports), Statistics	Analyze students who spend the most and the least time accessing course materials Find the greatest and least amount of time spent	Include reminders in learning strategy tips about importance of allocating regular, dedicated study time to reviewing materials

Note. Tool availability may vary by the LMS version, institutional LMS policy, and whether enabled by LMS administrator.

As also illustrated in the upper right-hand quadrant of Figure 5.2, early use of predictive analytics captures entry behaviors, preknowledge, and skills. Use of these analytics results requires early action to develop and implement immediate interventions such as providing feedforward, clear expectations, and instructions. Feedforward is the opposite of feedback. We typically provide feedback to students after they have performed or, perhaps, as they are performing. Feedforward is a proactive attempt to prevent a potential learning problem based on early use of predictive analytics that identifies students who likely will experience learning challenges based on, for example, their preknowledge or skills. When students first become engaged in course activities, faculty can emphasize clear expectations and instructions if, for example, the LMS data log shows low levels of student interaction with the materials. To address this concern, a course announcement could be released to highlight the expectation that students need to access and review course materials more regularly in order to achieve better in the course.

Use of Formative Analytics (Real-Time) in a Course

Formative assessment is essential for monitoring students' progress in a course to determine when "corrective" actions are needed to mitigate learning difficulties (Guskey, 2007). The types of LMS data usable for employing LA for formative assessment are discussed next.

Students' Performance Levels

Students' performance levels on quizzes, tests, homework, and other means of assessment identify (a) their progress toward achieving stated course learning outcomes as well as (b) the kinds of challenges they face as they learn. Data about student performance on various kinds of assessment throughout a course help faculty determine when they need to intervene with individual students or if they need to develop new strategies to assist student learning, as illustrated in the lower right-hand quadrant in Figure 5.2 and further summarized in Table 5.3.

If quizzes are used for administering formative assessments, faculty can analyze the questions to identify the topic(s) with which students had the most difficulty. Most LMSs provide an item analysis tool. In Moodle or Blackboard, for example, such a report can be attained by accessing the quiz reports, quiz responses, or quiz statistics (Muljana & Placencia, 2018). Figure 5.4 illustrates one of those reports on test item analysis. Based on item analysis results, for example, faculty can then plan for immediate interventions, such as creating a short video providing a topic(s) briefing; providing a remedial module; or assigning an additional task to ensure students' understanding of a challenging topic(s).

TABLE 5.3

Apply a Formative Analytics Approach Using LMS DATA to Develop Interventions to Improve Current Students' Performance on Assigned Tasks

LMS Data	LMS Tools	What and How to Analyze	Intervention
Results of formative assessment such as tests, quizzes, or exams	Blackboard: Test, Grade Center, Item Analysis, Retention Center Canvas: Quiz, Quiz Statistics, Gradebook Item Analysis Moodle: Quiz, Grades, Quiz Reports, Quiz Responses, Quiz Statistics	Analyze item difficulty to reveal the most difficult topics	Create and release a short video providing a quick overview or remedial module or assign an additional task to ensure students understand the topic(s)

(*Continues*)

TABLE 5.3 (*Continued*)

LMS Data	LMS Tools	What and How to Analyze	Intervention
Current assignment scores or grades	Blackboard: Gradebook	Analyze the scores	Scaffold students' time management skills by providing time-management tips
	Canvas: Gradebook	Analyze the submission timestamps	Reflect on the current assignment instructions and revise instructions as necessary to clarify expectations and include tips to complete the assignment
	Moodle: Grades	Identify students who submit assignments early and on time	
		Identify students who submit assignment late and miss the submission deadline	Release instructions for the next assignment as early as possible to allow students to prepare early
		Correlate these data: • Do students with higher scores submit a high-quality product and submit early/on time? • Do students with lower scores submit a lower quality product and submit last-minute or late?	

LMS Data	LMS Tools	What and How to Analyze	Intervention
Total hits occurring in the LMS course site during each week	Blackboard: Course Reports Canvas: Course Statistics, Analytics Moodle: Logs (within Reports), Statistics	Identify students who frequently access the LMS course site Identify students who rarely access the LMS course site Correlate these data: • Do students who frequently access the LMS earn better grades? • Do students who rarely access the LMS earn lower grades?	Include a reminder in the learning strategy tips about the importance of allocating regular, dedicated study time to reviewing materials
Total time spent accessing LMS course site during each week	Blackboard: Course Reports Canvas: Course Statistics, Analytics Moodle: Logs (within Reports), Statistics	Identify students who spend more time in the LMS Identify students who spend less time in the LMS Correlate these data: • Do students who spend more time in the LMS earn better grades? • Do students who spend less time in the LMS earn lower better grades?	Include a reminder in the learning strategy tips about the importance of allocating regular, dedicated study time to reviewing materials

(*Continues*)

TABLE 5.3 (*Continued*)

LMS Data	LMS Tools	What and How to Analyze	Intervention
The number of discussion posts	Blackboard: Discussion Board, Performance Dashboard Canvas: Discussions, Analytics Moodle: Forum, Logs, Activity Reports	Monitor participation in discussions and find forums with low participation Identify how many students actively participate in discussion Identify students who are less active in discussions Identify similar questions posted in the Q&A forum	Encourage more dialogue by giving probing questions or adding resources in low participation forums Add a reflective component such as assigning students a reflective diary detailing their own contributions to the discussions Evaluate the discussion prompts and improve future ones by providing more explicit, specific discussion prompts using relevant topics

Note. Tool availability may vary by the LMS version, institutional LMS policy, and whether enabled by LMS administrator.

Figure 5.4. Test item analysis provided by Blackboard.

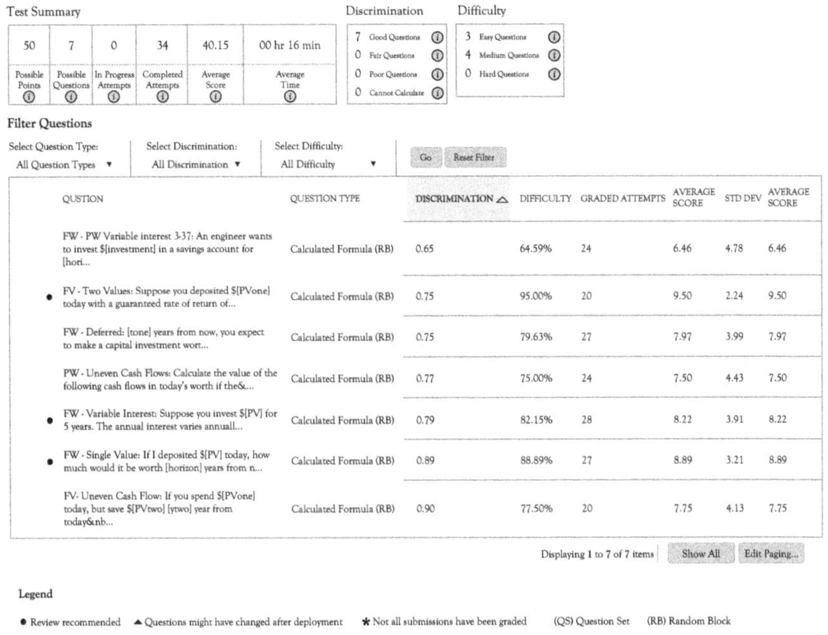

Test Summary

50	7	0	34	40.15	00 hr 16 min
Possible Points	Possible Questions	In Progress Attempts	Completed Attempts	Average Score	Average Time

Discrimination

7 Good Questions
0 Fair Questions
0 Poor Questions
0 Cannot Calculate

Difficulty

3 Easy Questions
4 Medium Questions
0 Hard Questions

Filter Questions

Select Question Type: All Question Types ▼ Select Discrimination: All Discrimination ▼ Select Difficulty: All Difficulty ▼   Go   Reset Filter

QUSTION	QUESTION TYPE	DISCRIMINATION △	DIFFICULTY	GRADED ATTEMPTS	AVERAGE SCORE	STD DEV	AVERAGE SCORE
FW - PW Variable interest 3-37: An engineer wants to invest $[investment] in a savings account for [hori...	Calculated Formula (RB)	0.65	64.59%	24	6.46	4.78	6.46
FV - Two Values: Suppose you deposited $[PVone] today with a guaranteed rate of return of...	Calculated Formula (RB)	0.75	95.00%	20	9.50	2.24	9.50
FW - Deferred: [tone] years from now, you expect to make a capital investment wort...	Calculated Formula (RB)	0.75	79.63%	27	7.97	3.99	7.97
PW - Uneven Cash Flows: Calculate the value of the following cash flows in today's worth if the$...	Calculated Formula (RB)	0.77	75.00%	24	7.50	4.43	7.50
FW - Variable Interest: Suppose you invest $[PV] for 5 years. The annual interest varies annuall...	Calculated Formula (RB)	0.79	82.15%	28	8.22	3.91	8.22
FW - Single Value: If I deposited $[PV] today, how much would it be worth [horizon] years from n...	Calculated Formula (RB)	0.89	88.89%	27	8.89	3.21	8.89
FV- Uneven Cash Flow: If you spend $[PVone] today, but save $[PVtwo] [ytwo] year from today&nb...	Calculated Formula (RB)	0.90	77.50%	20	7.75	4.13	7.75

Displaying 1 to 7 of 7 items   Show All   Edit Paging...

Legend

● Review recommended   ▲ Questions might have changed after deployment   ✱ Not all submissions have been graded   (QS) Question Set   (RB) Random Block

Note. This report can help instructors identify the most difficult topics for students in a test, for example. Used with permission from Blackboard, Inc.

Patterns Associated With High and Low Performance

An LMS activity log for a course also documents the time students spent reviewing the materials. Analyzing time spent reviewing materials might reveal a temporal pattern such as the peak day(s) and time(s) when students access a course. This temporal pattern further informs faculty of the best time(s) to update and adjust instruction and course content, thereby reducing the likelihood of students missing updates.

Another source of data that can be used for formative analytics is the submission timestamp that may correlate with a student's quality of work and grades. For instance, if students who earn high grades are likely to submit high quality of work on time, that pattern may suggest faculty would do well to scaffold lower performing students' time management skills, such as including time-management tips in the next assignment prompt.

If faculty members employ online discussions, the report pertinent to these discussions can be retrieved and analyzed to identify active versus reticent students. This report additionally provides data-informed insights about student-to-student engagement that may prompt faculty to develop interventions that promote student engagement in the discussion forum.

Figure 5.5. The Performance Dashboard tool (Blackboard) showcasing student discussion activity.

USERNAME	ROLE	LAST COURSE ACCESS	DAYS SINCE LAST COURSE ACCESS	REVIEW STATUS	ADAPTIVE RELEASE	DISCUSSION BOARD
Student1	Student	Aug 9, 2019 3:59:51 PM	44	0	☑	11
Student2	Student	Aug 27, 2019 11:36:20 AM	26	0	☑	12
Student3	Student	Aug 10, 2019 12:55:35 AM	43	0	☑	12

Note. This report can help instructors identify the "quietest" student(s). Review status is a Blackboard function that allows students to mark if they have reviewed particular course materials and consequently allows instructors to track whether students have reviewed the material. Adaptive Release is a Blackboard feature that allows instructors to selectively release particular course materials based on specified conditions such as date, time, test scores, assignment scores, review status, and so on. The Discussion Board column within the Performance Dashboard page displays the number of discussion posts generated by the student. Used with permission from Blackboard Inc.

The Performance Dashboard tool in Figure 5.5 tool provided by Blackboard provides such a report as do other LMSs. It is important to note that students who display passive social interactions may have a poor sense of belonging, which is a predictor of student attrition (Muljana & Luo, 2019; Nistor & Neubauer, 2010). If that is the case, the instructor of the course plays an important role mediating active interaction among students, especially when students may be shy or uncomfortable about offering their insights. Instructors may intervene by asking probing questions or adding resources to trigger further in-depth dialogue.

Instructors can further modify the discussion environment in subsequent discussions by dividing students into smaller groups and providing a more explicit, specific discussion prompt. To help students reflect and improve their own contribution to group discussions, assigning a postdiscussion reflection journal/diary encourages students to reflect on how active or passive they have been in discussions and why they have been active or passive (Center for Teaching Excellence, n.d.). Additional questions for considerations include the following: (a) Are the topics sufficiently interesting? (b) Is there synergy within the group itself? (c) Do the resources provided encourage active discussions? (d) Can faculty contribute more significant insights into the subsequent discussion sessions? Journal or diary submissions (if employed) can further be analyzed qualitatively to identify issues that inhibit student engagement. For an additional example, faculty can provide a special discussion forum for questions (commonly known as Q&A). An instructor might also need to clarify an assignment when multiple students raise similar questions about it.

Uses of Summative Analytics in a Course

Administering summative assessments and evaluations is typically conducted at the end of a unit of a course or at the end of a course representing, according to Taras (2005) "a judgment which encapsulates all the evidence up to a given point . . . [and] is seen as a finality at the point of the judgment" (p. 468). This summative phase is an opportunity for faculty to evaluate students' levels of attaining learning outcomes within the context of the components of a course, including strategies or interventions used. The types of LMS data used for this faculty reflective process are discussed in the following sections.

Summative Assessment Capturing the Attainment of Learning Outcomes

Although grades are helpful in understanding overall learning outcomes at the end of a semester, faculty can also reflect on the most difficult topics that semester, any improvements in students' learning after specific interventions, and interventions that could be improved in the next term. If there are multiple course sections, assessment results can be compared across sections to identify interventions that did or did not work and the similar or different ways they affected student learning in each course section (Ifenthaler & Widanapathirana, 2014).

Patterns Associated With High and Low Performance

As aforementioned, drawing correlations among students' final grades and other related data such the number of LMS accesses, time spent in the LMS, timestamps of assignments and quiz/exam submissions, item analyses of test or quiz items, the number of questions, or the number of discussion posts can provide additional clues regarding the difference between high-performing and low-performing students. Faculty can encourage behaviors associated with high performance in the subsequent semesters to help low-performing students perform better.

Reflection on Past Interventions and Future Improvement

The LMS data can also inform design decisions when redesigning courses for subsequent terms. For example, faculty can identify the least engaging course components. Figure 5.6 illustrates a visualization of the total hits/accesses that occurred on each module of a free course for instructional designers (IDs). Data were retrieved from an LMS called Canvas, capturing accesses by the participants. The course coordinators used the tools and followed the steps discussed in a free online course titled Analytics in Course Design: Leveraging Canvas Data ("Analytics in Course Design," n.d.). To visualize the data, a Sankey diagram was built using a free online tool available at http://sankeymatic.com/build/ to depict module access.

Figure 5.6. A Sankey diagram depicting course access flows in each module.

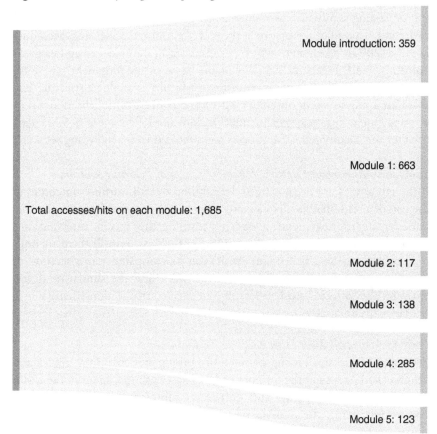

Note. These data were obtained from a free course for instructional designers, hosted in an LMS called Canvas, by following the steps listed in a free online course titled Analytics in Course Design: Leveraging Canvas Data ("Analytics in course design," n.d.). After organizing the data in Microsoft Excel, the diagram was built using a free Sankey diagram builder (http://sankeymatic.com).

This kind of visualization is helpful in understanding which part of a module receives the least student-content engagement. Many faculty also reflect on how crucial this component is to students' subject mastery. If it is crucial, how can the course be redesigned so that this important component will be more engaging in the future term? When redesigning a course, collaborating with an ID is highly recommended because each professional will bring specialized expertise and experience to improve the course.

Comparison of Various Cohorts
Last, but not least, it is important to ask students for feedback about their learning experiences, the efficacy of educational practices, and their

satisfaction levels by administering an exit survey. As a part of a continuous learning process improvement cycle, student feedback specifically helps faculty identify instructional strategies that have or have not worked within a cohort, thus prompting them to determine either how they can improve or redesign those strategies students identified as ineffective or how they might design new strategies (Ifenthaler, 2017).

Analyzing these kinds of data can support the summative evaluation informing faculty about the types of (a) exemplary student learning behaviors that can be encouraged in the next cohort or (b) interventions that made a significant impact on students' learning that can be used again with the next cohort. If the interventions did not effectively enable students to achieve an outcome or improve their achievement, faculty can brainstorm with colleagues or with the campus ID about ideas for more successful approaches in the next offering of that course. The lower left-hand quadrant in Figure 5.2 represents the use of data to refine or enhance practices in that next course offering. Table 5.4 displays the kinds of LMS data that can be analyzed for summative purposes and examples of how to use analyzed results to improve future iterations of a course.

Following up on the second part of this chapter, part three provides an example of how engineering faculty have integrated LA approaches into a topic in an undergraduate engineering course. These approaches have assisted them identify and predict potential risks that students encounter as they learn material addressed in that topic.

Part Three: Integration of Learning Analytics Into an Engineering Course

Identifying the potential risks students face in learning course content and determining how faculty can help students avoid those risks or alleviate them through strategic interventions should be a central consideration in course design. Because the primary purpose of implementing LA is to gain insight into student's learning within their learning context (Gašević et al., 2015), applying LA approaches to courses enables faculty to identify and, thus, predict risks students face along the trajectory of each course. Using a topic in an undergraduate engineering course, this part of the chapter describes the following LA approaches faculty have used to (a) predict potential issues students face learning statistical analysis; (b) project the short- and longer-term severity of those risks if not addressed; and (c) determine the probability that those risks will surface again in students' work. One approach involves faculty's collaborative identification and prediction of potential failure points in students' learning process and the consequences of those failure points for

TABLE 5.4

Applying a Summative Analytics Approach Using LMS Data to Develop Interventions for Future Iterations of a Course

LMS Data	LMS Tools	What and How to Analyze	Ideas on How to Follow Up
Results of overall summative assessment such as final grades	Blackboard: Grade Center, Retention Center	Analyze overall student learning outcomes	Reflect on interventions you conducted: • What type of interventions did you do that helped students perform better? • Is there anything that you could have done more to help low-performing students?
	Canvas: Gradebook, Analytics	Analyze high-performing students regarding success and failure points throughout the semester	
	Moodle: Grades, Activity Completion Report, Logs (by activity)	Analyze low-performing students for their "roadblocks" and about which topics they achieved poorly	
		Did students who submitted assignments last minute improve? Did timestamps on their later submissions improve?	
		Correlate these data again: • Do students with higher scores submit high-quality products and submit them early/on-time? • Do students with lower scores submit lower quality products and submit them last-minute or late?	

Total hits occurring in the LMS course site	Blackboard: Course Reports	Identify students who frequently accessed the LMS course site	Discover exemplary learning behaviors executed by high-performing students; if high-performing students access materials more frequently, plan to create brief course orientation modules in the next course that include learning strategies
	Canvas: Course Statistics, Analytics	Identify students who rarely accessed the LMS course site	
	Moodle: Logs (within Reports), Statistics	Correlate these data again: • Do students who frequently access LMS earn better grades? • Do students who rarely access LMS earn lower grades?	Reflect on most accessed materials and least accessed materials: • Were topics that were more difficult accessed more frequently? • Why were some materials less accessed by students? Did technical issues bar access?
		Identify which materials were accessed more or less frequently by students	

(*Continues*)

TABLE 5.4 (*Continued*)

LMS Data	LMS Tools	What and How to Analyze	Ideas on How to Follow Up
Total time spent in the LMS course site	Blackboard: Course Reports	Identify students who spent more time in the LMS	Discover exemplary learning behaviors executed by the high-performing students; if high-performing students accessed materials more frequently, prepare a brief course orientation module that includes learning strategies
	Canvas: Course Statistics, Analytics	Identify students who spent less time in the LMS	
	Moodle: Logs (within Reports), Statistics	Correlate these data: • Do students who spend more time in the LMS earn better grades? • Do students who spend less time in the LMS earn lower grades?	Reflect on the materials that were accessed briefly: • Were these materials lengthy? If so, consider segmenting them into smaller chunks
		Identify which materials were accessed briefly or for a longer time	

The number of discussion posts	Blackboard: Discussion Board, Performance Dashboard	Evaluate participation in discussions and reveal any forum with low participation	For forums with low participation, consider revising prompts with more explicit instructions and timely, relevant issues
	Canvas: Discussions, Analytics	Identify students who actively participated in discussions	
		Identify students who were less active in the discussions	
	Moodle: Forum, Logs, Activity Reports	Identify similar questions posted in the Q&A forum	
Results of exit survey	Blackboard: Survey	Analyze students' insights regarding the learning experiences	Reflect on both positive responses and constructive feedback and plan to incorporate this feedback in future iterations of course design
	Canvas: Survey	Categorize any open-ended responses	
	Moodle: Choice, Feedback		

Note. Tool availability may vary by the LMS version, institutional LMS policy, and whether enabled by LMS administrator. Collaborating with an ID can be very beneficial during course development and administration.

students' future performance; the other involves the use of formative analytics, specifically item analysis, to establish the probability that these risks will continue to surface or not based on faculty interventions.

Beginning with agreement on student learning outcomes for the topic of a specific engineering course, the following sections describe the steps that were taken.

Foreseeing Potential Learning Issues by Identifying Failure Points

Industrial and systems engineering (ISE) commonly uses failure mode and effects analysis (FMEA, read as "fah-me-ah") as a tool to reduce adverse events in industry. When integrated into the teaching and learning process, potential failures in the learning process can be examined ahead of time. Faculty can determine the most common failure scenarios (often by topic) and break them down into "modes" by which the failure occurs, their cause(s), and the short- and long-term consequences of students' inability to overcome learning issues they face. Severity of the effect(s) and mitigation(s) are also often included in the analysis. An example used in this context is a course covering human engineering factors offered to undergraduate students. One of the topics, called human factors experimental design and analysis, includes statistical analyses. In this context, faculty created a course syllabus broken down into learning outcomes and associated learning processes that help students achieve outcomes. We examined these processes as smaller learning outcomes to identify potential failure points or learning risks. Faculty often express these risks as scenarios and list the risks in bulleted points. For instance, one risk can be the steps that students may take incorrectly while performing a learning task. If we identify the learning outcome as "students can justify design changes by evaluating whether a change results in a statistical difference," failure points in achieving that outcome can be students use of an incorrect *t*-test, *t*-score, or *t*-value. In other words, we align a list of failure points or risks with the learning outcomes. Listing up to three failure points for each learning outcome is sufficient in the instructional context. Establishing these failure points helps us foresee which learning problems the students will potentially face, in line with an intent of a predictive LA approach: predicting and detecting students at-risk, early on.

Identifying the Effects of Each Failure Point

Once faculty create their risk list, they can start determining the consequences and the severity of effect(s) on students' attainment of the learning outcome. A consequence is a situation that occurs when taking wrong steps while performing a learning task. For example, when a student uses an incorrect *t*-test, that student will fail to compare the correct t-score, which is also a failure to achieve the corresponding learning outcome. If we analyze this failure from the course curriculum level (which is also called course-level effect), students who fail at this point also fail to establish a statistical significance in data and, consequently, fail to evaluate project designs appropriately. At a higher departmental curriculum level, students would likely fail to evaluate human engineering factors components in their senior projects as required in the curriculum (also called curriculum-level effect). Conducting an effect analysis from multiple lenses—learning outcome, course level, and curriculum level—is helpful for weighing and determining the potential interventions. Ideally, these interventions should be integrated into a revised course design whereby faculty foresee the risks. Course design revisions can include integrating supplementary materials specifically designed to explain problematic issues better. If this cannot be achieved, briefing students about the risk, its severity, and consequences is acceptable, but supplementary material should be included that can assist students with poor understanding of prerequisite materials.

Estimating the Probability That Risks May Occur

The final step is to establish a probability of how often a risk occurs. Faculty often use their intuition to estimate the probabilities of these risks, such as high or low. Conducting an LA approach provides quantitative values to help establish whether or not learning outcomes improve because of good process change. Even though this can be considered optional, we highly encourage the use of an LA approach, such as analyzing the test/quiz items, to establish actual probabilities to help faculty create a risk matrix. A risk matrix plots risks based on their severity and probability. This matrix enables faculty to focus efforts on improving the design of areas in their courses that have both high probability of failure and high negative consequences. That is, highly probable failures with severe effects should be prioritized and deserve immediate interventions.

Table 5.5 illustrates a matrix that represents the predictive and analytic approaches faculty use to identify students' risks, failure effects, and detection methods, leading to interventions to assist students improve the outcome: students evaluate whether or not a single product design change results in a statistical difference that justifies a product redesign.

Course data specifically from the item analysis in formative quizzes can be used to establish the frequency of the failure modes based on student performance. Such data could continually be updated for other classes and sessions within a curriculum. Additionally, we can use these data during summative assessment to compare values quantitatively to see whether improvements have occurred because of specific interventions.

TABLE 5.5

Example of Risk Identification, Effects Analysis, and Detection Method Using an LA Approach

Course Title: Basic Human Engineering		Identified Risk		Failure Effects			Detection Method	Severity	Intervention
Topic	LO	Failure Mode	Failure Cause	LO-Level Effect	Course-Level Effect	Curriculum-Level Effect			
Human Factors, Experimental Design, and Analysis	Students justify design changes by evaluating whether a change results in a statistical difference	Student uses incorrect t-test	Fail to recognize difference between within-subject and between-subject t-test	Incorrect evaluation	Fail to establish statistical significance in data Fail to evaluate project design correctly	Fail to evaluate human factors components in senior project	Formative quiz to identify correct test (formative analytics/item test analysis)	High	Demonstrate differences between within- and between-subject test
		Student uses incorrect t-score	Calculate incorrect t score	Compare incorrect t score			Formative quiz with known values to calculate t-values (formative analytics/item test analysis)	High	Facilitate in-class exercise finding t-score

Student uses incorrect t-value	Calculate incorrect DoF	Compare incorrect t value		Formative quiz with known value to calculate DoF (formative analytics/item test analysis)	High	Facilitate in-class exercise finding DoF
	Use incorrect α value			Formative quiz with known DoF to identify t-values by known α value (formative analytics/item test analysis)	High	Facilitate in-class exercise finding α
	Select incorrect t-value on t-table			Formative quiz with known α value & DoF to identify t-value (formative analytics/item test analysis)	High	Facilitate in-class exercise finding t-value

Note. For the detection method, test item analysis can be conducted in each formative quiz.
DoF = degree of freedom; LO = learning outcome

Caveats

Even though LA offers tremendous benefits, adopters should be aware of caveats. As noted, LMSs are but one system that can trace vast amounts of data generated by course user interactions. Moreover, datasets obtained through an LMS may look overwhelming, and data heterogeneity may cause inaccurate data assessment. Therefore, sorting and assessing relevant and meaningful information to align with proposed goals are crucial (Bienkowski et al., 2012; Li et al., 2017; Verbert et al., 2012). As Johnson (2017) astutely asked, "If we cannot make sense of the data, then how can we carry our mission to help people learn?" (p. 21). In the examples provided in this chapter, we, therefore, paired an LA approach with educational constructs, such as backward design, course design principles, Bloom's taxonomy, and risk analysis (FMEA) commonly used in ISE.

Although LA is a data-driven approach, an analysis should go beyond numbers derived from grades and totals hits. Gašević et al. (2015) verified that although education can provide plentiful data, those data may not capture both internal and external learning conditions such as cognitive load, goal achievement and orientation, instructional design, social context, and interpretation of findings. Existing studies have already recommended investigating multiple variables beyond numbers such as students' traits, including study habits, time management, financial issues (Campbell & Oblinger, 2007), and connecting findings with learning theories before determining an intervention (Gašević et al., 2015; Li et al., 2017). We, therefore, consider all these variables carefully. In our implementation ideas, we recommend promoting learning behaviors associated with course achievement (e.g., time management and metacognition) and designing pedagogically sound course structure.

Most LA researchers and experts acknowledge that privacy and ethics are important ongoing issues (Bienkowski et al., 2012; Campbell & Oblinger, 2007; Dietz et al., 2018; Ferguson, 2012; Nachmias, 2011; Verbert et al., 2013). Exactly who can and should access data in academia is an open question that can lead to resistance or "push-back" to implementing LA (Greller & Drachsler, 2012). One recommendation has been to consult the Family Educational Rights and Privacy Act (FERPA) before using student data (Dietz-Uhler & Hurn, 2013). We reemphasize, though, that the implementation practices presented in this chapter employ data collected within most LMSs and thereby are readily available to the course instructor and are effectively non-intrusive. However, we do encourage being open with students about how these data collection efforts are intended to improve their individual performance and informing them of any institutional policies related to their rights and privacy.

References

Abeysekera, L., & Dawson, P. (2015). Motivation and cognitive load in the flipped classroom: Definition, rationale and a call for research. *Higher Education Research & Development, 34*(1), 1–14. https://doi.org/10.1080/07294360.2014.934336

Analytics in course design. (n.d.). Canvas. https://learn.canvas.net/courses/1176

Anderson, L. W., & Krathwohl, D. R. (2001). *A taxonomy for learning, teaching, and assessing: A revision of Bloom's taxonomy of educational objectives.* Longman.

Bienkowski, M., Feng, M., & Means, B. (2012). *Enhancing teaching and learning through educational data mining and learning analytics: An issue brief.* US Department of Education, Office of Educational Technology.

Bloom, B. S. (1976). *Human characteristics and school learning.* McGraw-Hill.

Campbell, J. P., & Oblinger, D. G. (2007, October 15). *Academic analytics.* EDUCAUSE Publications. https://library.educause.edu/resources/2007/10/academic-analytics

Center for Teaching Excellence. (n.d.). *Collaborative online learning: Fostering effective discussions.* https://uwaterloo.ca/centre-for-teaching-excellence/teaching-resources/teaching-tips/developing-assignments/blended-learning/online-discussions-tips-instructors

Dietz, B., Hurn, J. E., Mays, T. A., & Woods, D. (2018). An introduction to learning analytics. In R. A. Reiser & J. V Dempsey (Eds.), *Trends and issues in instructional design and technology* (pp. 104–111). Pearson.

Dietz-Uhler, B., & Hurn, J. (2013). Using learning analytics to predict (and improve) student success: A faculty perspective. *Journal of Interactive Online Learning, 12*(1), 17–26.

Ferguson, R. (2012). Learning analytics: Drivers, developments and challenges. *International Journal of Technology Enhanced Learning, 4*(5/6), 304–317. https://doi.org/10.1504/IJTEL.2012.051816

Firat, M. (2016). Determining the effects of LMS learning behaviors on academic achievement in a learning analytic perspective. *Journal of Information Technology Education: Research, 15*, 75–87.

Gašević, D., Dawson, S., & Siemens, G. (2015). Let's not forget: Learning analytics are about learning. *TechTrends, 59*(1), 64–71. https://doi.org/10.1007/s11528-014-0822-x

Greller, W., & Drachsler, H. (2012). Translating learning into numbers: A generic framework for learning analytics. *Educational Technology & Society, 15*(3), 42–57.

Guskey, T. R. (2007). Closing achievement gaps: Revisiting Benjamin S. Bloom's "learning for mastery." *Journal of Advanced Academics, 19*(1), 8–31. https://doi.org/10.4219/jaa-2007-704

Ifenthaler, D. (2017). Are higher education institutions prepared for learning analytics? *TechTrends, 61*(4), 366–371. https://doi.org/10.1007/s11528-016-0154-0

Ifenthaler, D., & Widanapathirana, C. (2014). Development and validation of a learning analytics framework: Two case studies using support vector machines. *Technology, Knowledge, and Learning, 19*(1–2), 221–240. https://doi.org/10.1007/s10758-014-9226-4

Johnson, T. E. (2017). Using data analytics to drive performance and instructional decision-making. In F.-Q. Lai & J. D. Lehman (Eds.), *Learning and knowledge analytics in open education* (pp. 21–30). Springer International. https://doi.org/10.1007/978-3-319-38956-1_3

Li, Y., Bao, H., & Xu, C. (2017). Learning analytics: Serving the learning process design and optimization. In F.-Q. Lai & J. D. Lehman (Eds.), *Learning and knowledge analytics in open education* (pp. 31–40). Springer International. https://doi.org/10.1007/978-3-319-38956-1_4

Lu, O. H. T., Huang, J. C. H., Huang, A. Y. Q., & Yang, S. J. H. (2017). Applying learning analytics for improving students' engagement and learning outcomes in a MOOCs enabled collaborative programming course. *Interactive Learning Environments, 25*(2), 220–234. https://doi.org/10.1080/10494820.2016.1278391

Miller, G. A. (1956). The magical number seven, plus or minus two: Some limits on our capacity for processing information. *Psychological Review, 63*(2), 81–97. https://doi.org/10.1037/h0043158

Miller-First, M. S., & Ballard, K. L. (2017). Constructivist teaching patterns and student interactions. *Internet Learning, 6*(1), 15–32. https://doi.org/10.18278/il.6.1.3

Muljana, P. S., & Luo, T. (2019). Factors contributing to student retention in online learning and recommended strategies for the improvement: A systematic literature review. *Journal of Information Technology Education: Research, 18*, 19–57. https://doi.org/10.28945/4182

Muljana, P. S., & Luo, T. (2020). Utilizing learning analytics in course design: Voices from instructional designers in higher education. *Journal of Computing in Higher Education. Advanced online publication.* https://doi.org/10.1007/s12528-020-09262-y

Muljana, P. S., & Placencia, G. V. (2018). Learning analytics: Translating data into "just-in-time" interventions. *Scholarship of Teaching and Learning, Innovative Pedagogy, 1*, 50–69. https://digitalcommons.humboldt.edu/sotl_ip/vol1/iss1/6/

Nachmias, R. (2011). Web mining and higher education: Introduction to the special issue. *Internet and Higher Education, 14*(2), 65–66. https://doi.org/10.1016/j.iheduc.2011.01.001

Nistor, N., & Neubauer, K. (2010). From participation to dropout: Quantitative participation patterns in online university courses. *Computers and Education, 55*(2), 663–672. https://doi.org/10.1016/j.compedu.2010.02.026

Richey, R. C., Klein, J. D., & Tracey, M. W. (2011). *The instructional design knowledge base: Theory, research, and practice.* Routledge.

Sclater, N. (2017). *Learning analytics explained.* Routledge.

Siemens, G., & Long, P. (2011). Penetrating the fog: Analytics in learning and education. *EDUCAUSE Review, 46*(5), 30–32, 34, 36, 38, 40.

Simunich, B., Robins, D. B., & Kelly, V. (2015). The impact of findability on student motivation, self-efficacy, and perceptions of online course quality. *American Journal of Distance Education, 29*(3), 174–185. https://doi.org/10.1080/08923647.2015.1058604

Swan, K., Shea, P., Fredericksen, E., Pickett, A., Pelz, W., & Maher, G. (2000). Building knowledge building communities: Consistency, contact and communication in the virtual classroom. *Journal of Educational Computing Research, 23*(4), 389–413. https://doi.org/10.2190/W4G6-HY52-57P1-PPNE

Sweller, J., Van Merriënboer, J. J. G., & Paas, F. G. W. C. (1998). Cognitive architecture and Instructional design. *Educational Psychology Review, 10*(3), 251–296. https://doi.org/10.1023/A:1022193728205

Taras, M. (2005). Assessment—summative and formative—some theoretical reflections. *British Journal of Educational Studies, 53*(4), 466–478. https://doi.org/10.1111/j.1467-8527.2005.00307.x

Thille, C., & Zimmaro, D. (2017). Incorporating learning analytics in the classroom. In J. Zilvinskis & V. Borden (Eds.), *New directions for higher education* (Number 179, Fall 2017, pp. 19–33). Pearson.

Verbert, K., Duval, E., Klerkx, J., Govaerts, S., & Santos, J. L. (2013). Learning analytics dashboard applications. *American Behavioral Scientist, 57*(10), 1500–1509. https://doi.org/10.1177/0002764213479363

Verbert, K., Manouselis, N., Drachsler, H., & Duval, E. (2012). Dataset-driven research to support learning and knowledge analytics. *Educational Technology & Society, 15*, 133–148.

Wiggins, G. & McTighe, J. (2005). *Understanding by design.* Association for Supervision and Curriculum Development.

Yen, C. H., Chen, I., Lai, S. C., & Chuang, Y. R. (2015). An analytics-based approach to managing cognitive load by using log data of learning management systems and footprints of social media. *Journal of Educational Technology & Society, 18*(4), 141–158. https://doi.org/10.2307/jeductechsoci.18.4.141

You, J. W. (2016). Identifying significant indicators using LMS data to predict course achievement in online learning. *Internet and Higher Education, 29*, 23–30. https://doi.org/10.1016/j.iheduc.2015.11.003

Zimmerman, T. D. (2012). Exploring learner to content interaction as a success factor in online courses. *International Review of Research in Open and Distance Learning, 13*(4), 152–165. https://doi.org/10.19173/irrodl.v13i4.1302

6

DATA-INFORMED ONLINE DISCUSSION FACILITATION

Using Data From a Social Network Analysis App to Improve Students' Online Interactions

Jing Qi

Active learning methods, such as group projects and collaborative learning using asynchronous discussions, provide opportunities for students to participate in academic discourse and apply what they have learned. But inspiring students to participate in online discussion interactions and evaluating the degree of their discussion engagements can prove challenging for many instructors. This chapter addresses that important issue by describing how social network diagrams and quantitative data mined from within a learning management system (LMS) course enabled faculty to identify levels of interaction among students. Furthermore, this chapter demonstrates data-informed facilitation approaches with which the quality and quantity of online discussion may be increased using visualizations from a social network analysis app.

For many instructors, the value of in-class discussion is in the reception of informal feedback of student understanding. The "informal" is due to the fact that instructors often find it difficult to log participation and assess performance; in-class participation is generally little more than a fudge factor in the final grade where students are assumed to have participated if they attended (Bean & Peterson, 1998). In contrast, when academic discourse exists in online discussion forums where logging participation is automated, assessing performance is made significantly easier. For instance, most LMSs have built-in technology and capacity to gather and store data about student participation in online discussions.

Online discussion platforms provide instructors and students with a forum for asynchronous (and sometimes near-synchronous) academic communication. They also offer opportunities for students to reflect on what they have learned in a course or educational experience as well as contribute to and learn from others. A number of studies on asynchronous communication suggest that students benefit from online discussions. One recent study on online discussion facilitation strategies validated instructor prompts; frequent and continual probing yielded discussions that were more focused with higher participation than those with minimal to no instructor activity (Ming & Baumer, 2011).

However, unlike in-classroom discussion activities, where instructors can easily observe student behavior and provide immediate intervention, it can be quite challenging for instructors to see how students interact in an online discussion forum and, thus, facilitate online discussions effectively. In an attempt to address this issue, I worked with faculty and built a discussion visualization app using social network analysis (SNA) methods that easily allow instructors to examine interactions among students and identify engagement patterns. Typically, there tend to be three levels of student engagement in online discussions. The first level includes minimally engaged students, also called *peripheral students*, who do not respond to peers' posts or generate discussion threads that elicit peers' responses. The second level includes *information providers*, who actively contribute to online discussions by providing feedback or solutions to peers' posts or questions. The third level includes heavily engaged students, also called *influential participants*, who develop posts that tend to catch attention and elicit many responses from peers. They also read and comment on peers' postings. Using SNA-based visual and quantitative analyses, instructors can monitor these levels of interactivities and the role played by each participant in online discussions. Furthermore, instructors can leverage the information and adapt online discussion facilitation strategies accordingly to promote collaborative learning and community building.

An In-House Developed SNA App

SNA refers to the methods applied to map and measure connections and flows between network nodes (Hanneman & Riddle, 2005). Generally speaking, nodes in a network refer to individual participants, and the link between two network nodes corresponds to the immediate interaction between two participants (Hanneman & Riddle, 2005). The in-house SNA app I developed uses social network analysis to model discussion interactions. Social network diagrams generated in this app, together with textual analysis of students' discussion entries, provided our faculty with previously inaccessible data that helped faculty develop evidence-based interventions to improve students' online discussions and increase their levels of engagement in them. Based on using the SNA app, I will discuss the measurement concepts behind SNA-generated diagrams represented for online discussion interactions in a class of 47 students and in a subgroup of 21 students from another large class. Capital letter S followed by a number represents a specific student in a class.

Representation of Student Online Interactions

Figure 6.1 represents student online discussion interactions in a class of 47 students. Each circle corresponds to an individual student who either

Figure 6.1. Online discussion interactions in a class of 47 students.

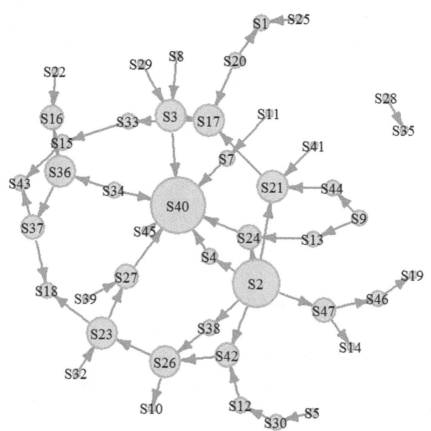

provided or received one discussion reply. The directed link represents an interaction between a sender and a receiver.

When using SNA to analyze online discussion interactions, each node represents a student and the lines between nodes represent either sending a comment on a peer's post or receiving a reply to one's own thread. SNA mapping provides faculty with a visual representation of direct interactions among students in a social network diagram, as well as the direction of an interaction. Perhaps most importantly, SNA diagrams represent the structural location and grouping of participants in a network, which sheds light on roles within a network: the "leaders," "bridges," "peripherals," and "outsiders" (Csardi, n.d.; Qi, 2017). These roles, illustrated in Figure 6.1, are further described as follows:

> *Leaders* (e.g., S40, S2): The most active individuals in online discussion forums, posting well-thought-out threads that welcome peers' comments and providing feedback to peers' posts
> *Bridges* (e.g., S2): The individuals who connect different subgroups, which otherwise may become isolated subsets within a network
> *Peripheries* (e.g., S19. S5): The least active individuals in an online discussion forum
> *Outsiders* (e.g., S28, S35): Isolated yet connected subgroups with few to no interactions outside the group or with the rest of the class

Although these role descriptors are commonly applied in the field of social network analysis to identify behaviors, in an online discussion forum those terms may not necessarily reflect the actual learning taking place, because some students may choose not to engage. Certain individuals, for example, may not feel comfortable sharing feedback and interacting with a group in online discussion forums. In fact, choosing to nudge peripherals and outsiders in an attempt to increase their levels of interaction with peers might not only fail to deepen their engagement but also actively decrease their involvement.

Measurement of Network Activity

The following sections describe the measures the SNA app uses to generate students' network activity and levels of engagement visually and then discusses how faculty have used this data-informed approach to increase online discussion participation based on the visualizations. Network activity for a student is determined by identifying student groupings based on what are referred to as *centrality measures*, the number of connections a node (a student) has. These measures are referred to as the degree centrality measure and the betweenness centrality measure. *Degree centrality* identifies the students who have more immediate interactions with their peers, including the peripherals who have fewer interactions within a network. *Betweenness centrality* identifies a group of students who are relatively closely connected (in a subset) but have fewer interactions with other groups.

Results of the Degree Centrality Measure
When we use SNA degree centrality to model student online discussion interactions, we can define the degree for student activity as the number of replies that a student provided to or received from other students. The link between two students suggests a relation between a sender and a receiver. When a student sends a response to another student, the interaction is counted as out-degree; when a student receives a reply from a peer, the interaction is considered as in-degree. The app uses the in-degree and out-degree measures to calculate the number of replies that a student receives from other students and the number of comments that a student sends to their peers.

Social network diagrams also represent students' degree of interaction in a discussion group. Figure 6.1 shows levels of interaction among 47 students in an online discussion forum. Each circle corresponds to an individual student who either provided or received at least one discussion reply. The lines represent interactions and direction of interactions between a sender and a receiver. The size of a node corresponds to the total number of interactions for a student. Instructors can leverage students' in-degree and out-degree measures to analyze their types of participation and interaction. When discussion interactions for a student yield high in-degree and low out-degree centrality, that means that specific student received many replies but provided few comments to peers' postings. The visualizations produced by the app help course instructors easily identify the peripheral student(s) who initiated few responses to their peers (e.g., S5, S19, and the isolated subgroup of S28 and S35 in Figure 6.1). A comparison of in-degree and out-degree measures for S40 and S2 is shown in Table 6.1. It reveals that S40 received 7 replies but provided no response to peers, and S2 sent 6 comments to peers

TABLE 6.1
Comparison of Two Students' In-Degree and Out-Degree Measures

Degree Mode	S2	S40
In-Degree	0	7
Out-Degree	6	0
Total-Degree	6	7

but received no replies to his posting. Thus, S40 has a high in-degree central-ity, and S2 yields a high out-degree centrality.

Results of the Betweenness Centrality Measure
The betweenness centrality measures the extent to which a node lies on paths between other nodes. Nodes with high betweenness may have consider-able influence within a network because they control information passing between others (Franceschet, n.d.). As such, when a node falls on the geo-desic paths between other pairs of nodes (Ognyanova, 2016), even though it may have less degree centrality (i.e., fewer direct connections), it can still be in a "favored" position to the extent that it bridges other groups, clusters, or nodes in the network. Conceptually, high-betweenness nodes lie on a large number of nonredundant shortest paths between other nodes; they can thus be thought of as "bridge" (Csardi, n.d.). In the app, we applied a specific betweenness centrality measure for community detection to identify densely connected students with fewer interactions with other groups. This between-ness centrality measure also helps identify students who act as "bridges" and connect subcommunities.

Cohesion and interdependence are key concepts of collaborative learn-ing, and monitoring group density can uncover an important aspect of col-laborative behavior at the group level (Rabbany et al., 2014). This SNA community detection approach provides insight into the cohesiveness of col-laborative groups. The results of community detection can inform educators about the status of collaboration and allow them to take data-driven inter-ventions when needed (Saqr et al., 2018). Using the community detection approach, Figure 6.2 represents loose interactions with isolated subsets of students in an online discussion—an extension of face-to face activities—of a group of 21 out of 62 students in a class.

Data-Informed Interventions to Improve Student Engagement in Online Discussions

As a first step to draw in independent subgroups that had few or no interac-tions with other groups, such as those identified in Figure 6.2, faculty decided to identify a student facilitator to connect them intentionally. Unsurprisingly, the student facilitator, S1, played a bridge and leader role by connecting the four subgroups, establishing immediate interactions with S10, S11, S15 and S51. A comparison of pre- and postintervention diagrams (compare Figure 6.2 to Figure 6.3) reveals that postintervention group interactions became more cohesive and interactive.

Figure 6.2. Community detection approach results for a subset of students in a discussion forum.

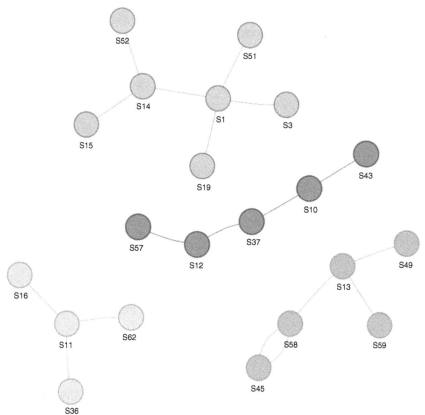

Concerned that some students interacted strongly with one another while other students isolated themselves from the broader class, as illustrated in Figures 6.1 and 6.2, faculty refrained from nudging students to participate and, instead, attempted to incentivize them based on the work of Hecking et al. (2017). According to Hecking et al., when an online discussion forum is designed to provide students with deep learning opportunities to think critically and share exemplars of their learning, instructors can incorporate incentives into the discussion forums to motivate learners to participate in discussions in a constructive manner. Our faculty reached out to those less communicative students, identified in our network visualizations as peripherals and outsiders, to motivate them to participate and contribute to the discussions. Specifically, faculty developed helpful critiques for those students, focusing on how they could demonstrate their knowledge and learning to

Figure 6.3. The community detection diagram after the intervention.

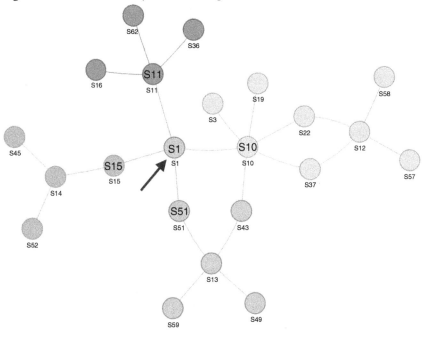

benefit their peers as well as reflect on their own experiences as a way to engage collaboratively with peers.

We coupled our SNA results with textual analysis of students' responses or reactions to discussion prompts or other students' contributions to deepen our understanding about the kinds of posts that generated peers' responses. Results of our textual analysis of students' initial threads suggested that along with other factors, such as time (when a thread was posted) and sequence of a posting, threads that used first-person narratives tended to get more comments from peers than postings that used many complex academic words. Popular threads that received many responses were the "right" length (neither too long nor too short in terms of word length) and typically were written in the first person, such as "I think," "I feel," or "I believe." These threads also asked other students directly what they might think or feel about the post. These posts often pertained to general aspects of the learning tasks or shared information. Conversely, the students in the class with the fewest responses often had the longest posts and tended to use more formal, or academic, writing.

In addition to the efficacy of a student facilitator, we had a few other takeaways from our initial experience using network diagrams and study of textual analysis. Namely, if instructors want students to converse with each other in a discussion forum, they should do the following:

- Construct discussion prompts that ask students about the nature of their experiences.
- Establish clear expectations for students by articulating the goals of an online discussion.
- Set a word limit for the length of a posting.
- Encourage students to comment on peer posts. (Schroer, 2016)

Student engagement is best assured when students understand what is expected of them in the online environment.

The boxplots in Figure 6.4 represent the quantity of reply activities in a course in so-called topic 1 and topic 2 respectively. The X-axis represents discussion topics: topic 1, before the interventions, and topic 2, after the interventions. The Y-axis corresponds to the number of replies provided by individual students to peers' initial threads. Comparing the two shows a statistically significant increase in mean number of replies in topic 2 after the interventions compared to topic 1, before the intervention.

In addition, comparing the visualizations of discussion interactions among topics and forums can prompt instructors to pay more attention to the design of online discussion prompts. In our case, for example, faculty reconstructed the composition of discussion prompts for the second iteration of the same course to include audio as well.

Implications

Our app employs centrality measures and produces network diagrams that help instructors identify students' participation rates and interaction types in online discussions. Based on the visual presentation of discussion data, instructors can provide early-on interventions to encourage less active students to demonstrate their knowledge, read peers' postings, and share feedback. Furthermore, using the community detection approach to show a network diagram with subgroups' information allows course instructors to locate student groups relatively closely connected (in a subset) with fewer interactions with other groups. Faculty may leverage this information to facilitate a cohesive learning community and explore the evolution of student online interactions across discussion topics.

Although it is relatively easy to model online discussion interactions using SNA, the current version of our app fails to present the dynamics of

Figure 6.4. Boxplot representing total replies contributed per student to a discussion topic.

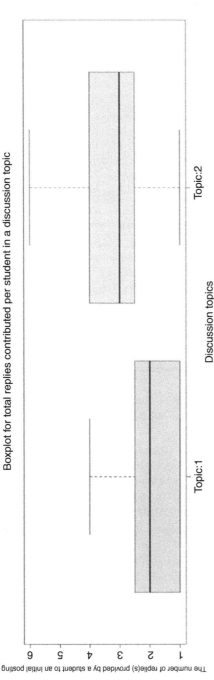

Boxplot for total replies contributed per student in a discussion topic

● The top and bottom lines of the rectangle are the 3rd and 1st quartiles (Q3 and Q1), respectively. The length of the rectangle from top to bottom is the interquartile range (IQR). ● The line in the middle of the rectangle is the median (or the 2nd quartile, Q2). ● The top whisker denotes the maximum value or the 3rd quartile plus 1.5 times the interquartile range (Q3 + 1.5*IQR), whichever is smaller. ● The bottom whisker denotes either the minimum value or the quartile minus 1.5 times the interquartile range (Q1 − 1.5*IQR), whichever is larger.

```
Tukey multiple comparisons of means
  95% family-wise confidence level
  factor levels have been ordered

Fit: aov(formula = contribution ~ topic, data = discussion.activity.data)

$topic
                  diff       lwr      upr    p adj
topic:2-topic:1 1.085714 0.6357268 1.535702 8.6e-06
```

online interactions over time and to help identify the temporal indicator. Yet, our exploration in using SNA to analyze and visualize student online interactions at the course level is novel. The implication of using SNA to model student online interactions naturally lends itself to a time-varying graph formalism, which prompts us to explore the temporal analysis and visualization of social networks in the future.

References

Bean, J. C., & Peterson, D. (1998). Grading classroom participation. *New Directions for Teaching and Learning, 1998*(74), 33–40.

Csardi, G. (n.d). *Igraph R manual pages.* iGraph. http://igraph.org/r/doc/betweenness.html

Franceschet, M. (n.d.). *Betweenness centrality.* https://www.sci.unich.it/~francesc/teaching/network/betweeness.html

Hanneman, R. A., & Riddle, M. (2005). *Introduction to social network methods.* University of California, Riverside. http://www.faculty.ucr.edu/~hanneman/nettext/

Hecking, T., Chounta, I. A., & Hoppe, U. H. (2017). Role modelling in MOOC discussion forums. *Journal of Learning Analytics, 4*(1), 85–116. https://doi.org/10.18608/jla.2017.41.6

Ming, N., & Baumer, E. (2011). Using text mining to characterize online discussion facilitation. *Journal of Asynchronous Learning Networks, 15*(2), 71–109.

Ognyanova, K. (2016, January 10). *Network analysis with R and igraph: NetSci X Tutorial.* kateto.net/networks-r-igraph

Qi, J. (2017, December 6). *Role modeling in online discussion forums.* Analytics in Instruction Design. https://sites.dartmouth.edu/learninganalytics/2017/12/06/role-modeling-in-online-discussion-forums/

Rabbany, R., Elatia, S., Takaffoli, M., & Zaïane, O. R. (2014). Collaborative learning of students in online discussion forums: A social network analysis perspective. *Educational data mining: Studies in computational intelligence, 524,* pp. 441–464. Springer, Cham. https://doi.org/10.1007/978-3-319-02738-8_16

Saqr, M., Fors, U., Tedre, M., & Nouri, J. (2018). How social network analysis can be used to monitor online collaborative learning and guide an informed intervention. *PLOS One.* https://doi.org/10.1371/journal.pone.0194777

Schroer, K. (2016, November 28). *Community-based approaches: Using data from online discussion boards, part 3.* Analytics in Instructional Design. https://sites.dartmouth.edu/learninganalytics/2016/11/28/community-based-approaches-using-data-from-online-discussion-boards-part-3/

7

TEACHING, TECHNOLOGY, AND BUILDING TRUST

What I've Learned About How Artifical Intelligence Can Improve Student Writing

Jamey Heit

Before YouTube existed, I tried to teach myself how to play guitar. I would read a book, fumble about with my fingers to figure out basic chords, and usually be so frustrated that I would put the guitar away for a while. Not surprisingly, I didn't learn to play very well.

Learning to play an instrument is a lot like learning how to write. The skill is difficult and requires extensive practice. A crucial part of that practice is feedback loops that can help the learner identify mistakes. These positive feedback loops drive the acquisition and refinement of the skill in question. If I had simply taken lessons, I expect my guitar teacher would have pointed me in the right direction. This, in turn, would have likely encouraged me to work through my mistakes rather than set the learning process aside.

Positive feedback loops are the foundation of a successful learning environment. In my role as cofounder and CEO of Ecree, I aim to provide these feedback loops to students who are learning how to write successful outcomes. Ecree provides automated assessment in a formative context for students who are learning how to write. Students access this technology via the web. Through Ecree's technology, students received unlimited human-quality feedback in real-time. It is, in effect, a virtual teacher that can provide targeted feedback on the key skills of good writing: organization, analysis, clarity, and logic. The technology has been built to mirror what a human teacher does with students: provide positive feedback loops to help those students learn an invaluable skill.

The Problem

Positive feedback has a clear impact on student learning, but it is important to situate this resource within the broader context of how students typically learn to write in a formal education system. In my roughly 20 years of teaching (it's closer to 30 if I count by credit hours), I settled on a basic model for how I taught my students. This model is easy to visualize as represented in Figure 7.1.

Presentation is what occurs in the classroom. I teach students a concept or concepts. As an example, assume the class for the day is going to talk about thesis statements. I would present information to my students both on what the concept means and why it is important as a component of good writing. After explaining the concept, I would then assign my students practice. They need to write to develop the skill; the specific exercise I would assign would be designed to work on that skill.

Thus far, the process is running smoothly. Most teachers can recognize some version of these steps and wouldn't suffer undue headaches in thinking about this as part of the teacher's role. Things grind to a halt, however, during the third step. Assessment, or the evaluation of the practice, is where the way

Figure 7.1. Basic teaching model.

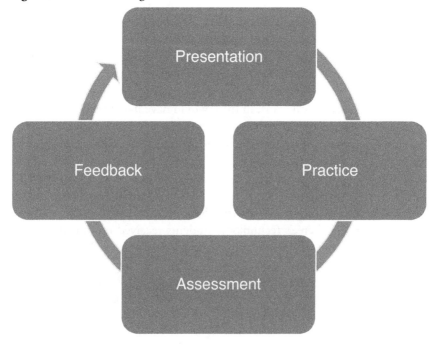

Figure 7.2. Typical assignment timeline.

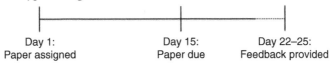

| Day 1: | Day 15: | Day 22–25: |
| Paper assigned | Paper due | Feedback provided |

students learn to write breaks down. Assessment takes a tremendous amount of time. As a result, the fourth and most crucial step, the feedback that helps students improve, reaches the student in a problematic state.

Time is a crucial factor in how my cofounder and I set about developing Ecree for two reasons. The first is obvious: Teachers have only a limited amount of time to do any task, and the average teacher who assigns writing will have dozens, if not a hundred, students to teach in a given term. This means less time for assessment per student. This reality points to the second problem: either the feedback students do receive is incomplete, or the time needed to give sufficient feedback stretches onward. This is the original negative feedback loop.

It is helpful to diagram the assignment process in a bit more detail to understand the way the teaching cycle breaks down. Figure 7.2 illustrates how practice and feedback unfold.

The gap between an assignment being due and feedback being provided is too long for effective learning to take place. To return to the guitar example, those long breaks taken in frustration meant that anything I did learn while practicing began to atrophy. Picking up the guitar again meant starting over in a sense. There was more effort needed to maintain the same aptitude level. If getting back to the same spot is the typical experience, then we should very much expect students not to be good writers.

That point was the key motivation for founding Ecree. I was part of a negative feedback loop: I and my students were not getting what they needed. Based on this realization, two key things informed my thinking about how to design technology that could help students become better writers:

1. This is a problem of scale, so technology has to be part of the solution.
2. Students need practice and feedback on that practice.

Principles of Design

The starting point for designing Ecree was the impact of time on the learning process—the framework for designing a viable automated assessment resource. Recall the timeline in Figure 7.2. As constructed, this way of teaching students how to write locates the most important step in the learning

Figure 7.3. Default target for student learning.

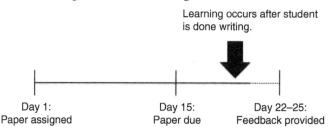

process at a point that is not optimal for building skills. When feedback occurs *after* the exercise is complete, the learning process is stunted. Figure 7.3 illustrates this timing within the general learning paradigm.

My great-great aunt had a sweet roll recipe that has subsequently been passed down through my family. Growing up, those sweet rolls were a favorite treat for my siblings and me. Now that I have two daughters of my own, the sweet rolls are back. My mom makes them whenever I bring the girls for a visit. Inevitably, the girls will ask me to make the sweet rolls once we've returned from our visit. Though I have the recipe, I simply cannot get the rolls to turn out well. Somewhere in the process I make a mistake. That mistake is baked into the rolls. The outcome is less than ideal, and I can't fix it because I don't know when the error occurred. I only get confirmation of that outcome in the form of my daughters' feedback that "the rolls don't taste as good as grandma's." I have spoken with my mom multiple times to try to figure out what I'm not doing correctly, and we still can't find the error. This is what happens when feedback occurs after the task itself is complete.

If I were to make the sweet rolls with my mom in the kitchen, chances are she would spot the mistake immediately, and we would be able to correct it. This is why the point in the learning process at which feedback is delivered matters. If feedback can be provided when the task is being done, the skill being learned is far more likely to improve. Rather than the timeline represented in Figure 7.3, Figure 7.4 shows Ecree's feedback for learning.

This jump in when feedback is delivered was the fundamental design principle at Ecree. From the outset, we knew that effective use of automated assessment technology would require a shift in how feedback is delivered. If we could provide students with positive feedback loops as they were writing, they would be far more likely to become better writers. Just like having my mom in the kitchen watching me make the sweet rolls, having an expert writing instructor with students as they write would result in improved skills.

As with solving for the realities of time, this straightforward process is impossible for humans to practice. Simply, humans don't scale. The best

Figure 7.4. Ecree's learning timeline.

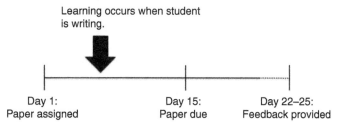

writing teachers in the world can work with only so many students at any one time. Any attempt to add students to a teacher's purview will, beyond a certain point, trigger the negative feedback loops associated with time. Technology, however, can scale. An influx of thousands at students at once would overwhelm a person, but technology can maintain its service to students when faced with a surge. This is the second principle we had for building Ecree's technology.

Technology and Human Psychology: Not a Match Made in Heaven

We anticipated (and still encounter frequently) two key resistance points from teachers when discussing the role of Ecree in helping students become better writers. The first point is some version of a claim that technology cannot "do what humans do." The second point is not a claim so much as a concern. If technology *can* do most of what humans can do, then are we inviting a hostile takeover into the teacher's classroom? Won't technology just replace teachers?

The first point is far more important to discuss, because in defining the scope of what automated assessment technology can do, a clear framework for resolving the second concern comes into focus. To address this first concern, it is helpful to briefly step back and describe in a bit more detail what Ecree does. Ecree uses a standard writing rubric to deliver targeted feedback on every paragraph the student writes. We designed this rubric to be similar to most rubrics that are used in a variety of institutions and educational contexts. To define Ecree's rubric, we collected more than 200 rubrics from different institutions, departments, and standardized tests to identify the key elements of good writing that are most common. To determine what should be included in the Ecree rubric, we set a goal of being at least 90% similar to every sample rubric in that set of 200.

The use of a rubric is an important consideration in light of a common critique that artificial intelligence (AI) cannot "read" papers. Systems that use a machine learning approach to assess writing are pattern-based. This approach relies on a large training set of papers, curated by humans, to train the algorithms. Algorithms look for patterns within subsets of papers (e.g., all papers of score 4 have qualities X and Y). The algorithms then look for X and Y in subsequent papers; if found, the paper gets a score of 4.

This approach is righty critiqued as not doing what humans can do. There are several reasons the critique is legitimate. First, a pattern-based algorithm relies on highly domain-specific elements to evaluate papers. Language is not domain-specific. Second, pattern-based algorithms either measure fixed topical elements or are trained to find elements that are merely correlated with prespecified essays (e.g., a thesis statement must be the last sentence of the first paragraph). Third, with pattern-based algorithms, the basis for determining quality (a rubric or standards-aligned set of metrics) is not shared. Students and teachers therefore do not know the actual elements of an essay the algorithm is using to generate scores and feedback.

These considerations point to an additional critique of the pattern-based approach. As quality of writing and argumentation are not directly measured, pattern-based algorithms generate results without clear textual justification. This limits the accuracy of scores and does not identify the specific area of a text where a student needs to improve. This is not how formative teaching works. Effective formative engagement must directly measure the quality of the essay before offering students feedback on how to improve their essays.

Ecree's technology uses a *rules-based* approach to assess a paper. The Ecree algorithm understands the rules of good writing and uses those rules to determine if the paper is good or not. Ecree uses a rubric that states what is expected of a paper *before* the paper is assessed. This is the same process humans use: A departmental or institutional rubric is established and then used to determine a paper's quality. The Ecree rubric can be shared widely, so that students and teachers know exactly what elements of good writing Ecree is assessing.

Ecree's approach thus lives on the *master system* branch of the AI family tree. This term means that Ecree mirrors the performance of the best human scorer based on the same rules that scorer uses. Thus, to claim that Ecree is not reading a paper is to claim that the best humans are not reading a paper. Ecree uses the same metrics people do (e.g., thesis statement, use of evidence, analysis). Because Ecree uses a clearly defined set of rules to assess a student's writing, feedback for any metric on the rubric is tied directly to the text. The result is that students get more granular and justifiable results.

The elements of the rubric will sound familiar. In an introductory paragraph, students are expected to provide relevant background information, then provide a thesis statement. In the body paragraphs, students are expected to introduce a point for discussion that follows from the thesis. That point should be the main idea developed in the paragraph. The student is then expected to elaborate on that point as it relates to the thesis using evidence and analysis. In the conclusion, the student is expected to summarize their argument, then provide some final thoughts. All of these steps should be completed in a focused manner and without grammatical mistakes.

These basic elements of good writing do not include higher-order conceptual considerations. Content-specific feedback (e.g., the implications of claiming that the adults in *Romeo and Juliet* engender conflict in a way that dooms their legacy) is not something Ecree does. Ecree focuses on basic elements of organization and argumentation.

In one respect, then, Ecree can very much do what humans can do. More accurately, Ecree can do a significant portion of what humans do. The good news is that the things Ecree can do tend to be the types of things that really grind down teacher morale. The point at which Ecree cannot engage with student work is, essentially, the point at which the teacher gets to engage with students on ideas. In my own experience, this is the part of teaching I liked the most.

This distinction provides the basis for thinking about the second resistance point. Can Ecree (or any technology) replace teachers completely? Of course not. There will always be higher-order tasks that are part of the learning process that cannot be reduced to an algorithm. Effective technology requires a design that acknowledges the limits of what that technology can do. The tradeoff is that humans should return the favor and acknowledge what technology is capable of doing and embrace that capability as a learning resource.

Research and Results

Having defined the scope of Ecree's technology, the next point to address is: How well does it actually work? Can it compare to humans? To answer these questions, Ecree worked with a senior professor at the University of North Carolina at Chapel Hill (UNC) to evaluate how well Ecree's automated assessment technology compared to humans. Using a three-part study, we reached a clear conclusion regarding Ecree's performance: It is not just reliable, it is *more reliable than humans* (Edmonson et al., 2018).

In the first phase of the study, we set out to compare human scores on student papers to Ecree scores. We took the papers from a large introductory philosophy class with 250 students. The course was taught by a senior philosophy professor with the help of five teaching assistants (TAs). Before the student papers were scored, the professor hosted inter-rater reliability (IRR) sessions to ensure the five TAs were applying the departmental rubric consistently. After multiple IRR sessions, the professor dismissed the TAs to complete their grading. The motivation for dismissal was not that IRR was achieved. Rather, the professor was *unable* to achieve IRR among the TAs after several hours reviewing student papers. The average numeric gap between TA scores using the same rubric was 10 points. Some pairs of TAs were as much as 15 numeric points different in their application of the same rubric to the same student papers. Even though the TAs were unable to reach consensus, they still had to provide students with official scores on the assignment. In order to provide students with their scores in the standard assessment model, the professor asked the TAs to grade 50 papers each. These papers were distributed randomly to each TA. The grading took slightly longer than a week.

For each TA, we generated a grading profile, which conveys the distribution of grades assigned by each TA for their respective stack of 50 papers. The grading profile can be understood as characterizing how each TA interpreted and applied the department rubric to student papers. We graphed each TA's grading profile in Figure 7.5, which demonstrates the intrinsic variability that defines human scoring.

Figure 7.5. TAs' grading profiles.

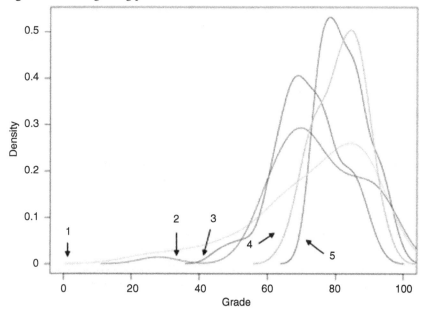

The graph depicted in Figure 7.5 makes clear the variability in how individuals interpret and then apply the same standard rubric. In a set of papers, this graph indicates that student scores depend on the random assignment to a specific human grader. Several patterns are also clear in the TA grading profiles. Profiles 4 and 5 exhibit the "Mercy D" approach to grading. If the student at least turns the paper in, the TA will not fail the paper (this approach does not adhere to UNC's grading scale, which defines clearly when a paper should receive a failing grade). Profiles 1 and 2, however, pose a more stringent grading experience for the student. The TAs are willing to assign failing grades, and the average grade is also noticeably lower.

Students should rightly be concerned with the implications of this graph. The TAs are certainly capable of grading papers. The problem is not the possibility of a justifiable score based on the rubric being used; the issue is variability across TAs. A student who is unfortunate enough to be assigned TA 3 is most likely to get a D grade, whereas a luckier student who is assigned TA 4 is much more likely to get an A grade. Because each profile is based on a TA having graded 50 papers, we can take these patterns as statistically significant. These different profiles make clear that each TA sets their own unique probability distribution for assigning scores; thus, there are different probabilities for each TA of assigning a range of scores even when a standard for scoring papers exists.

In an attempt to understand the variation in how TAs scored student papers, we proceeded to the second phase of the study. In this phase, 10 papers were randomly selected from the full batch of 250 papers. The TAs were then asked to rank the papers in order of quality to measure *general consistency* in scoring based on quality as defined by the department rubric. Figure 7.6 shows the results of this second phase.

Not a single paper achieved consensus with respect to ranking papers based on general quality. In order to capture the lack of consensus, we generated a disagreement score for each paper. To generate the score, we calculated the distance between a ranking where there was agreement between at least two TAs and the rankings that varied from this point of consensus. For example, Paper 1 had a consensus point at 7, then a gap of one plus a gap of two (the difference between rankings 7 and 6 and 7 and 9 respectively).

If there was no consensus, we added the difference in ranking between the highest and lowest rankings in quality, and then multiplied the distance by 2. For example, Paper 3 has no consensus ranking and a gap of four spots between the highest and lowest ranking. Thus, Paper 3 has a score of 8. This multiplier served to amplify that the spread in rankings did not include a single point of consensus. Table 7.1 summarizes the variability in how papers were ranked.

Figure 7.6. Human variability in ranking papers by quality.

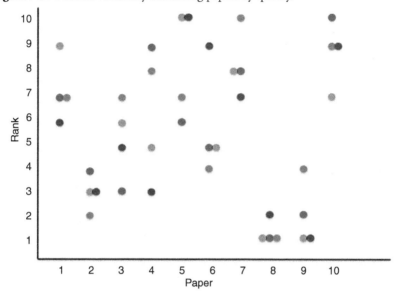

Only two papers (2 and 8) achieved relative *consensus*, which we defined as a having a score of 2 or less. Importantly, both papers were among the poorest quality papers. These papers are evident in the clustering at the lower end of the quality-ranking axis in Figure 7.6. A third poor-quality paper,

TABLE 7.1
Variability in How Papers Were Ranked

Paper	Variability Score
1	3
2	2
3	8
4	18
5	7
6	5
7	3
8	1
9	4
10	3

9, showed signs of clustering at the lower end of the rankings, but one TA deemed it good enough to be in the middle of the rankings. Similarly, there were a few papers that trended toward agreement at the top of the rankings. Papers 1, 7, and 10 had a score of 3, which, like the poor-quality papers, showed that general signal was still not enough to generate strong clustering in the rankings.

Even when removing the granularity of numeric grades, there is still intrinsic variability in the way humans interpret and apply rubrics. This clarifies the problem that surfaced during Phase I of the study when the professor hosted the IRR sessions with his TAs. There is simply no evidence that the TAs in this study could consistently interpret and apply a defined standard.[1] Even when the humans involved are top performers, they will produce fundamentally inconsistent and unfair results. A student's grade should not depend on who is grading the paper, yet there was consistent evidence during the first two phases of the study that this is exactly what happens.

Given the trends during the first two phases of the study, our third phase was designed to test whether humans could determine quality between drafts of the same paper. For this phase, we gave five teachers 50 sets of papers. Each set contained two versions of the same paper. We labeled the papers according to their set: 1A and 1B, 2A and 2B, and so on. We then asked the teachers to read each set of papers and assess whether paper 1A or 1B was the higher quality paper. The goal was to measure whether humans can agree on general quality within a single paper. In some cases, the difference was clear (e.g., when the B paper was an initial outline and the A paper was a fully written draft). In other cases, there was very little difference between papers.

For the first analysis of the results, we separated the 50 sets into one of the following three categories:

1. Unanimous Consensus: All five humans agreed on which in the set was the higher quality paper. For example, all five humans agreed Paper 1B was the better paper in the first set.
2. Strong Consensus: Four out of five humans agreed on which paper in the set was the best. For example, four humans agreed that Paper 4B was the better quality paper in the set.
3. Weak Consensus: Three out of five humans agreed on which paper was the better paper of the set. For example, three out of five humans agreed paper 10A was the better paper in the tenth set.

In Table 7.2, we show the number of papers that fell into each category.

The results suggest that, on average, humans can differentiate quality within two drafts of the same paper, though the results show a high *error rate*

TABLE 7.2
Distribution of Papers According to Categories

Consensus Category	Amount
Unanimous Consensus	54% (27 out of 50)
Strong Consensus	28% (14 out of 50)
Weak Consensus	18% (9 out of 50)

(defined as a case where there was weak consensus and thus was not a reliable determination of which paper is better quality).

After calculating these figures, we used Ecree's automated assessment technology to complete the same exercise. The papers were assessed in real-time to determine which paper in each set was better. We then looked at how often Ecree's determination of the better paper agreed with the human consensus. The results are shown in Table 7.3.

Ecree's performance is clearly in line with human experts' ability to differentiate between a better or worse paper. The software never missed the mark when there was clear agreement (unanimous or strong consensus) among the humans. Notably, not a single human performed as well; every human disagreed at least once with the majority in strong consensus sets.

The final question to explore in light of these results was who or what is the most reliable source for differentiating quality when there is weak consensus? As these papers are likely to be the so-called problem cases where variability in performance would be most likely, we calculated which party—one of the humans or Ecree—was in agreement most often with the majority in a weak consensus set of papers. These results are shown in Table 7.4.

Several important takeaways are evident in Table 7.4. The first takeaway is that there exists among humans a clear average performance level when assessing drafts of the same paper without a clear difference in quality. Sixty percent of the humans were in agreement, with the consensus two times out of three. The second takeaway is that in this group, and likely in any given

TABLE 7.3
Ecree's Agreement With Human Consensus

Ecree Agreement With Human Ratings	Rate
Unanimous Consensus	100% (27 out of 27)
Strong Consensus	100% (14 out of 14)
Weak Consensus	89% (8 out of 9)

TABLE 7.4
Results of Human and Ecree Agreement With the Majority

Assessor	Percentage Agreement With Majority
Human 1	78% (7 out of 9)
Human 2	67% (6 out of 9)
Human 3	67% (6 out of 9)
Human 4	22% (2 out of 9)
Human 5	67% (6 out of 9)
Ecree	89% (8 out of 9)

group, there is a *poor performer* as defined by the inability to agree with the consensus. This suggests that in addition to intrinsic variation in the assessment process, there is likely to be an outlier who can amplify the effects of subjective assessment. Finally, there is similarly a top performer in the group who is in agreement with the majority more than average. Within these trends, the key takeaway from the third phase is clear: Ecree provides *the most reliable assessment most consistently.* In ambiguous cases, Ecree matches the majority more often than the top-performing human. This claim finds further support in the fact that Ecree is the only assessor that matched strong consensus majorities 100% of the time.

Conclusion

Across the three phases of this study, we saw a clear answer to our initial question. *Humans are not reliable* when it comes to assessment at scale. At a more granular level (i.e., differentiating quality within drafts of the same paper) humans perform better, but there is still a pronounced variability in human performance. Two results follow: First, Ecree's technology is reliable, and second, expecting technology to mirror human performance is not really possible because human assessment varies too much.

In terms of assessing the quality of student work, this conclusion indicates an important shift in how we should think about automated assessment technology. The question is no longer whether technology can mirror humans, but, rather, how humans can build on the baseline that technology provides. With respect to issues of quality teaching and fairness to students, the effects of automated assessment technology, if accepted as an evidence-based viable substitute for assessment, will be pronounced. Further, these improvements can be realized in a more efficient manner. Ecree returned all results in this study in real-time. The consistent and quality feedback it provides is also more accessible to the student in that it eliminates the need for a human to complete the process. The typical waiting time for a student to receive feedback from a teacher is one week or more.

This chapter closes with a question that became obvious as we analyzed these results. Rather than ask whether automated assessment can do as good a job as a human expert, we should be asking why so many of us continue to resist the impact this technology can have on education?

Note

1. We have found similar results in a previous study (Heit et al., 2015). In that study, we asked five college professors to grade the same 20 papers.

References

Edmonson, T., Bundesen, K., Goldsberry, W., Donaldson, R., & Heit, J. (2018, October 23). *Who's better at assessment—humans or algorithms? A three part analysis comparing humans and automated assessment technology* [Presentation]. Assessment Institute National Conference, Indianapolis, IN, United States.

Heit, J., Donaldson, J., & Rudemiller, N. (2015, Fall). *How automated assessment and feedback can improve L2 student outcomes* [Presentation]. Symposium on Second Language Writing Annual Conference, Auckland, New Zealand.

8

HOW WE MAY LEARN

Cybersecurity Awareness Training as a Model for Future Learning Platforms

Peter Shea and Bora Aytun

A common definition of *learning* is "a relatively permanent change in behavior brought about by practice or experience" (Lachman, 1996, p. 477). This behavioral view of learning has often been undervalued in higher education. Demonstrations of academic knowledge through the creation of written artifacts (e.g., student essays and exams) is the traditional manner of assessing student learning in colleges and universities. This contrasts with the culture of the workplace, which identifies successful learning outcomes through performance improvement and the application of knowledge in specific real-world contexts.

For decades it was assumed that the two conflicting views could coexist in relative harmony, each maintaining dominance in the separate spheres of academia and the workplace. However, significant cultural disruptions due to technology advances and the evolving global economy have led many to think that this discontinuity in learning values is no longer sustainable. Higher education, critics insist, must do more to deliberately prepare students for the new world of work (Weise et al., 2018).

One of the shortcomings of the higher education establishment is that although there have been many decades of fruitful research related to teaching and learning, applied learning science is rarely found in colleges and universities. The force of tradition—and the preference of many college instructors to employ the teaching methods they encountered when they were students—has often barred the door of college classrooms to pedagogical methods that research has shown to be more impactful on student learning than the standard college lecture. One place where learning science has found a receptive audience is professional education. A common workforce training technique grounded in the neuroscience of learning is simulation (Cardoza, 2011). Although the idea of learning simulations in higher education is not unknown (Hertel & Millis, 2002), simulation-based learning is more frequently found in career paths where practitioners are required to make decisions that have potential life and death consequences. Soldiers, firefighters, police, and medical personnel have a long tradition of employing simulations as learning tools, allowing students to make decisions in dynamic environments and then seeing the effects of their actions without incurring real-life consequences. Simulations used for nursing education, for example, have seen a large impact on the psychomotor domain as a consequence of simulation-based learning (Kim et al., 2016).

One of the fastest growing areas of simulation-based learning is cybersecurity awareness training. In an age where more and more activity takes place in a cloud-based environment, cybersecurity has grown exponentially, with a projected market value of $300 billion by 2024 ("Global Cybersecurity Market, 2019–2024," 2019). A significant portion of this market is dedicated to preventing cybercrime by enhancing awareness of the risks of attacks by malicious hackers and cybercriminals. Because cybercrime affects everyone, cybersecurity awareness is seen as an essential 21st-century competency. In the United States, October has been designated National Cybersecurity Awareness Month (The University of Rhode Island, n.d.). As in the case of other professions mentioned, cybersecurity deals with potential cybersecurity threats; thus it is crucial that effective cybersecurity awareness education be rooted in quality learning science and evidence-based practices. In this chapter we describe the design of a specific cybersecurity awareness product, explain how the design is supported by learning theory, and discuss ways the design may be adopted to promote learning in more traditional academic subjects.

The cybersecurity awareness learning series *Agent Surefire* was released in 2008 by Mavi Interactive, a company founded by one of this chapter's contributors, Bora Aytun. *Agent Surefire* games take the learner through an interactive story in which the learner plays the role of a top cybersecurity agent investigating a cybercrime at various organizations. In the course of trying to solve the case, the learner is put through a series of challenging scenarios related to cybersecurity practices and protocols.

Another novel element of assessment that cybersecurity awareness training programs like *Agent Surefire* possess is their integration with phishing simulations. *Phishing* is a type of email-born cyberattack designed to trick the user into taking an action, such as clicking on a link then entering login credentials or opening a malicious attachment, in order to escalate the attacker's access to sensitive information. Phishing is typically done by hackers who send falsified email messages to unsuspecting people. A phishing simulation, by contrast, is a false attack generated typically by an information technology (IT) department to assess whether a member of an organization is susceptible to the fraudulent tactics of cybercriminals. The phishing simulation allows organizations to assess which of their members need to be trained or retrained to resist cyberattacks. For example, Mavi Interactive partnered with Keepnet Labs to integrate their cybersecurity awareness mini games (*Info Sentinel*) with Keepnet Lab's phishing simulation system. When a user fails a particular phishing test, a relevant mini game is assigned automatically to assess those weak points.

Agent Surefire incorporates three important elements of contemporary learning design. First is the virtual environment, which uses game mechanics and contextualized challenges to lead to greater learner engagement (Dawley & Dede, 2014). Second are adaptive pathways of the simulation, which respond to the users' decisions rather than forcing them into one linear path of progression. Third, the performance data capture allows for an instructor to assess the performance of the learner in ways that traditional learning assessment approaches cannot. For example, *Agent Surefire* captures data on how long a learner took to solve a particular challenge, which is extremely difficult, if not impossible, to record in a traditional classroom environment. Taken together, these three elements comprise a unique form of educational technology, something which would not have been possible until a few short years ago. Its potential to change our dominant teaching and learning paradigm is profound.

Engaging the Learner Through Virtual Environments Using Game Mechanics and Contextualized Challenges

There is a considerable body of work that supports the effectiveness of using game mechanics and immersive simulations as a means of creating learning experiences to engage and sustain the learner's interest (Aldrich, 2009; Gee, 2005; Squire, 2008). By presenting information in the highly contextualized setting of a crime scenario, *Agent Surefire* draws on the insights of Jean Lave and Etienne Wenger's (1991) surefire learning theory. Two of the key ideas presented in Lave and Wenger's theory are that "knowledge needs to be presented in an authentic context, i.e., settings and applications that would normally involve that knowledge [and] learning requires social interaction and collaboration" (Instructional Design.org, "Situational Learning," para. 6).[1]

In *Agent Surefire* the learner interacts with several nonplayer characters (NPCs) who provide information and give advice, essentially simulating social interaction and as represented in Figure 8.1.

Figure 8.1. NPC in *Agent Surefire*.

Another aspect to bear in mind is that when learners are developing knowledge by moving through a simulation, they are demonstrating their skills and knowledge by making decisions rather than providing answers. This change in context can promote a sense of agency in the learner that is not achieved through standard academic exercises.

Adapting Pathways for Individual Learners

As noted earlier, *Agent Surefire* is an example of an adaptive learning tool. A brief article published by *EDUCAUSE* titled "7 Things You Should Know About Adaptive Learning" provides the following succinct definition of *adaptive learning technology*: "Adaptive learning systems use a data-driven—and, in some cases, nonlinear—approach to instruction and remediation" (EDUCAUSE Learning Initiative, 2017, p. 1). The element of choice intrinsic to adaptive learning systems increases the learner's sense of control and autonomy, which can have an impact on the learner's engagement (Reeve & Tseng, 2011). The possibilities of adaptive learning systems suggest a paradigm shift equivalent to that which occurred in the early 1990s with the introduction of web pages. Before that time, reading was entirely a linear experience; the direction of the text was guided by the author's intention and not by the reader's choices. *Hypertext*, defined as a type of document that allows the reader to select from multiple ways to read a text, was only an experimental model available in a few formats such as Apple's Hypercard program or the *Choose Your Own Adventure* book series for elementary and middle school students. After the invention and widespread adoption of the World Wide Web, hypertext web pages became a dominant mode of publishing reading material. Arguably, today, more people read online today than traditional printed material. Adaptive learning systems could conceivably bring about an equivalently significant cultural shift.

Agent Surefire games employ various methods of adapting the user's path of exploration in accordance with their previous actions. The games provide users with a series of nonlinear scenarios. Users can face any one of numerous challenges and uncover related clues, in any order. These clues together lead to unlocking the next key discovery. The following are the three elements of adaptive learning found in the *Agent Surefire* games:

1. *Adaptive narrative.* Both NPC interactions and the user's character's (the titular Agent Surefire) inner monologue change based on the order in which the user discovers each clue. The narratives appear in comic book–style speech or thought balloons.
2. *Key performance indicators (KPIs).* KPIs document potential mistakes and failures. The (in)actions and (in)correct KPI are mapped into the game space. When the user chooses a faulty action or ignores an important element, undesirable outcomes result and the user is made to feel the repercussions via multisensory dramatization. This system is also known as the *repercussion engine.*
3. *Scenario branch.* A scenario branch occurs at a crucial decision point. The user must decide between multiple "no-win" options, revealing the user's character through handling tough situations.

One of the long-standing critiques of the traditional classroom-based education model is that it assumes that a group of age-equivalent learners in a room having the exact same instructional input will achieve roughly the same educational progress over a set period of time (a semester). This fails to acknowledge obvious differences among students in regard to prior knowledge, preparation, motivation, or natural ability. Adaptive learning systems can be seen as a long-overdue corrective to this flawed model.

Assessing Mastery Through Performance Data and Phishing Campaigns

Another compelling aspect of *Agent Surefire* is the performance data capture. Computational learning media can capture aspects of a learner's performance that are difficult to record in conventional educational settings. In their article, "Big Data Analysis in Higher Education: Promises and Pitfalls," Chris

Dede and Andrew Ho, Harvard University, and Piotr Mitros, cofounder and (then) chief scientist at Edx, described how the collection of large and diverse educational data sets could impact our instructional practices. As an example of using big data to support learning and assessment, they mentioned "using game-based environments for learning and assessment, where learning is situated in complex information and decision-making situations" (Dede et al., 2016, para. 7).

Agent Surefire games assess a number of relevant performance points related to developing cybersecurity awareness. For example, these games assess whether the user can identify a cybersecurity risk (and, if so, what category of risk it is). These games can also measure how long it takes a user to solve a particular challenge—an important data point which can suggest whether certain types of problems bedevil a learner more than others. At the conclusion or cessation of game play, *Agent Surefire* displays performance data on dashboards that can be accessed by an individual user (i.e., the person who is learning) or by an instructor who wishes to assess individual and group performances, as illustrated in Table 8.1.

Application of the Cybersecurity Awareness Model to Other Subjects: Challenges and Potential

Perhaps the greatest difference between traditional academic learning objectives and the educational paradigm represented by a computer-based learning game series like *Agent Surefire* is that, in the case of the latter, the focus is not predominantly on knowledge transfer. In cybersecurity awareness training, both knowledge acquisition *and* behavioral change are valued. The distinction between *education* (creating new mental models and schemata to understand the world) and *training* (behavioral change intended to help the learner accomplish specific tasks) is blurred. Widespread adoption of learning games like the *Agent Surefire* series may result in a greater appreciation of applied knowledge. One of the reasons that such a change has not already occurred in the mainstream educational establishment relates to the expense that has often come with the adoption of quality interactive learning media. The commitment to funding complex, high-impact learning technology has often been restricted to domains where significant risks are involved. For example, the desire to prevent costly mistakes that can result in loss of life (e.g., medicine, military, aviation) or the loss of critical organizational data or financial resources (e.g., cybersecurity) has led these industries to make significant commitments to complex, immersive learning tools.

TABLE 8.1
Partial Admin Dashboard View

Vulnerability: Improper disposal of documents				Vulnerability: Improper handling of documents or media containing valuable intellectual assets				Vulnerability: Improper handling of information that can be used in Social Engineering				Vulnerability: Using predictable PIN numbers and passwords			
Correctly Categorized	Mis-categorized	Discovery Rate	Accuracy Rate	Correctly Categorized	Mis-categorized	Discovery Rate	Accuracy Rate	Correctly Categorized	Mis-categorized	Discovery Rate	Accuracy Rate	Correctly Categorized	Mis-categorized	Discovery Rate	Accuracy Rate
2	3	100%	40%	2	3	23%	40%	0	4	36%	0%	0	1	25%	0%
0	0	0%	-	0	0	0%	-	0	0	0%	-	0	0	0%	-
1	0	20%	100%	1	1	9%	50%	1	2	27%	33%	1	0	25%	100%
3	0	60%	100%	10	0	45%	100%	1	3	36%	25%	2	0	50%	100%
4	0	80%	100%	6	0	27%	100%	0	1	9%	0%	0	1	25%	0%
2	2	80%	50%	3	2	23%	60%	0	2	18%	0%	2	0	50%	100%
0	0	0%	-	0	1	5%	0%	0	0	0%	-	0	0	0%	-
4	1	100%	80%	3	8	50%	27%	0	3	27%	0%	1	0	25%	100%

Accuracy Rate Legend:

NO DATA	No items in this category were discovered
SUCCESS	At least one item in this category was correctly categorized
FAILURE	None of the items discovered in this category were correctly categorized

Although there have been some promising pilot programs in which adaptive learning providers and higher education institutions have created partnerships to explore the potential application of immersive learning technology (Fain, 2014), such programs are far from the norm. The cost of building and sustaining such learning technologies has proved prohibitive for many colleges and universities, to say nothing of allocating professional development resources to prepare faculty for adopting such technologies. A possible way forward would be for state and federal organizations to use public funds to create and maintain a centralized immersive learning resource open to all state-funded schools and colleges. Although managing costs and securing a reliable source of funding are obstacles to consider, making such a resource freely available to schools and colleges would enable the collection of large data sets related to student learning, thus realizing the vision of data-informed educational progress (Dede et al., 2016).

Perhaps the ultimate significance of learning tools such as the *Agent Surefire* series is that they fuse the instructional and assessment functions in ways we have never seen before. As Lou Pugliese wrote in his 2016 *EDUCAUSE Review* article on adaptive learning, "Our current didactic, transactional digital learning solutions are designed around the concept of *sameness*. It's like the lull before a storm" (para. 1). It is possible that the most important educational technology to emerge in the coming years will be those tools that place a near-equal emphasis on promoting learning *and* gathering data for performance assessment.

The potential advantages, including the promotion of deeper, more rigorous learning for all postsecondary learners, are too great to ignore, particularly in the 21st century when people need to learn and retain what they learn quickly and effectively in order to cope with a world that is more dynamic, fast changing, and complex than ever before.

Note

1. In their foreword to Lave and Wenger's (1991) book, *Situated Learning: Legitimate Peripheral Participation*, technology and education scholars Roy Pea and John Seely Brown wrote, "In changing situations of knowledge acquisition and use, the new interactive technologies redefine—in ways yet to be determined—what it means to know and understand" (p. 12), thus anticipating the rise of learning technologies of which *Agent Surefire* is an example.

References

Aldrich, C. (2009). *The complete guide to simulations and serious games: How the most valuable content will be created in the age beyond Gutenberg to Google.* John Wiley & Sons.

Cardoza, M. P. (2011). Neuroscience and simulation: An evolving theory of brain-based education. *Clinical Simulation in Nursing, 7*(6), e205–e208. https://doi.org/10.1016/j.ecns.2011.08.004

Dawley L., & Dede C. (2014). Situated learning in virtual worlds and immersive simulations. In J. Spector, M. Merrill, J. Elen, & M. Bishop (Eds.) *Handbook of research on educational communications and technology* (pp. 723–734). Springer. https://doi.org/10.1007/s10758-014-9231-7

Dede, C., Ho, A., & Mitros, P. (2016, August 22). Big data analysis in higher education: Promises and pitfalls. *EDUCAUSE Review.* https://er.educause.edu/articles/2016/8/big-data-analysis-in-higher-education-promises-and-pitfalls

Design.org. (2020, August 20). *Situated learning.* https://www.instructionaldesign.org/theories/situated-learning/

EDUCAUSE Learning Initiative. (2017, January). *7 things you should know about adaptive learning.* EDUCAUSE. https://library.educause.edu/-/media/files/library/2017/1/eli7140.pdf

Fain, P. (2014, October 10). Online and in control. *Inside Higher Education.* https://www.insidehighered.com/news/2014/10/10/emerging-adaptive-software-puts-faculty-members-charge-course-creation

Gee, J. P. (2005). Learning by design: Good video games as learning machines. *E-Learning and Digital Media, 2*(1), 5–16. https://doi.org/10.2304/elea.2005.2.1.5

Global cybersecurity market forecasts, 2019–2024. (2019, November 22). *Businesswire.* https://www.businesswire.com/news/home/20191122005417/en/Global-Cybersecurity-Market-Forecasts-2019-2024---Market

Hertel, J. P., & Millis, B. (2002). *Using simulations to promote learning in higher education: An introduction.* Stylus.

Kim, J., Park, J., & Shin, S. (2016). Effectiveness of simulation-based nursing education depending on fidelity: A metaanalysis. *BMC Medical Education, 16*(52). https://doi.org/10.1186/s12909-016-0672-7

Lachman, S. (1996). Learning is a process: Toward an improved definition of learning. *The Journal of Psychology, 131*(5), 477–480. https://doi.org/10.1080/00223989709603535

Lave, J., & Wenger, E. (1991). *Situated learning: Legitimate peripheral participation.* Cambridge University Press. https://doi.org/10.1017/CBO9780511815355

Pea, R., & Brown, J. S. (1991). Series foreword. In J. Lave & E. Wegner *Situated learning: Legitimate peripheral participation* (pp. 11–12). Cambridge University Press. https://doi.org/10.1017/CBO9780511815355

Pugliese, L. (2016, October). Adaptive learning systems: Surviving the storm. *EDUCAUSE Review.* https://er.educause.edu/articles/2016/10/adaptive-learning-systems-surviving-the-storm

Reeve, J., & Tseng, C.-M. (2011, October). Agency as a fourth aspect of students' engagement during learning activities. *Contemporary Educational Psychology, 36*(4), 257–267. https://doi.org/10.1016/j.cedpsych.2011.05.002

Squire, K. D. (2008). Video games and education: Designing learning systems for an interactive age. *Educational Technology: The Magazine for Managers of Change in Education, 48*(2), 17–26. https://doi.org/10.1007/s10648-010-9128-5

University of Rhode Island. (n.d.). *National cybersecurity awareness month* 2019. https://security.uri.edu/ncsam2019/

Weise, M. (2018). *Robot-ready: Human+ skills for the future of work* [White paper]. Strada Institute for the Future of Work. https://www.economicmodeling.com/robot-ready-reports/

PART THREE

ADOPTION AND INTEGRATION OF LEARNING TECHNOLOGIES ACROSS THE INSTITUTION: CASE STUDIES

9

ENABLING A SOLUTION
FOR ASSESSMENT
AND TECHNOLOGY

Ruth Newberry, Robin Robinson, and Adriana Botha

I n the previous chapters, a key focus has been the intersection of educational technologies—those digital tools and systems used to facilitate, support, and collect data on teaching and learning—and learner success, instruction, and evaluation of learner performance at the course level. In this chapter, we intend to focus on the assessment of learner performance at the program and institutional level and its intersection with assessment technology (AT) systems. For the purpose of our discussion, an AT system is software that helps institutions and programs facilitate and/or manage their assessment processes. That is, it can do some or all of the following tasks:

- Store the various types of learning outcomes (institutional, program, accreditor, and course) needed for assessing curricular and student performance
- Align these outcomes to course learning activities that are the sources of direct or indirect evidence and produce curriculum maps and assessment plans
- Collect evidence of student performance through commonly used assessment approaches, such as
  - juried or secondary review of artifacts through rubrics aligned to learning outcomes by a committee of reviewers; and/or
  - primary or direct review of student performance by instructors using course-embedded rubrics with rows or tests with questions aligned to learning outcomes for instructors to score

- Provide reports and analysis of student performance on learning outcomes by course, across sections of courses and disciplines, and by individual student with statistical analysis for inter-rater reliability and reliability of the measurement tool
- Enable the creation and monitoring of action plans for improvement
- Capture and facilitate the assessment narrative for accreditation reports

Some AT systems attempt to do all of the previously listed tasks, and others focus on specific parts of the assessment process. Some manage the documentation, the action plans, and the reporting for internal and external accreditation, and others focus specifically on evidence collection, analysis, and reporting of student performance on learning outcomes. It's important to note that most AT systems operate externally to the learning management system (LMS). That is, they are separate applications and must be managed and supported as independent applications. Only a few are part of the LMS itself, directly leveraging the activities that students and faculty already do in the LMS for teaching and learning.

Our intent in this chapter is not to adjudicate the functional capabilities of the many assessment and accreditation systems available today—that is a focus for another time.[1] Our purpose is to present an AT adoption framework (ATAF), or a set of practices to enable a technology solution for program and institutional assessment.

ATAF

We offer a perspective derived from our experiences and observations in educational technology, assessment, and consulting that has resulted in a methodology framework of insights and practices.[2] When this framework is embraced by those involved in the process of program and institutional assessment and by the institution's educational technology support unit in collaboration with a consultant for an AT solution, the result can be a successful, scalable, sustainable, and cost-effective implementation of an AT for broad adoption at an institution. As seen in Figure 9.1, our framework has four primary areas, which we will refer to as quadrants, that, when working in partnership with each other, can achieve a successful implementation and adoption of an AT to help improve learning for students.

The aim of our ATAF model is to move beyond the implementation of an AT to achieve sustainable and broad adoption for the AT system. The

Figure 9.1. ATAF partnership.

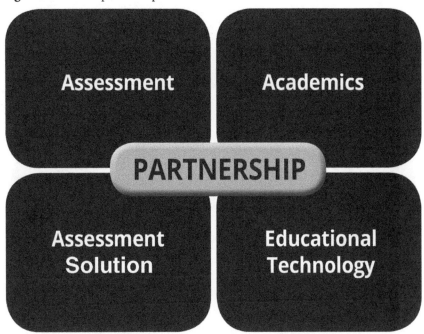

indicator for success is when the AT is supporting and facilitating the assessment processes of multiple academic units and providing actionable results for improvements in teaching and learning.

In our ATAF model, each quadrant participates in the process of technology adoption, as shown in Figure 9.2.

This five-stage process of adoption, to be described in more detail in this chapter, begins with defining a mutually understood and defined vision for a scalable, sustainable, and systemic use of an AT system to support the evaluation of student performance on institutional and program level learning outcomes so that the academic and assessment quadrants have actionable information to develop plans for improvements. This shared vision of sustainability and broad adoption is both result and foundation for the *partnership relationship*—a partnership based on collaboration, trust, respect for the other's expertise, and the interchange among the four quadrants necessary to achieve the vision of successful and sustainable AT adoption (EDUCAUSE-Jisc Working Group, 2015).

Additionally, our ATAF model acknowledges two essential considerations for the adoption of an AT:

Figure 9.2. ATAF process.

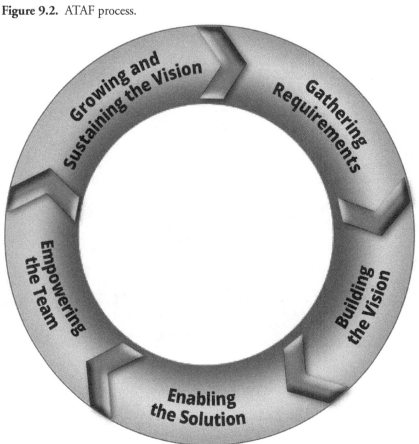

1. Achieving full implementation of the technology across the institution might take 3 to 5 years, given the size of an institution or program, the cohesion of the institution's or program's assessment processes and structure, the depth of the institution's or program's technology support staff, and the commitment of the institution's or program's administrative leadership to the overall vision of sustainable adoption.

2. Achieving the shared vision of sustainable and scalable adoption is more about working collaboratively and developing trust among the individuals in each quadrant and managing and facilitating the change that will occur in processes and sometimes practices than it is about the specific functionality of an AT.

Therefore, our ATAF combines people, roles, and practices with a process of adoption in order to execute a shared vision for effectively implementing a technology to assist with evaluating learning outcomes at the institutional and program level to improve learning and learner success. In Figure 9.3, the adoption process encircles the four key quadrants to illustrate how each stage in the adoption process involves all quadrants and their interactions as they move through the five stages.

We offer this ATAF as a guide, understanding that institutions will share some of the challenges and opportunities we will discuss, as well as have some unique challenges and opportunities of their own that need consideration. Our intent in this chapter is to present our ATAF as a model for successful adoption of an AT in a broad sense. Given tightening budgets, shrinking resources for support staff, increasing demands on faculty to "do more" across higher education, and the uncertainty of COVID-19, it is especially important for institutions that any technology selection is intentional, and implementation is cost-effective, scalable, and sustainable. We believe

Figure 9.3. ATAF partnership within the process.

our ATAF model can assist institutions with meeting these aims. Finally, as we describe our ATAF model, we will reference at each stage two case studies—Framingham State University in Massachusetts (Case 1, found in Appendix 9A) and the University of Pretoria in South Africa (Case 2, found in Appendix 9B)—and direct readers to a site that lists additional resources and examples to further support our model.

Enabling a Solution Through the ATAF

In today's digitized world of teaching and learning, most institutions use their LMS to supplement their campus courses and deliver their blended and online courses. During COVID-19, institutions were forced to move nearly all active courses into their LMS. In these conditions, the LMS becomes a container for a wealth of direct evidence of learning with course-embedded authentic activities of students' performance on institutional and program learning outcomes stored digitally in the LMS through the work students submit to their LMS courses. Even though the use of technology for teaching and learning delivery has mostly been embraced by institutions, programs, and faculty, the field of institutional and program assessment has struggled with the use of technology to facilitate its practices, as evidenced by the following far-too-common scenarios:[3]

- Assessment coordinators ask faculty to provide thumb drives, zip files, and printed copies of student work that they then print multiple copies of for reviewers to score on printed rubrics.
- Assessment coordinators ask instructors to meet for 1 or 2 designated days to sit in a room to read and score printed artifacts on paper rubrics and then meet again 3 to 6 months later to discuss the findings.
- Chairs ask instructors to fill out an Excel file to capture how each student in their courses performed on particular exam questions (a practice that inadvertently reveals the number of faculty who have never used an Excel file). The chairs then spend days collating and creating pivot tables and charts for the program's annual report on student learning.
- Program coordinators ask instructors to send them their Word file rubric results or complete a rubric form on Google Docs to capture the individual student's performance on signature assignments in courses.
- Institutional effectiveness staff spend weeks trying to merge each general education instructors' assessment data for the year's one or two assessed institutional learning outcomes.

Surely, we can "save some trees" and better use the time, resources, and efforts of instructors and assessment coordinators by leveraging an AT system to accomplish these data collection and reporting tasks. Surely there are AT systems that can help

- facilitate various methods of collecting and reviewing course-embedded, authentic student work to determine the extent to which students have met expected program and institutional learning outcomes;
- generate reports on student performance against program and institutional learning outcomes and assist with data analysis and trending of performance longitudinally by academic areas, by program, by course, and by student;
- connect institutional and program assessment processes to the day-to-day teaching of faculty and the learning and performance of students;
- prioritize decision-making options for curricular change and program quality;
- identify instructional approaches across various delivery modalities and educational models that best support learning;
- monitor improvements and steps taken to improve learner success within program or institutional contexts; and
- monitor the effectiveness of resource allocations made to programs and units to support assessment across the institution.

Resoundingly, yes we can! Many ATs exist to assist programs and institutions with the tasks. An AT can save time—the essential resource we all lack—through automating tasks, adding efficiencies (and accuracy) to reporting and analysis, and providing reports in a timely fashion so decisions regarding improvements and interventions can be made sooner.

Although institutions and programs are beginning to embrace assessment technologies, the field of assessment seems to be following a trajectory similar to that of online learning. Like online learning, assessment is also a "disruptive innovation" (Clayton et al., 2006; Meyer, 2011) in teaching and learning. In its best uses, assessment of student achievement of learning outcomes is causing faculty, administrators, and support units to rethink what they do, how they do it, and why they do what they do in teaching to promote and support learning and learner success. Even though institutional and program assessment has been around for several decades and does not appear to be leaving higher education, the role of institutional and program assessment continues to elicit healthy debate regarding its legitimacy and purpose as a field of practice, as did initial forays into online teaching.[4] The practice of assessment has added new roles (e.g., assessment coordinators and directors, data managers) as did online teaching (e.g., instructional designers, remote faculty) to institutions that some would say has led to further administrative bloat, and for many institutions, adding additional support services or repurposing existing support roles has been required. Graduate degrees can now be obtained for educational technology administration, instructional design, and online teaching and learning, and the professionalization of assessment is also starting to occur, with certificates and institutes emerging and graduate degrees in assessment, measurement, and evaluation beginning to appear.

Just as early adopters of online teaching struggled with tedious workarounds in the technology to facilitate the virtual learning environment they envisioned, so it seems adopters of assessment technologies struggle to find technologies to fit their current practices.[5] More important, early adopters of online teaching found that merely transferring what was done in the physical classroom to the online was not very successful—a rethinking of practices and strategies occurred. A similar rethinking or evolution of current practices may also occur as technology is adopted. Finally, there is the issue of broad adoption. Today, online education has been embraced by most disciplines, with technologies able to facilitate a wide variety of pedagogical and discipline-specific needs. The online modality is accepted as a viable method of teaching and learning and used by institutions to attract and expand their educational brand and access by students. Assessment and its technologies, however, still struggle with acceptance and adoption across an institution. Like online learning, assessment confronts a wide variety of methodologies and philosophies, discipline-specific needs, and faculty skepticism. Thus, broad adoption of assessment technologies has been elusive. But with broad adoption comes economies of scale for resources and investments, or the necessary return on investments to justify licensing and support resource costs for institutions.

ATAF: The Quadrants

Our ATAF has four quadrants that represent the key stakeholders in the implementation and adoption of an AT to support practices for assessing institutional and program learning outcomes. As noted in Figure 9.1, our framework is as much about people and roles as it is about process and technology.

The first three quadrants are specific to the institution and to its organizational culture and structure.[6]

Assessment Quadrant

Even though any one or combination of the three institutional quadrants could be the initial evangelist for adopting an AT at an institution, our ATAF model purposely begins with the assessment quadrant. Whether institutional effectiveness vice presidents, institutional assessment directors, general education directors or committee chairs, department chairs, or program coordinators, it is this group of assessment administrators whose needs the AT should address and support. Individuals in these roles are typically responsible for coordinating, supporting, guiding, and even facilitating and supervising assessment practices and policies for the institution or a program. They facilitate the development of curriculum maps, assessment plans and cycles, and measurements and evaluation processes; analyze report findings and action plans; and monitor progress to demonstrate improvements for student learning at the institutional level or within a program. They guide and support the assessment practices of others and ensure the institution is meeting its various reporting responsibilities and improvement actions.

The most common reasons for using an AT are to (a) move away from time-consuming paper-and-pencil or manual processes, (b) have more dynamic reporting capabilities for decision-making, and/or (c) more efficiently manage the end-to-end process for external accreditors and internal reviews. In general, the AT should be able to help with

- identifying and facilitating the methods for determining what will be assessed, from where student work will be collected, and how it will be measured;
- generating reports in a timely and efficient manner, assisting with analysis of the findings, and distributing results to instructors and others for review and discussion;
- developing and monitoring improvement plans and managing changes;
- repeating the assessment process by efficiently facilitating each step for each learning outcome in the assessment cycle; and
- curating the assessment evidence and assisting with supporting the narrative for internal and external assessment reports.

It is the assessment professionals at the institutional and program level that must make evident and explicit how the institution or program is systematically and periodically conducting a programmatic assessment of student learning performance across all teaching modalities (online, campus, hybrid/blended) on general education (transdisciplinary skills and abilities) and discipline-specific learning outcomes. It is these practices for evidence collection, analysis, and reporting that the AT should address. And, it is especially important that individuals in these assessment roles understand that they will be the primary managers or operators of the AT, aware of its functionality and able to support and facilitate its use with others on campus.[7]

Academics Quadrant
Institutional assessment directors and program assessment coordinators work very closely with the academic units to support the discipline-specific units with their assessment efforts. These academic units, or their faculty, are the second quadrant in our ATAF model. The academics quadrant consists of various roles, such as department chairs, program and quality assurance coordinators, and the faculty in the discipline charged with facilitating the discipline's assessment efforts for internal program review and participation in institutional assessment and/or for external discipline-specific accreditor review. Even though institutional and program assessment representatives typically act as guides and coaches for assessment practices and processes, the academic disciplines and their faculty are the "owners and drivers" of the assessment process, particularly at the program level. They are the designers, deliverers, and assessors of the program's curriculum and must be involved in the design of the assessment plan and methodology. They are responsible for

- identifying the learning expectations for students;
- designing the curriculum (what is required and optional) and its sequence (the order of courses), the content, and the formative and summative learning activities for students;
- determining how they will deliver the curriculum, its instructional approach (pedagogy), and the modalities (online, blended, classroom) that will be offered;
- designing the external events (internships and cocurricular events) needed to expand and supplement course-level student learning; and
- designing the measurements to determine the extent to which students achieve expected learning outcomes.

More often than not, however, the academics quadrant can be a skeptical and/or resistant stakeholder in the assessment process and the adoption of an AT system.

For successful adoption and use of an AT, it is essential that the academics quadrant is fully vested in the process of assessment of learning outcomes if any technology is to be successful. Faculty often express concerns that institutional and program assessment requirements interfere with academic freedom, are not relevant to their course level instruction and student learning, are time-consuming and additional work, and are simply another bureaucratic demand imposed by administration and outside agencies on their already overstretched lives. In 2013, the National Institute for Learning Outcomes Assessment (NILOA) surveyed provosts and deans in the United States to identify the role of learning outcomes assessment at the institutional and program level. A major finding of their report was that provosts and deans saw it as a necessity to involve faculty in the entirety of the assessment process in order "to improve teaching and learning and to enhance institutional effectiveness" (Kuh et al., 2014, p. 7). At the same time, these provosts and deans acknowledged that it "is not just or primarily an obligatory response to demands from outside the institution but a challenge within the institution" to foster, support, and sustain a culture of improvement within academic units" (Kuh et al., 2014, p. 7). Exploring the reasons behind academics' feelings of reluctance and skepticism toward assessment is outside the scope of this chapter but others, such as Scott and Danley-Scott (2015) and Wang and Hurley (2012) have. However, the continuing debate on the purpose, value, and perception of institutional and program assessment mentioned earlier suggests more research is needed in this area.

Educational Technology Quadrant

Our third quadrant brings into the conversation another critical voice: educational technology, or those involved in assisting the academic units with their technology needs for teaching and learning. Whether represented by an individual or a team, they are typically instructional designers or technologists in educational technology units but may also be educational consultants in Centers of Teaching Excellence (Kinzie et al., 2019). They have significant insight into the institution's broader use of technology for teaching and learning and particularly the comfort level and skills of the faculty that will be important for adoption. They also voice concerns for data security, data integrations with other systems, ease of use, and operational and sustainable management of the technology and are often asked to assist with technical tasks like system set up, configuration, data integration, and training and support of technologies used by faculty. Even though they may or may not be familiar with specific practices for program and institutional assessment, because they have this "broader" institutional view of the teaching and learning with technology landscape, their participation throughout the ATAF process is vitally important for successful implementation, adoption, and sustainability.

Assessment Solution Quadrant

The assessment solution quadrant is outside the institutional context but is a key component of the adoption of an AT. This quadrant represents the technology application and the activities of the consultant for the technology solution. The majority of AT solutions available to institutions and programs will be commercial products that, when purchased, will provide varying types of implementation and support services to its users for effective use of the technology. Along with commercial products, open source AT solutions may also be available. Open source technologies assume the institution or program has sufficient internal technical expertise in application management and development to further develop the base technology to meet the institution's or program's needs. For open source solutions, instead of a consultant, a user-community is typically available to provide input on the technology's implementation. Home-grown or internally developed systems are similar to open source technologies—development and support are dependent upon internal resources, time, and funding. Because the most likely scenario would be a technology vendor and consultant, we will be discussing the consultant's role in the ATAF from this perspective.

The AT's consultant has, along with the company, a significant investment in the successful use of an AT. The consultant's primary responsibilities are to help the institution and its users learn how to effectively use the technology to support their assessment needs. The consultant should make every attempt to understand the assessment practices and philosophies of the institution, its use cases, and the situation and culture of the institution. Additionally, the consultant will need to understand the relationship among the three quadrants as he or she works with them to construct a roadmap for effective and sustainable implementation within their specific context. A "one size fits all approach" may be preferred by the technology company but is not very satisfactory for the institution. The consultant is a critical piece of the implementation and adoption process, not because of expertise in the AT solution but for their understanding of assessment and thus ability to align the technology with the needs and requirements of the three institutional quadrants to assist with identifying sustainable practices and relationships among the quadrants for an AT's use. Another critical motivating factor for the consultant is developing satisfied and successful institutions which, in turn, increases the value of an AT solution in the market and the institution's ROI.

AT Adoption Framework Stages

We have identified five stages in the adoption of an AT with dependencies and relationships that influence the success of the adoption. Each stage is discussed in the following sections.

1: Gathering Requirements

From what we and others have experienced in higher education and according to the literature on technology adoption, a technology system is most effective and broadly adopted when it is relatively easy to use and when it can solve a specific problem, such as automating a particular procedure, bringing efficiencies to a process, or enabling users to accomplish something they could not do previously (Hevner et al., 2004). Too often, however, we find technologies mismatched to instructional needs and educational models, mismatched to teacher and student digital competencies, or limited to a very small number of users even when the technology is not necessarily a niche tool. The mismatch of an AT solution to user needs is often the result of an imperfect vetting process and lack of communication, collaboration, understanding, and vision among the three institutional quadrants. In a recent qualitative study on educational technology purchasing decision-making, Fiona Hollands, associate director of the Center for Benefit-Cost Studies of Education at Teachers College, addressed this mismatch of technology to user need: "I thought more institutions would start with a need or a problem and then figure out the solution, rather than starting with solutions and finding problems to solve with them" (McKenzie, 2019, para. 11). Nothing is more frustrating for everyone involved than to discover in the post-purchase stage that significant gaps in the functionality of an AT exist or additional requirements by the institution or program prevent an AT from adequately addressing the institution's or program's needs. For instance, the assessment and academic quadrants may have understood that an AT was supposed to facilitate a particular data reporting method when in fact it cannot, leaving them frustrated and the educational technology and technology consultant quadrants scrambling for a work-around that could be costly to all in resources, development, and support. The key to success in our ATAF model is to establish as early as possible the partnership relationship among the four quadrants—assessment, academics, educational technology, and technology consultant—to address any mismatching of requirements to an AT.

This partnership among the four quadrants begins with the first step in our ATAF process. This first stage is the process of gathering the requirements for an AT. In this stage, the institution or program seeking an AT identifies the needs or problems the AT should address: What assessment problems should it solve? What does the technology need to do specifically? Ideally, whichever institutional quadrant is the evangelist for an AT, this evangelizing quadrant should partner with the other two units to define the problems, needs, and specific requirements the AT should address. As the three institutional quadrants—assessment, academics, and educational technology— engage technology vendors, each quadrant will become more focused and precise regarding the requirements and more self-reflective on the current processes and practices an AT needs to support. Although the prepurchase process can be lengthy and even tense given expectations, assessment timelines, budgetary concerns, and internal vetting procedures, this selection process is crucial because it is where the partnership begins between institution and vendor, as each does its due diligence to ensure that the AT product will be able to meet the institution's or program's assessment requirements.

During these discussions, the seeds are sown for collaboration, trust, and respect, as all quadrants look for signs of success and opportunity and for challenges and risks in the postpurchase implementation work ahead. Table 9.1 lists some typical questions the institutional quadrants and the technology vendor consider as they engage in the prepurchase phase to identify key risks and opportunities for successful implementation of an AT. Harrison and Braxton (2018) and Anstey and Watson (2018) also have some additional questions for selecting academic technologies that could be useful considerations.

Too often, the prepurchase vetting process is done by a small internal group missing one or more key stakeholders or so localized to the needs of one discipline that adoption beyond that discipline would be difficult. Successful AT adoption is not a build it and they will come approach. The successful adoption of an AT hinges on how well the AT solution addresses multiple methods for collecting evidence, applying measurements, evaluating student

TABLE 9.1
Key Prepurchase Questions in Selection of an AT

Institution or Program	*Technology Solution*
• Will it solve our "problems" or meet our needs with assessment? • Where are the gaps? Can we live with these gaps? • How well does it fit our processes? • How easy is it to use? Configure? • How easy will the vendor be to work with? • Will the vendor provide us with support now and later? • Does the cost align to needs, budget, and the functionality the tool provides?	• Do the assessment and academic representatives know what they want the technology to do? Do they articulate needs and requirements clearly and realistically? • Where are the gaps? Can we be successful with those gaps? • How mature are their assessment processes? • Do they seem organized and focused? • Do they have a clear vision for implementation and scaled adoption? • Do they have sponsorship and budget?

work, and generating reports for the institution or program. For institutional adoption, an AT must be able to facilitate complex but often disjointed processes and assessment philosophies, meet the distinct requirements of external accrediting agencies, and accommodate the needs of smaller as well as larger programs. Most important, because an AT is meant to be operationalized at the institution level, it must support incremental growth and adoption over several years while still providing immediate efficiencies and results for decision-making for its early adopters. ATs are meant to scale across the institution, bringing efficiencies to multiple practices and the benefits of longitudinal insights for program performance over 5 to 8 to 10 years. The more attention paid to the prepurchase conversations of requirements, needs, and uses, the greater the likelihood of a successful implementation and broader adoption of the selected AT and thus better ROI for resources, time and effort, and expenditures for the institution or program.

In the example of our first case study, Framingham State University in Massachusetts (Appendix 9A) conducted a vetting process that included key stakeholders from the three institutional quadrants and with various technology vendors only to have a curveball thrown at them during initial decision-making when the needs of their College of Education (CoE) trumped their broader focus. Framingham State University successfully hit that curve ball by using the CoE opportunity to develop and strengthen the partnership among representatives from the four quadrants. They have built from the CoE opportunity internal processes to assist other disciplines with using the selected AT. Our second case study (Appendix 9B), however, from the University of Pretoria in South Africa, did not arrive at an AT with the luxury of an institutional vetting of needs. Instead, a specific assessment need from an external discipline-accreditor and budgetary concerns drove them to explore how technologies already available to them in their LMS could meet this need. Nonetheless, because they brought all their key quadrant stakeholders together during an early workshop with the technology consultant, they recognized how the existing LMS's AT could, with some adjustments, support the assessment practices of several academic units as well as those of the initial discipline if they could move sponsorship from the specific unit to the institutional level. In both cases, these very early conversations among all four quadrants about the requirements of an AT established working principles for everyone's success: collaboration, communication, and respect among all four quadrants.

2: Building the Vision
The second stage in our ATAF process is perhaps the most important: building the vision. This post-purchase stage initiates the collaboration, trust, and

respect between the institution's or program's assessment project team and the AT solution's consultant(s). Even though the implementation of the technology may have a defined time period (1 year or more), the initial in-person or webinar sessions among the institution's three quadrants and the AT consultant set the tone for what is to come. The key objective during these early sessions is to establish a mutually shared vision among all four quadrants for the eventual role an AT will have at the institution. This shared vision identifies what success factors and levels of adoption should be achieved by 1 year, 3 years, and 5 years of using an AT. If the institution has a strategic plan that clearly identifies institutional and program assessment as a key initiative, then aligning that initiative with the implementation roadmap and success indicators for an AT is ideal. This alignment clearly communicates to the institution's community the value of the project and administrative and academic sponsorship that will become important for supporting change management, resource needs, and considerations for any policy and procedure changes as the assessment project proceeds.

The shared vision that evolves from the four quadrants should also define what *operational sustainability* means to the institution and program(s): Will all programs be using the technology in 3 years, or only half? What is the implementation roadmap? Which programs will go first? Why? Which programs are next? How ready are these programs for using technology to facilitate their assessment processes? Will additional personnel positions be needed, or can existing positions be leveraged, or will certain positions need revised responsibilities? What new policies and/or procedures might be necessary? And what support, training, or assistance is needed for not only the technology administrators but also instructors and perhaps for students? As these questions and others get discussed, the four quadrants evaluate each other's skill-sets and develop ways to collaborate, communicate, and contribute to their mutually shared vision for success. From these discussions and activities, the makings of a "partnership" mentality should form that will enable the four quadrants to work as colleagues, each vested in the vision and its success, through the remaining adoption phases.

In the Framingham State University case study, this partnership initially existed only between the CoE's assessment team and its educational technology office. The two quadrants were committed to solving education's very urgent need to replace its existing AT (the curve ball) with a new AT selected for implementation. During a visit to campus early in the project by the AT consultant to establish the shared vision and define the roadmap for achieving it for the CoE, the institutional assessment quadrant was added to the conversation to expand the vision, the requirements, and the processes to be supported by the new AT. From these discussions among the four quadrants, a partnership emerged as each quadrant participated in defining an immediate, a short-, and a long-term vision and success indicators.

The notion of partnership and a shared vision for the University of Pretoria evolved more slowly among the three institutional quadrants because each saw the technology as a "silver bullet" for meeting their separate needs instead of a more holistic or comprehensive approach that contained their separate requirements. The assessment quadrant wanted an AT that would address and facilitate specific institutional student assessment needs outside program assessment concerns while the academic quadrant wanted an AT that would make it easier to collect evidence on student learning within their large lecture, team- and campus-based educational delivery model and external accreditor requirements. However, during early consultation the sources of evidence of student learning and alignments to learning outcomes were not consistent across courses and sections, making it nearly impossible for the LMS's AT to capture student performance data at program or institutional levels. Additionally, the educational technology unit wanted the AT to drive deeper adoption of the LMS across the programs. During the workshop, the technology consultant redirected the focus from the role of an AT and the LMS to an examination of current assessment practices. Through these collaborative discussions and a developing understanding among the four quadrants that each quadrant could achieve its objectives by working together, a shared vision and evolving partnership emerged. The shared vision involved a revision of course-building practices to include program assessment needs. This change in design process has led to more consistent, robust, and effective use of the LMS for teaching and learning and for programs to extract the required data on student performance from the LMS. A significant benefit of this early collaboration has been the University of Pretoria's internal review of its assessment processes and model of institutional and program assessment.

3: Enabling the Solution

Partnership and shared vision are the desired outcomes of ATAF's second stage, "building the vision," and can be achieved through purposeful inclusivity of voices from each of the quadrants. In the third stage of the ATAF process, enabling the solution, this shared vision and partnership is tested and will either be strengthened or could begin to crumble. In this stage, the three institutional quadrants—assessment, academic, educational technology—begin to use an AT with the guidance and support of the technology consultant, the fourth quadrant, to facilitate the assessment practices of the program and/or institution. Ideally, a happy marriage of practice and technology should occur, as an AT adds efficiencies to the assessment process by facilitating what was once done by paper and pencil, seat-time, and manual data collation to an AT for automatic collection of student evidence, facilitation of measurement and evaluation of student performance, and more timely generation of assessment reports for review and decision-making. Almost always to some degree, the honeymoon is short-lived, as newly articulated requirements come to light or manual processes do not translate as expected to an AT. In fact, it is advisable that the initial implementation of the AT should be (a) a very focused with a targeted roll-out in order to locate any key gaps in expectations and functionality of an AT, (b) identify or raise awareness of possible new procedures or policies related to assessment, (c) and experience how the AT facilitates and addresses the needs of the assessment processes and practices before it is rolled-out on a larger scale. If a solid partnership has been established, even when an AT may be less than adequate at its inception, the partnership of the quadrants remains as one or the other or all make adjustments to the implementation tasks to achieve their shared vision. However, if the partnership is not sound, it is easy for one or more of the quadrants to walk away disgruntled and frustrated when the implementation does not go as planned.

In both case studies, the partnership among the four quadrants expanded and strengthened during the initial implementation. In the situation of the University of Pretoria, it was clear early in the project that some pre-AT assessment processes needed to be developed. For example, the academics quadrant needed to identify its assessment approach for data collection and sources of evidence in its large-course environments and improve faculty use of the LMS for it to be the assessment data collection point. Working collaboratively with each of the three institutional quadrants, the AT consultant helped them understand how the individual interests of each quadrant intersected and supported their combined, shared vision. By revising some of their assessment processes and committing to consistent course design within the LMS, each quadrant could reap the efficiencies and benefits an AT could provide. This collaboration among the four quadrants is helping to expand the sponsorship of the project from a single program to across the campus use with varied programs.

At Framingham State University, the challenges were not with the assessment processes but with missing functionality in the AT, as new requirements were articulated for an AT during the implementation process. As the academics quadrant, or CoE, became acquainted with the functionality of the AT, it saw another potential application of the technology they had not voiced previously and was not articulated in the shared vision for success. Their original need was to capture course-embedded assessments of student performance on learning outcomes from within the LMS. Their new requirement was to collect student performance assessment data from external sources, such as supervising teachers, who would be outside the

LMS. Because of a strong partnership and shared vision among each of the quadrants, this new requirement did not become a sticking point. Instead, educational technology worked with institutional policies for granting access to the LMS for these supervising teachers and with an AT vendor to create a temporary solution to address CoE's new requirement. After initial implementation of this new enhancement that included a more in-depth scrutiny by the CoE of their current paper and postal processes, the new, temporary technology feature was replaced by a different, long-term technology that better addresses their revised processes. Because of the strong partnership that existed, this potential setback actually strengthened the partnership as each quadrant worked collaboratively to find the best solution for the situation.

These two case studies demonstrate the importance of developing and curating a strong partnership among the four quadrants because of the risk involved for each quadrant when the implementation does not go as planned. At the University of Pretoria, the assessment team had to ask the academics quadrant to do more and new work to revise its assessment processes to account for data collection by an AT. The assessment team also asked the educational technology team to devote additional resources to support a more developed course-building process. Both of these requests needed to happen before the benefits of an AT could be realized. At Framingham State University, all four quadrants had to review the CoE's newly articulated assessment requirement to determine how it impacted each quadrant's resources for implementation and the shared vision and indicators for success. In both cases, the AT consultant was asking the three institutional quadrants to review current processes in order to improve the benefits they could receive from an AT. Framingham State University was further asked to invest its educational technology resources to address a previously undefined need. Because there was a mutually shared vision of success and foundation of respect, trust, and collaboration among all four quadrants, the risk of an AT implementation stalling or ending was averted.

4: Empowering the Team

During the stages of building the vision and enabling the solution of the ATAF process, management responsibility for the AT is discussed in nonspecific terms in regard to long-term use and operational sustainable actions. In the fourth stage, empowering the team, the four quadrants evaluate collaboratively if the success factors defined in building a vision were met. In this stage, the AT consultant engages the three internal quadrants in a plus/delta activity. This activity asks all four quadrants to reflect on the value of what has occurred during the previous three stages of gathering requirements, building the vision, and enabling the solution. In general, the consultant asks each quadrant to identify the following:

- What worked well in process, practice, and use of the AT?
- What did not work well or could be improved in process, practice, and technology?
- What gaps or challenges still exist to meet success indicators?
- What new requirements, challenges and opportunities were discovered?
- What adjustments or refinements should be made to the shared vision, success indicators, and timeline for adoption?

This collaborative exercise in self-reflection calls attention to the achievements and progress that have been made toward achieving the vision; reiterates the value of their shared vision; and identifies in positive ways necessary refinements to practices, processes, and to the use of an AT. This fourth stage is intended to reinforce the shared vision with an emphasis on sustainability and long-term objectives taking precedence over short-term achievements.

In our case studies, the University of Pretoria is still in Stage 4, enabling the solution, as it implements its revised assessment and course development processes. Framingham State University, however, has completed this fourth stage and found it very empowering for its three institutional quadrants. The plus/delta approach enabled the CoE team to acknowledge the significance of the successful transition it had made from the institution's previous AT to the new one without any significant disruptions to its processes. Moreover, Framingham State University's CoE and educational technology office acknowledged the unsustainability of the technology work-around developed for CoE's additional requirement during the enabling the solution stage. Indeed, the work-around prompted them to review their current processes and consider improvements that eventually led them to adopt a technology they already had in-house. Due to a state-mandated work stoppage that delayed the institutional assessment team's use of the AT, the educational technology office was able to focus solely on the CoE and develop a model from this experience for expanding AT adoption across campus. Additionally, the plus/delta exercise allowed the AT consultant to identify gaps in the technology that could impact long-term sustainability.

5: Growing and Sustaining the Vision
The fifth stage in the ATAF process is growing and sustaining the vision. In this final stage, the focus is on operational management of an AT, and the AT consultant moves from primary guide to a supporting role. In this stage, the

assessment, academics, and educational technology quadrants take ownership of the AT application. In the earlier stages of the ATAF process, application ownership discussions are subordinate to the primary concerns of configuring, understanding, experiencing, and aligning the AT to institutional and program assessment practices. As mentioned earlier, the AT quadrant, which comprises the technology and the consultant, is meant to support the processes and practices of the assessment and academic quadrants. The overall aim is to have the AT embedded in the institution's and each program's teaching and learning processes to help facilitate more efficiently their assessment practices for evidence collection, measurement, evaluation, reporting, and analysis and review that lead to improvement actions.

A particularly successful arrangement for sustainable operational management of an AT is when the assessment and academics quadrants leverage their partnership with the educational technology quadrant to assist with expanding an AT's use across the campus. When an AT is seamlessly embedded in the LMS, this partnership among the assessment, academic, and educational technology quadrants is particularly valuable. Most ATs operate external to the LMS in their evidence-gathering and reporting functionality, which typically means the following tasks happen outside the LMS:

- Storing institutional and program learning outcomes
- Creating relationships between learning outcomes and course-embedded authentic learning activities
- Creating associations of students and their attributes to their degree programs and learning outcomes
- Measuring student performance on learning outcomes outside the LMS course
- Generating reports on and analysis of the performance data

When programs use the LMS for teaching and learning, this separation of assessment evidence collection and evaluation from the learning activities in the LMS can cause duplication of work for instructors and students, as students submit in two places (the LMS and AT) and instructors grade in the LMS and evaluate in the AT. Although this separation may be a preferred approach for assessment purposes, it causes more work for students and instructors and disrupts the teaching and learning process. When the collection of evidence and evaluation processes are embedded in the LMS and, if necessary, assessment and grading can continue to be separate activities in the LMS, then the process is more streamlined, transparent, and less disruptive for both students and faculty.

Neither of the two case studies, Framingham State University or the University of Pretoria, has reached campus-wide adoption for their ATs, or the aim of this fifth stage. As mentioned earlier, a full adoption of an AT is a 3- to 5-year process, and at the time of this chapter, both institutions were only 2 years into their implementations. The long-term expectation for success, however, is that each is developing an onboarding process to grow AT adoption based on its initial experiences with the process and the technology. Framingham State University's educational technology quadrant has created an intake form that identifies the requirements for assessment practice and LMS use that positions a program for effective use of the AT. This form will be used to initiate conversations with interested programs to assist them with using the AT to meet assessment needs. The educational technology unit is positioned to be a vital player in developing sustainable operational practices for their AT. At the University of Pretoria, the four quadrants continue to strengthen their partnership and in the process are identifying strategies for implementing an AT among its targeted academic units. Campus-wide adoption is still a future endeavor.

This partnership of collaboration, respect, and trust among the four quadrants is the key success factor for institutions and programs moving through the ATAF. Because of the interrelationship of assessment practice and process, teaching and learning, and technology, each quadrant brings expertise along with specific requirements that can best be achieved when the four quadrants work collaboratively to define and achieve a shared vision for institutional and program assessment processes being facilitated through a selected AT. Achieving success is a path with twists and turns as our two case studies demonstrate. At the same time, because of the strong partnership among the four quadrants, each institution is successfully working its way through the ATAF process to enable its specific AT solution to address their institutional, program, and accreditor assessment requirements so more timely and data-driven actions can be achieved for improving student learning.

Contributors' Note

Readers can visit http://bit.ly/enablingsolutions to access additional resources we have used in our work to enable a solution to assessment and technology.

Notes

1. Visit our additional resources site at http://bit.ly/enablingsolutions for a matrix of the various types of assessment technology available.

2. See the contributors' full biographies at the end of the book. This framework has developed from practices derived from Ruth Newberry's 14 years and Robin Robinson's 17 years as a director of educational technology at their respective institutions and Adrianna Botha's 5 years as an instructional designer and educational consultant at her institution. Newberry's recent 5 years working as a principal education consultant for Blackboard Inc., assisting more than 100 institutions in higher education internationally and nationally with assessment and competency-based education has only confirmed the importance of the framework described in this chapter for successful AT implementations.

3. These scenarios are drawn from attendance at the Assessment Institute at Indiana University-Purdue University conference, Higher Learning Commission Conference, and Association of Assessment of Learning in Higher Education and from conversations with prospective and current clients in which they describe their current situations.

4. Assessment has been much in the news recently regarding its value and especially its usefulness to faculty. For instance, see Gilbert (2018, 2019) and Worthen (2018) and Linda Suskie's (2018) replies to Gilbert and Worthen's 2018 posts.

5. With artifacts to be collected and reviewed, common requests are for redaction of identifying information; ability to cost-effectively capture in-class handwritten, demonstration, or performance student work; and to facilitate multiple reviews and specific methods of reviews.

6. The organizational structure of an institution can pose significant barriers to adoption. For instance, a statewide system with multiple locations or a community college with its diversity of programs can prove challenging for scalability and centralizing (if desired) processes, policies, and assessment methodologies. Additional challenges for assessment adoption are expectations for union versus nonunion and full-time versus part-time instructors and the roles and responsibilities of chairs and assessment directors and program coordinators, particularly when it comes to data governance and supervision of the assessment process. Finally, in international institutions, we find the assessment quadrant to be a formalized office of quality assurance that manages the overall process of program assessment in the institution. Each college in the institution has a quality assurance officer that oversees the programs' process of assessment. The academic units further have quality assurance positions within each program or department. This position is typically a faculty member tasked with working with colleagues on course level assessment activities to ensure that faculty have ownership of the assessment of learning within their programs.

7. An anecdotal observation is that people in these roles on campus have been less willing overall to take on the responsibilities associated with supporting, training, and managing an AT system. Too often, these tasks fall to those in the educational technology quadrant or to individuals in institutional research who are "more comfortable" with technology systems. More research is needed in this area to determine if this separation of responsibilities is a contributing factor to the growth and adoption of assessment systems on campuses.

References

Anstey, L. M., & Watson, G. (2018). A rubric for evaluating e-learning tools in higher education. *EDUCAUSE Review*. https://er.educause.edu/articles/2018/9/a-rubric-for-evaluating-e-learning-tools-in-higher-education

Clayton, C. M., Baumann, H., Ruggles, R., & Sadtler, T. M. (2006). Disruptive innovation for social change. *Harvard Business Review*, *84*(12), 94–101, 163. https://www.ncbi.nlm.nih.gov/pubmed/17183796

EDUCAUSE-Jisc Working Group. (2015, April 15). Technology in higher education: Defining the strategic leader. *EDUCAUSE Review*. https://er.educause.edu/articles/2015/4/technology-in-higher-education-defining-the-strategic-leader

Gilbert, E. (2018, January 12). An insider's take on assessment: It may be worse than you thought. *The Chronicle of Higher Education*. https://www.chronicle.com/article/An-Insider-s-Take-on/242235

Gilbert, E. (2019, April 5). Assessment is an enormous waste of time. *The Chronicle of Higher Education*. https://www.chronicle.com/article/Assessment-Is-an-Enormous/245937

Harrison, J. M., & Braxton, S. N. (2018). *Technology solutions to support assessment*. NILOA Occasional Paper #35. National Institute for Learning Outcomes Assessment. https://files.eric.ed.gov/fulltext/ED590513.pdf

Hevner, A., March, S., & Park, J. (2004). Design science in information systems research. *MIS Quarterly*, *28*(1), 75–106. https://pdfs.semanticscholar.org/b84f/b58a59aeb5151bfed8ecfd005347daeeea9e.pdf

Kinzie, J., Landy, K., Sorcinelli, M. D., & Hutchings, P. (2019). Better together: How faculty development and assessment can join forces to improve student learning. *Change: The Magazine of Higher Learning*, *51*(5), 46–54. https://doi.10.1080/00091383.2019.1652076

Kuh, G. D., Jankowski, N., Ikenberry, S. O., & Kinzie, J. (2014, January). *Knowing what students know and can do: The current state of student learning outcomes assessment in U.S. colleges and universities*. National Institute for Learning Outcomes Assessment. https://www.learningoutcomesassessment.org/wp-content/uploads/2019/02/2013SurveyReport.pdf

McKenzie, L. (2019, August 21). Examining the limited role of research in ed-tech adoptions. *Inside Higher Ed.* https://www.insidehighered.com/digital-learning/article/2019/08/21/examining-limited-role-research-ed-tech-adoptions

Meyer, K. A. (2011). Is online learning a disruptive innovation? It isn't the technology per se, but the new thinking it inspires, that can be disruptive. *Planning for Higher Education, 39*(4), 44–53.

Roger, E. M. (2003). *Diffusion of innovations* (5th ed.). Free Press.

Scott, G., & Danley-Scott, J. (2015). Two loops that need closing: Contingent faculty perceptions of outcomes assessment. *The Journal of General Education, 64*(1), 30–55. https://doi.org/10.5325/jgeneeduc.64.1.0030

Suskie, L. (2018, March 4). *What do faculty really think about assessment?* Linda Suskie. https://www.lindasuskie.com/apps/blog/categories/show/2167986-state-of-assessment

Wang, X., & Hurley, S. (2011). Assessment as a scholarly activity? Faculty perceptions of and willingness to engage in student learning assessment. *The Journal of General Education, 61*(1), 1–15. https://doi.org/10.5325/jgeneeduc.61.1.000

Worthen, M. (February 23, 2018). The misguided drive to measure "learning outcomes." *The New York Times.* https://www.nytimes.com/2018/02/23/opinion/sunday/colleges-measure-learning-outcomes.html

Appendix 9A: Case 1: Framingham Case Study

Enabling A Technology Solution

In the fall of 2017, the Education Technology Office (ETO) at Framingham State University led an initiative to deliver a university-wide assessment solution as part of a larger learning management system (LMS) review process. Choosing the platform relied on faculty-authored use cases to ensure the technology platform met the assessment needs on campus. After the dust settled and the ink was dry on the vendor contract, the plan was to pilot the solution with a single department. What transpired was a very different outcome.

Events on campus often influence technology decisions. Such was the case with the assessment platform selected to address a need for juried and direct assessment projects. At the same time that plans were moving forward to pilot the solution, the College of Education (CoE) was searching for a platform to collect Council for the Accreditation of Education Preparation (CAEP) accreditation data. The choice was to either renew an existing platform, but at a cost that would directly fall to students, or take a chance on an unknown but supported technology.

The perfect storm of circumstances (in this case, a spontaneous conversation and a newly purchased assessment platform) created the opportunity for collaboration, but it was a shared vision, mutual understanding of the goal, and trust among the project team and the technology vendor that shaped a successful rollout of the assessment solution and influenced the projects that followed.

Reflecting on the project from the ATAF lens, all quadrants in Figure 9.1 were present in Framingham State University's application of the ATAF as follows:

- Assessment quadrant: The CAEP Coordinator articulated her needs clearly, and garnered support from the university provost, the COE dean, and other administrators for regularly scheduled project meetings.
- Academics quadrant: As a faculty member herself, the CAEP coordinator was also influential in bringing faculty on board to participate in training sessions and to integrate the technology into their courses.
- Educational technology quadrant: The vendor consultants were instrumental in the success of the project, listening to user needs on both the technical aspects and implementation of the tool and providing instruction and guidance at the appropriate times when it was needed most.

- Assessment solution quadrant: Members of the ETO were welcomed at the conversation, based on past collaborations, to provide both pedagogical and technical support on an ongoing basis.

In the end, the ETO team enabled the solution not by focusing on the technology, but rather by supporting a collaborative process and creating opportunities for partnership among the teams. What we learned from the experience is that it is beneficial to begin with a conversation to understand goals, identify a mutual understanding of roles, take advantage of good consulting practices, and then leverage the technology platform to enable a solution. We developed an intake form (available at http://bit.ly/enablingsolutions) to aid this process, and it is being used to document assessment projects on campus moving forward.

Appendix 9b: Case 2: University Of Pretoria Case Study

Internal Quality Assurance Initiative Utilizing Technology

An emerging hybrid university in South Africa, the University of Pretoria (UP) has taken initial steps to develop program-level assessment across the university. The educational consultant for the faculty of Engineering, Built Environment, and Information Technology (EBIT) began an intensive research study to investigate the usability and possible implementation of an existing goals tracking and reporting tool integrated into the university's learning management system (LMS). Due to the extensive number of available programs accredited by professional bodies, the education consultant (EC) at UP decided to begin with a department in the School of Information Technology (SIT) that had already committed to a process for implementing technology as part of their improvement plan for 2018–2019. Specifically, the Department of Informatics fully embraced this journey, as it was required to present a self-evaluation report to the Accreditation Board for Engineering and Technology (ABET) in 2019.

In the absence of a university-wide approach or way to perform program assessment using the available LMS Goals tool, a 2-day workshop was conducted in collaboration with SIT, the Department for Education Innovation, and the LMS vendor's principal education consultant. The aim was to assist SIT in developing a systematic process for program-level accreditation review that incorporated the LMS Goals tool to meet the assurance of learning needs for accreditors.

The focus of the workshop shifted from the anticipated introduction of the LMS tool to a workshop on how to establish a program assessment practice that would help attendees effectively capture, report, and act on data that the LMS's technologies could provide them on student performance based on program and institutional learning outcomes. The aim shifted from using technology to simply "tick the box" to establishing a partnership that supported an annual process for accountable reporting on the assurance of learning.

Reflecting on the workshop, the research study, and the results, the ATAF quadrants were present in UP's case, but only in an emerging state with the hope of synergy to be established among the quadrants in the near future as the key stakeholders were starting to engage. To support the process of finding the synergy, the vendor consultant recommended a multiphased, multiyear approach in which the South African program review framework was fused with recommended program assessment best practices and UP's situational context. The key focus areas proposed for this process were to

- develop an assessment practice model for SIT (EBIT) and the university;
- clarify the institutional student learning outcomes to demonstrate association between institutional and program student learning;
- implement a phased approach to LMS technologies to support and sustain teaching, learning, and assessment initiatives; and
- assist the Quality Assurance and Academic Planning Office with enhancing internal program review to promote reflection and improvement.

To achieve these focus areas at UP, the EC in collaboration with key stakeholders are applying the ATAF model, represented in Figure 9.1, to strengthen program level assessment:

- Assessment quadrant: An established process and assessment professional role equipped with knowledge of LMS technologies linked to the role is not institutionalized on a macro level at UP. However, the educational consultant (EC) for EBIT is involved with the deputy vice chancellor's academic initiative (in progress) to use the LMS Goals tool to report on alignment, goals coverage, and students' performance of UP graduate attributes against program learning outcomes. The Department for Education Innovation is designing a program assessment course to expand the workshop recommendations to the wider UP academic community.
- Academics quadrant: The EC established a network and various partnerships with academic staff across UP Faculties through her work with the program faculty, her research study, and involvement in the 2018 workshop. Through continuous consultation and training opportunities, she communicated the importance of the academic and assessment processes that need to be in place before considering technology for assessment and reporting.
- Education technology quadrant: As in the case with Framingham State University, a long-standing professional and collegial partnership with the vendor's principal education consultant contributed to the success of the workshop and was influential in expanding this initiative to other universities in South Africa. It is essential to design and deliver the program assessment process with technology in mind but not as the driver of the process.
- Assessment solution quadrant: The Department for Education Innovation at UP allowed the EC to conduct her research on the LMS Goals tool. In collaboration with the instructional designer and

education consultant training teams, she proposed a fused model of South Africa's evolving assessment practices with the U.S. framework presented in the workshop with training in the LMS goals tool for the design and development of UP's future quality program review process.

In conclusion, workshop attendees and the broader UP community are informed over time about the quality program review framework that uses an assessment approach and strategies that are drawn from UP's assessment practices, the EC's research and design, and the AT consultant's broader set of best practices for program assessment communications further emphasize the usefulness of LMS efficiencies for operational sustainability of the AT to support assessment practices. Moreover, the requirements for UP are similar to other South African universities, that is, to create a cycle of review and process for analysis with a focus on improving student learning experiences.

IO

ADVANCING GENERAL EDUCATION ASSESSMENT THROUGH FACULTY AND STUDENT ENGAGEMENT WITH COLLEGE-WIDE ELECTRONIC PORTFOLIOS AND AN ASSESSMENT PORTFOLIO

Kem Barfield

Three Rivers Community College (Three Rivers), a community college serving southeastern Connecticut, did not have a long tradition of using electronic portfolios (ePortfolios) for assessing student learning outcomes. Our earliest ePortfolio efforts began in the nursing department to meet the department's accreditor requirement: evidence that our nursing students were meeting accreditation requirements. Before we had any technological means to store or present that evidence, we submitted paper assignments to the accreditor as evidence—not very many of them, and then only the best. In their most rudimentary form, the paper artifacts constituted the precursor to portfolios. At the time, no one would have called the department's collection of student work a portfolio, electronic or otherwise.

A grant-funded opportunity to build on this early work, however, launched our journey to expand this early commitment as well as build a foundation to advance general education assessment using college-wide ePortfolios and assessment technology. The history of our journey highlights the importance of (a) collaboratively exploring the capabilities and limitations of technology options within the context of institutional culture, behaviors or attitudes, and program- and institution-level needs, even if an option is successful elsewhere; (b) trying out an option to understand the technology and to get a sense of the inherent challenges in its use; (c) including students in early piloting of a promising option; (d) providing workshops for faculty and students that help them learn how to use the selected technology; (e) preparing students and faculty teaching general education courses to submit work samples that represent students' demonstration of general education outcomes; and (f) recognizing that technological issues can suddenly arise even in the best of situations.

Early ePortfolio Efforts and Growing Need

The earliest ePortfolio efforts began in our nursing department as part of a multi-institutional Fund for the Improvement of Postsecondary Education (FIPSE) grant administered by and in concert with the Connecticut Distance Learning Consortium (CTDLC), one of the first developers of an ePortfolio platform. The CTDLC's web-based platform had a number of good tools at the time. Early efforts to collect student work to meet accreditor requirements and the program's highly structured assignments and distinct learning objectives also made it easier for the program to generate artifacts for assessing student performance than other programs at the time (Pedersen & Williams, 2004). Generating artifacts is especially important, because the nursing program's accreditors require evidence that nursing students are mastering the key learning objectives listed in their nursing accreditation standards. Nursing students now build ePortfolios of their work in at least one of their courses, with continued ePortfolio development possible throughout their nursing program. ePortfolios, sometimes still called electronic portfolios, are valuable on several levels: Student artifacts are retained for program review purposes, and students in the nursing program benefit from being able to reflect on their collected work.

Several other programs, especially those that had external program accreditations, were also interested at that time in how their programs could benefit from the use of ePortfolios (Watson et al., 2016). Program coordinators whose programs required assessment and accreditation compliance were looking for better ways to manage their collection of artifacts and assessment so that, among other uses, visiting teams could view representative student work. The Technology Accreditation Commission of Accreditation Board for Engineering and Technology (TAC-ABET), for example, requires that visiting teams view student sample work in science, mathematics, and technical areas. The format of the sample work can be standard assignments or include laboratory reports, drawings, projects, and evidence of oral and written communications (ABET, 2009). The Early Childhood Education

Program's National Association for the Education of Young Children (NAEYC, 2018) also requires evidence of student teacher actions and learning. Evidence of some successful learning outcomes is difficult to show in descriptive written-only formats (e.g., teachers are expected to help children learn to regulate their emotions), thus supporting review of a range of artifacts. In addition, the standards of the accrediting organization for business programs, Accreditation Council for Business Schools and Programs (ACBSP), applied at Three Rivers also requires evidence of individual learning outcomes (ACBSP, n.d.).

In addition, there were college needs beyond the compliance requirements with program accreditation. Our general education assessment, which was mandated by our regional accrediting agency and our state board, was not progressing. The Commission on Institutions of Higher Education (CIHE, 2011), now the New England Commission of Higher Education (NECHE), required approximately one third of each of our associate degree programs to contain a common core of course work that was deemed general education. The core curriculum needed to include assignments that allowed students to display skill in the following areas: written and oral communication, scientific and quantitative reasoning, critical analysis and logical thinking, aesthetic and ethical principles, and historical and social phenomena (CIHE, 2011). The college's accreditation process involved a 5-year cycle during which a committee collected paper artifacts and assessed them at the end of the academic year.

Collection of student learning artifacts was, however, limited. Although committee members diligently worked throughout the year to solicit artifacts from fellow faculty at division meetings, few faculty were involved in the assessment process. Moreover, many faculty who were not on the accreditation committee did not have a clear understanding of the reasons for the assessment activity. Some faculty were suspicious of the process. They raised concerns about whether or not the artifacts collected could be used for evaluating their classes or their teaching performance. Consequently, these faculty wanted to provide only those artifacts that represented work by their best students.

Even after a year of attempting to get samples of student work from faculty, the committee rarely worked with more than a few artifacts. In addition, the artifacts that were put forward were generally drawn from the work of students whom the faculty considered exceptional. Because these artifacts were not representative of the average student and there was no way to assess oral communications or performances, the general assessment goal was undermined. It became clear that in order to address the general education issue we would need access to larger sample sizes and a greater range of student work.

Apart from the problem that only a few faculty were providing artifacts, we recognized that relatively few faculty had in-depth knowledge of assessment best practices. We believed, as we still do, in distributing institutional knowledge, especially in areas we considered preeminent in higher education such as assessment. We realized that any attempt to enhance our college's culture of assessment meant increasing general faculty knowledge about assessment.

ePortfolio Adoption: Early Stage Problems

Although the professors in the nursing department were committed to making ePortfolios work in their program, they faced challenges using the ePortfolio system. First, they wanted the system to expand to accommodate all nursing courses; however, the existing ePortfolio platform charged the college a per-student fee. The FIPSE grant paid for only a classroom's worth of student licenses. When the college calculated the cost of supporting our goal by recruiting and paying peer mentors, purchasing scanners, devoting lab assistant time to ePortfolio, and buying flash drives, we realized that also buying or licensing a new platform was cost prohibitive. The CTDLC web-based platform had a number of good tools at that point in time, but electronic systems require continuous development (National Center for Education Statistics, n.d.).

Second, the original platform was a fairly simple repository for folders and files owned and controlled by the student, and it had limitations. There was little ability to open and display the files in the system. The navigation was not intuitive. Consequently, students often experienced confusion and got lost in placing ePortfolio artifacts in different locations in the platform. Students also frequently made errors in the invitation process required to share the ePortfolio with faculty. Faculty had difficulty accessing previous invitations, which meant that students had to resend the invitations multiple times. Most importantly, there was a concern that artifacts would not be available after students graduated which would make using the ePortfolios for accreditation, counseling, and other student success areas challenging.

Third, there were digital space issues. Each student user of the system was allotted 25 MB of storage for a fixed cost to the institution. The storage in the homegrown system could fill up with student content from the first course alone! When electronic storage was exhausted, the student or the college was required to pay more. To accommodate each new class of nursing students, the college had to clear out the work created by previous students. If a student wanted to maintain the ePortfolio after leaving the college, the student needed to pay a fee directly to CTDLC. With only the nursing students participating, the college could not justify more funding to store old materials.

Fourth, the FIPSE grant allowed the CTDLC to design and implement an ePortfolio system, but it did not prove to be a viable enough model to warrant continued development. Additionally, the CTDLC had growing responsibility for a variety of eLearning initiatives beyond ePortfolios. With ePortfolio system management becoming a smaller portion of their core business, the CTDLC chose to refrain from future development of its ePortfolio platform. For these reasons, we concluded that CTDLC's ePortfolio platform was not the ideal platform for us to scale up the use of ePortfolio.

Seeking New Options: Initial Considerations

Once we decided to pursue a new software package, we explored a number of options. Both prepackaged software suites and customizable social media applications were considered.

Software Application and an LMS

Realizing we needed to search for a new ePortfolio option, we tried a promising assessment and curriculum management software application that colleagues at one of our sister institutions had success with. The application had an ambitious set of tools. The company that licensed the application was small but very customer responsive. Company representatives would meet with our campus team to support us when there were problems.

However, we did not have the same level of success as the other college had with the assessment application. Critically, the program required a great deal of manual entry. It was a Sisyphean task to both input program data and maintain platform uptime. Sometimes time-intensive technical fixes were needed, which set back the effort to get campus adoption. When attempting to demonstrate the program at the academic division meetings, the program crashed. (Sometimes the crashes were disastrous, which resulted in the loss of a great deal of data.)

Faculty were rightly skeptical and resistant to using the new assessment portal. In our implementation, we had hoped that faculty program coordinators would enter their own program data because they understood them best. After seeing the ongoing issues, the challenge of convincing faculty to enter their programs into the platform was greatly increased. After 5 years of paying licensing fees and attempting to sell the portal to faculty, there was only one academic program in the system, our early childhood education program. That program had been added through a Herculean effort of the institutional research director, who had championed the project. When it was done, the continued work to add student information proved daunting.

There was very little additional work done to enhance the early childhood data or use the information it then contained.

This experience left us looking for technology alternatives, but other platforms seemed equally ill-designed for the task. Our existing learning management system (LMS) was considered as both an LMS and an assessment platform. The LMS's ePortfolio component had recently been introduced to the campuses. All courses at the college had an LMS component. Online syllabi, handouts, discussions, grades, and assignments were added features even in on-campus courses. With student assignments already contained in the LMS, it was logical to examine the system's potential.

However, there were a number of challenges with the LMS. The nascent ePortfolio component of the LMS had only a few features. Also, the LMS had a problem in extracting artifacts. In our past experience with the LMS, aggregate data were never easy for reviewers or administrators. Program data would need to be stored and maintained outside the LMS's environment. Only individual instructors or someone in the instructor role who was enrolled in the courses could pull out artifacts, and that person could only do so one at a time. Without the ability to easily retrieve artifacts for review by the assessment committee, and with limited ePortfolio functionality, our consideration of the LMS was not promising.

Our technology issues with our assessment platform at the time of searching for new software had also made us leery of any platform that did not have strong around-the-clock performance. Unfortunately, our LMS had not been such a performer. Before the days of cloud-based LMSs, our implementation required constant server maintenance and cleaning to keep the performance optimal. If the server hosting the LMS was not cleared of old course data every 2 to 3 years, the overall performance for the students and faculty would slow down. Entering courses, viewing assignments, uploading and downloading materials, and so on would all slow to a crawl. Removing courses that contained artifacts was less than ideal for tracking performance over time. Just as critically, it meant that we were unable to show accreditors the artifacts after the students had graduated or after the artifacts themselves were gone. We concluded that our LMS technology was not the solution.

Social Media as ePortfolio Repositories

We also considered social media sites as alternatives to a campus-based ePortfolio platform. Several sites gave students control over their content and allowed them to present impressive displays of their work. Social media sites, such as Slideshare, Prezi, Squarespace, and even Facebook, offered possibilities for ePortfolio use. However, we soon recognized problems with this approach. Critically, although social media provided platforms for student work that would not expire when students left the college, these sites did not provide mechanisms for local administration. To be specific, social media made images and video easy for the students to upload, save, and share; however, there was no way to extract the artifacts and maintain program data. In addition, several people questioned the ethics of requiring students to use social media and the long-term reliability. Ultimately, social media options for ePortfolio were deemed unsecure. There was a distinct consensus that social media did not treat student work and data as securely as higher education is federally required to do. The lack of privacy in social media was particularly problematic. Student work placed in a social media platform was often freely available worldwide.

Another concern was the long-term viability of social media. Social media companies could rise and fall quickly. If the college built an ePortfolio assessment program within a social media platform that closed down without warning, it could be disastrous. Moreover, students themselves had complained about using social media in the classroom. The perception was that they were hackable, if not on the entire platform, then certainly at the individual level. Students described incidents in which the accounts of friends or their own accounts had been taken over by others. Social media was not the solution.

Movement to a New Platform

Our interest in ePortfolios was enhanced by our participation in the regional accreditor's annual meeting in 2012. At the meeting, the New England Association of Schools and Colleges (NEASC) provided workshops and activities important to the colleges throughout the region. At two presentations, colleges demonstrated how they used student ePortfolios as a means of assessing not only the individual student work but also the college as a whole. Among the vendors in attendance was the ePortfolio company Digication. In conversation with them, we described our goals and challenges and inquired how their platform might help.

Upon returning to campus, we met with the academic dean, the dean of information technology, and the president to talk about our approach to ePortfolio to get a sense of how amenable senior administrators were to making changes. It was a challenging case to make because we already had an ePortfolio platform through our affiliation with the CTDLC. The platform was important in the nursing program, but not yet to other programs, and we already had an assessment program that we were having a great deal of trouble getting off the ground.

However, the issues with the other systems were precisely the reasons to change to something new. There were several reasons that a new ePortfolio technology would benefit the colleges. If a new platform could solve the problems, its benefits would apply to the college in multiple areas. Based on our experiences and explorations, we realized that, if we were to introduce the benefits of ePortfolio college-wide, we needed an ePortfolio technology with an unrestricted number of licenses

Benefits of College-Wide ePortfolio Adoption

We made our case based on our intended use of the ePortfolio and the following evidence. The ePortfolio could make student learning vivid and evident, bringing into view and placing on display for others the students' quality of learning. We wanted to be able to assess the learning that is sometimes hidden and that we speculated occurred for all students. The ePortfolio as a tool to provide quality of learning information could offer the faculty more insight into student learning than standard quizzes and exams. Students who create well-designed ePortfolios actually learn better (Pedersen & Williams, 2004). ePortfolios cause students to consciously consider the quality of their own work as well as their own development (Pedersen & Williams, 2004). Typically, students share their ePortfolios only with the professor but could easily share with others in their course group or the whole class, creating a connection with other students. If only one department were to use it, we would be doing a disservice to the rest of our students and the faculty. We also emphasized to the deans and the president—to the extent possible for a community college—the importance of student involvement. The benefits of ePortfolios had been established at several institutions that we held as models. Rather than relying on the faculty selection of artifacts, students themselves provided their own artifacts, a much better representation of artifacts. Moreover, this would extend the learning culture to students. Students had to be partners in the use of ePortfolios or it would fail.

Further, we argued college-wide adoption of ePortfolios would yield data essential for our institutional assessment goals. In the past, efforts to collect aggregate information about our students' learning and development from their classwork yielded information that was not generalizable. The sample sizes were too small. Likewise, the information that was collected involved few individuals. A majority of the faculty and their students did not participate in the assessment process and, therefore, the knowledge about ourselves was concentrated in those few individuals. The individuals who collected the artifacts also analyzed and reported on their findings, and because so few were directly involved, the findings failed to have relevance for most and completely failed to have meaning for some. In reality, the institution was meeting the goal to assess but not the goal to help maintain and strengthen the learning community.

The Pilot

Because the college's management was not opposed to a new platform but not enthusiastic about it either, we ran a pilot semester with Digication. Before adopting any new platform, it is crucial to understand the technology and to get a sense of the inherent challenges in its use. Some departments were interested in how ePortfolio technology could benefit their programs, but the majority of them were not looking for this solution. Discovering that students were confused by the technology, that it was too time-consuming to use the ePortfolio, or that we had trouble extracting artifacts would have quickly ended a large-scale ePortfolio project. An initial poor experience with a wider audience could brand the effort and ePortfolios in general meaningless. The pilot allowed us to get our answers on a small scale.

In fall 2013, the Digication pilot was conducted with a few classes in first year experience and nursing programs. We created a handout to describe to students how to build ePortfolios. The team coordinating the pilot was able to train all instructors and all classes in the selected programs as well as the chair of the General Education Committee. The pilot effort required only nursing professor Lillian Rafeldt and me, Kem Barfield, to conduct the training. Because we both had been involved in ePortfolios for several years at that point, we did not require additional training. Scaling up, however, did require more training, which meant we needed to expand our training team to include Jodi Calvert, director of learning initiatives, and Amanda Caffary, coordinator for the Innovative Design in Educational Advancement (IDEA) Center. We brought in a trainer from Digication to show us how to use the platform. The four of us attended the training, and we invited Steven Neufeld, chair of the General Education Committee; Terence Delaney, chair of the Curriculum Committee; and Stephen Goetchius, dean of information technology. Later in the project, Michael Stutz, who became the chair of the General Education Committee, was trained. The four-member team handled the training of faculty and students, but the synergy of having other key members involved made the transition more possible.

The results were overwhelmingly positive. Students did not seem to wrestle with the new ePortfolio as they had in the previous system. We were able to pull assessment data from their submissions. It clearly showed that we could use ePortfolios to both support students' understanding of their own learning and get assessment data from their ePortfolios. The pilot was successful with many of the pilot instructors describing to the team how they thought they could use ePortfolios in future classes.

The Importance of Partnerships

Three Rivers had beneficial and supportive partners. We were members of the Connect to Learn project led by LaGuardia Community College, which allowed us to share ideas and get feedback from several other higher education institutions. As a group of universities and community colleges, we discussed in advance the merits and pitfalls of decisions such as scaling up our ePortfolios efforts so rapidly. Through Connect to Learn, we developed great relationships with key leaders in the field. Both Georgetown University's Randy Bass and Guttman Community College's Laura Gambino assisted us and inspired our work. Through their own work, writing, research, presentations, and advice, we hoped to use their experience to design a sustainable ePortfolio program.

If the ePortfolio project was going to remain alive, it had to meet an essential set of conditions. It was critical to monitor the interest of key stakeholders. The dean and the president were kept informed of our progress. The academic dean was onboard, but that was not guaranteed in perpetuity. In addition, there was a concern that faculty would perceive this project as a faculty mandate. At a minimum, we had to make sure that we had sufficient faculty adoption to make the general education student submission successful. We had to listen to faculty feedback. With the ePortfolio project intended to last years, one last potential pitfall was managing personnel in order to minimize team member loss to other projects.

General Vision

In adopting the new ePortfolio program, we had several goals. We wanted to improve the academic assessment process overall, not just general education. We hoped to support our accreditation requirements, not only regional but also professional. We wanted to expand the use of ePortfolios to all courses, not just those with professional accreditation requirements (which meant replacing less effective platforms). Finally, we wanted to continue our affiliation and collaboration with our Connect to Learning partners.

Practice Informed by Pedagogical Theory

In our planning, we discussed whether we should promote positivist or constructivist ePortfolios. Positivist ePortfolios would primarily be about assessment (Barret & Wilkerson, 2004). Constructivist ePortfolios would feature ePortfolios in which the students would construct their own meaning and decide their own content (Barret & Wilkerson, 2004). Our efforts throughout the pilot had been focused on constructivist aspects of ePortfolios. The concerted effort was to make students in the ePortfolio pilot aware of the benefits to their academic development by maintaining an ePortfolio. Rafeldt's work within the nursing department had been both constructivist and positivist but slightly more positivist. Student learning was emphasized, but their ePortfolio submissions were based on specific criteria. In our discussions with our colleagues, most were familiar with ePortfolios in which students collected artifacts representing the work the students felt was their best—in other words, constructivist ePortfolios. However, most also thought the positivist ePortfolio had the most value to the institution.

Challenges of College-Wide Adoption and Implementation

In the spring 2014 semester, the college adopted the new ePortfolio system. Originally, the plan was to have it in place at the beginning of the summer, but there were administrative delays that kept this from beginning until just before the fall semester. One problem was that we needed a way to fund the licensing of the new ePortfolio system. I advocated to end the use of both the previous limited ePortfolio system and the previous assessment portal. With the success of the pilot, we were able to make this change. Another problem was that the electronic login process was not developed in a timely fashion. We did not want students to have new and different usernames and passwords but rather to use their existing versions. This meant getting some external sources to help with the configuration.

Training now had to include many more classrooms and all faculty. Our small team needed to connect with 76 full-time faculty, 239 part-time faculty, and nearly 4,000 students. We hoped to enlist the support of some others after we trained them. Our core team began to meet on a weekly basis to ensure the training was going smoothly. We began to meet with various committees and governance units on campus to describe the work.

Measuring Success

We believed the success of the training component could be measured by several metrics, such as the following:

- Student participation numbers (indicating faculty support and valuation of the ePortfolio effort)
- Increased faculty workshop attendance numbers compared to previous workshops (indicating greater faculty participation and success in the effort)
- Faculty qualitative feedback

Training Students

Training had been made available to students via a few open workshop sessions. The capacity of the open workshops was insufficient to accommodate the increased number of our students who were now required to use ePortfolios. Members of the ePortfolio team scheduled short in-class demonstration sessions for the ePortfolio platform. We also trained several tutors from our tutoring center. This would allow students who did not receive the in-class training (or those who needed some additional assistance) to receive one-on-one support in the use of ePortfolios.

Training Faculty

Enticing faculty to come to professional development on campus has always been a challenge. The college was obligated to provide professional development opportunities, but few faculty attended other voluntary training sessions. The college always had many professional development activities, committees, meetings, and workshops vying for the time of faculty and staff members simultaneously. Our desire was that faculty would understand ePortfolio training's unique value, prioritize it above other activities, and fit it into their schedules. We believed that we had developed a successful plan, which involved communicating the potential impact of ePortfolios to many areas of the college.

The measure of success for our college-wide ePortfolio professional development activity was complicated because there was no direct comparison possible with past years. However, we did have a database for the past several years of technology workshops that have been offered on campus. We planned to use those participation numbers as a baseline to show that we were increasing the number of technology workshops significantly. If we were successful, the numbers should increase above standard training sessions. With the timelines of the training part of the project, significant results were expected in fall 2014 and spring 2015.

Faculty were given 1-hour training sessions throughout each semester, which were facilitated in a computer lab. The sessions were scheduled to fit within the common hour between classroom periods. This was important because faculty were more likely to participate if there was not a large time commitment. Each workshop had a maximum of 10 participants, to allow the facilitators to help everyone. Multiple facilitators (mainly ePortfolio team members) were present at each workshop, if possible. The facilitators were well-versed in the ePortfolio and general education processes. As much as possible, the workshops were conducted as a conversation that the faculty should lead with their comments and questions.

Initially, we called our workshops with faculty *training*, which we learned was loaded terminology for our faculty. The term had connotations of unidirectional speech, corporate intrusion into classrooms, and inequality among participants. From the beginning, our intent was to provide space for cross-communication. Although that was not the team's position and had not been in the planning, we decided to change the term after just a few "training" sessions. We called all future sessions with faculty *ePortfolio faculty consultations*.

One key aspect we discovered, partly through this conversational approach, was that we needed to clearly articulate the differences between *grading* and *assessment*. Grading had many purposes, including feedback to students regarding their educational improvement and measurement of student performance against course or program goals (Pedersen & Williams, 2004). However, high grades in a course did not necessarily correspond to high assessment scores. We communicated very clearly to the faculty that it was acceptable to the administration and the committee if assessment scores and grades appeared to disagree.

To give ePortfolios the most visibility possible, several nonworkshop activities were created. We showcased ePortfolio works in multiple venues, including in the nursing lab, an ePortfolio fair, and the classrooms. With student permission, we showed ePortfolio examples to the faculty at nursing curriculum meetings, the educational technology committee meetings, the Center for Teaching meetings, and later student workshops and faculty consultations. The continuous messaging helped to keep everyone aware of the change and the progress being made.

Onboarding the Students

Students were required to create at least one ePortfolio. The students were asked to choose the college template, which provided areas in which they could add artifacts including programs, courses, experiential learning, a self-description, and a general education section. The students could place any artifacts they wanted in the ePortfolio, but faculty would guide them in the artifacts for the general education section.

The General Education Committee was interested in assessment, particularly institutional assessment. We were seeking to learn how well students showed evidence of achieving the accreditation requirements. A pattern of lower assessment scores on the artifacts should translate to action plans for the institution or prompt overarching programmatic changes, not disrupt the work of an individual instructor. The ePortfolio had given us the ability to collect assessment artifacts from virtually every student throughout the institution. Therefore, the General Education Committee voted to require all students to maintain an ePortfolio using the college template for purposes of assessing that they were meeting the general education core requirements. This supported the accreditation agency's (NEASC's) requirements. The committee's recommendation was made to the academic dean and was solidified as policy for the institution. Faculty were asked to inform students at the beginning of their classes about the requirement. They were given the option of placing one of three statements in their syllabi. Their choice then could be based on their own plan for integrating ePortfolios into their coursework. Faculty could also opt to modify the statement. The three statements are presented in Figure 10.1.

The ePortfolio system was implemented in a way that required minimal faculty involvement. In our constructivist approach the faculty designated an assignment for the students to upload. Our faculty told the students which assignments to post to their ePortfolio and which to submit as evidence of achieving the general education core. It was never our goal to burden the faculty with tasks that lacked a connection to their classroom activities. We designed a process in which they could, if they chose, have zero involvement. They did not need to upload artifacts; their students did that. They did not need to create new assignments; they were to use assignments that they already had. They did not need to supervise the students' submissions; our committee, with the help of Digication, would do that. They did not have to determine their outcome rubrics; the committee had done that. The only requirement was to tell the committee the unique name of their assignments and tell their students to remove their names and upload the artifacts. At faculty meetings, we would often say that it required zero involvement if that is what they choose. Although it did require assignment alignment by faculty, many did take a mostly hands-off approach.

After some initial assessments, the team realized that the students' ePortfolios did not always provide a complete picture to the assessment committee. For example, an image submitted for critical analysis and logical thinking in a graphic design class, illustrated in Figure 10.2, does not necessarily show the assessing chemistry professor the steps involved or the thinking that went into developing that image.

In many cases, the assessment committee needed to understand the assignment itself in order to fairly assess the student submissions. After the first semester ePortfolios were launched, we asked full-time faculty to complete an assignment alignment sheet. They were to look at the general education rubrics and to tell us how one of their existing assignments aligned with the rubric. To help us connect the assignment to the submissions, we asked the instructors to give the assignment a unique and specific name (e.g., "Military's Role in the Spanish Flu" rather than "Essay 2"). At the time, we

Figure 10.1. Three syllabus statements.

Option 1: Basic
"All students are required to maintain an online learning ePortfolio in Digication that uses the college template."

Option 2: Traditional
"All students are required to maintain an online learning ePortfolio in Digication that uses the college template. Through this electronic tool, students will have the opportunity to monitor their own growth in college-wide learning. The student will keep their learning ePortfolio and may continue to use the Digication account after graduation. A Three Rivers General Education Assessment Team will select and review random works to improve the college experience for all. Student work reviewed for assessment purposes will not include names, and all student work will remain private and anonymous for college improvement purposes. Students will have the ability to integrate learning from the classroom, college, and life in general, which will provide additional learning opportunities. If desired, students will have the option to create multiple ePortfolios."

Option 3: Student Centered
"As a student, you will maintain an online learning ePortfolio using a college-designed template in Digication. Through this electronic tool you will have the opportunity to monitor your own growth in college-wide learning. It may even help you determine a major that is best suited to you. You will be able to keep and maintain your learning ePortfolio after graduation. A Three Rivers General Education Assessment Team will select and review random works to improve the college experience for all. If your work is selected and reviewed for assessment purposes, it will remain anonymous and private. Digication provides a 'place' where you will connect your learning from the classroom, college, and life in general. Sometimes when you review all of the work you have done and think about it, you end up learning something different and perhaps unexpected. Please review your course outlines to determine what assignments to upload into the TRCC Digication template and please post your own choices, as well. Have fun in learning!"

---

had a surplus of blue paper, and we printed the assignment alignment forms on that blue paper. The form came to be called the "blue form." The paper was submitted to multiple team members at various times during each semester.

Figure 10.2. Coffee ad for graphic design class.

When it became difficult to track the paper forms, we moved the process to the college's website. The assignment alignment form's background was made blue, and it was still called "the blue form." Since then, the electronic form has been changed several times to allow direct upload of the form and is no longer blue, but it is still known as the "blue form" (see Figure 10.3).

If one of our goals was to increase faculty and institutional knowledge, it may seem curious that we would design a process by which they could refrain from being involved. The team was pleased that most participating faculty wanted more information about how it worked. Many faculty wanted to be more involved, asking how they could help us. Whether the reason was suspicion about the project's motives or genuine enthusiasm for the new tool to help students learn, it worked to the advantage of the training.

Technology Recommendations
ePortfolios that can also assist with assessment should capture general student, faculty, course, and registration information with the submissions. This allows the connection of artifacts to students, faculty, and courses. Our vendor, Digication, allowed all of these elements to be uploaded into their platform using comma separated values (CSV) files. This is the way we initially uploaded content. We used Banner, our student information system, to

Figure 10.3. The blue form.

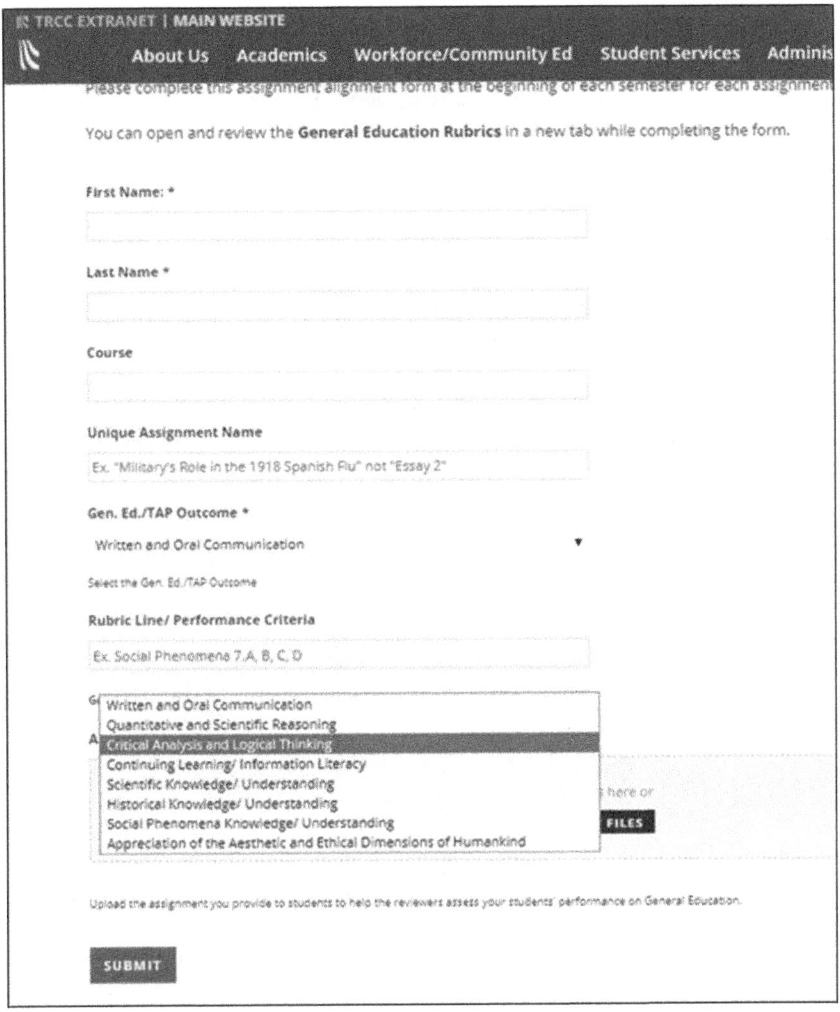

extract and gather data. The extracted data then had to be cleaned, stripped of nonessential information, placed in the correct format, and finally loaded into Digication.

A colleague at a sister institution developed a webpage that could take an upload consisting of a few standard extracts and complete the entirety of the manual work on our behalf. We persuaded him to make a modification that would do this for our college, which worked very well. The page was dubbed "Banner2Digication Live," illustrated in Figure 10.4. Ultimately, the

Figure 10.4. Banner2Digication Live.

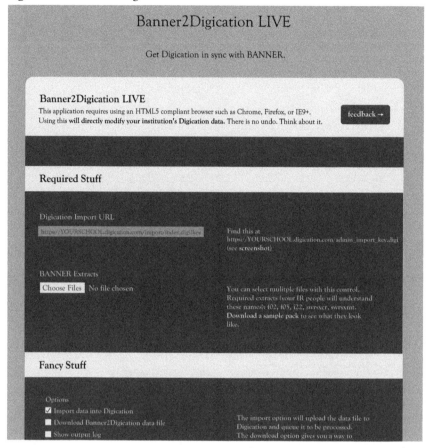

webpage was adapted and used to create a new webpage for all the colleges in our system.

Web browsers are not static, however. Frequently, they are updated. Sometimes, when they update, web pages that were designed for specific purposes are affected and thus need their own updating. At one point, coding across the four major browsers changed, and for several weeks we could only manually upload to the ePortfolio platform. Although our ability to upload with Banner2Digication was eventually restored, we realized that we were very dependent on it. During this time, we developed a backup method using a Microsoft Access database. The backup method would allow us to continue to work with ePortfolios the next time browsers changed.

In our pilot, securing students access was manageable but not easy. Members of the ePortfolio team had created and distributed usernames and passwords distributed by the instructors to the students, and we input those into the Digication platform. Because students are the only people who know their own passwords in our other applications, we could not make the passwords in Digication match what the students were already using. Pilot students had to have special electronic ePortfolio portal passwords. Sometimes we brought the information with us to class workshops. Members of the team also became the information technology (IT) support for the students when they lost or had trouble with passwords. Our approach at that time worked, because the student numbers were small, but the manual process would not work for very long once we scaled up. The team was too small, and not necessarily IT staff.

Within a short period, we had a solution. We worked with our central IT office to allow students to login with their existing student usernames and passwords. A few sister colleges in our state system had been using the Digication platform longer, but each had retained a manual username and password process to grant users access. We were pleased when we found that the ePortfolio platform already had a built-in connection, an application programming interface (API). It made login easier for faculty and students. To do so we connected our active directory (AD) login system to Digication's API using lightweight directory access protocol (LDAP).

The LDAP required us to create a webpage interface to allow students to login to Digication, which we did. The central IT office further developed another central webpage from which students at several colleges in our system could also login, so students did not need to remember an additional credential to access their ePortfolios. The only drawback was that the login process added a special login webpage rather than sending students directly to a site that could be found in search engines, a "Googleable" Digication web page. Students had to know the address of the page rather than being able to find the page when they needed it.

A couple of years later, an IT development in single sign on (SSO) solved that problem. With SSO we were able to send students once again to the searchable Digication web page but still have them login with their regular username and password. Our goal was to continue to improve the way that students accessed the portal. We wanted even easier login. Ideally, students would be able to login to our myCommNet student portal and, without logging in again, click to get into Digication.

Effects of College-Wide ePortfolio Adoption and Implementation
Our work in general education continued to improve as everyone grew more comfortable with the technologies. The assessment team had started as a small group of faculty that met each summer to assess a small group of

artifacts. The adoption of ePortfolios allowed us to use an assessment portal that contained our standards and rubrics. This allowed the committee members to work from different locations even outside the college. When the artifacts had been assessed, the portal could, in a matter of seconds, produce a spreadsheet containing tallies of all the scores. The ePortfolio had given us thousands of artifacts in the first year. The larger number allowed us to use random samples rather than convenience samples. The larger number also gave us the opportunity to increase institutional knowledge.

At a conference, two of our instructors, Stutz and Delaney, adapted an idea from a conference they attended: Assessment Days. We now have Assessment Days as an end-of-the-year event for faculty in May. All faculty are encouraged to attend the 2-day activity. We usually feature an expert external speaker or a respected internal faculty speaker who is there to inspire everyone and to talk about ways assessment can help the institutional mission. We cover the process of norming and we even norm an artifact as a group. Then the faculty are divided into group tables, which are assigned a certain number of artifacts to score. Because everything is web-based, scoring is done in the assessment portal using Chromebooks. We chose Chromebooks because they have long battery life and can open most types of submitted files. Although our analysis will continue into the fall semester, upon concluding the Assessment Day activities, we are able to generate aggregate data right away from the assessment portal.

Conclusion

In the end, many of the issues we hoped could be resolved through ePortfolios and our efforts yielded results. We effectively traded in platforms that were not being used campus-wide for one with which most are more familiar. Our faculty training has been overwhelmingly successful. We managed to have at least one consultative workshop with all the full-time faculty, even those who are not the strongest proponents of technology. We were able to satisfy the faculty that our intentions were student-centered and lasting. We were better able to assess oral communications with video artifacts. We wove ePortfolios into standard usage for the college. We better distributed assessment knowledge throughout the college. We simplified the use of the technology over time, making it easier for students and faculty to use.

There are still several aspects of both the technology and our processes that we would like to improve. Although we have continued to adapt technology or even create our own technology solutions, we must work with our vendor to move samples to an assessment portal, a procedure which is slower than we would like and that seems relatively inflexible. We would like it if the assessment sampling process were more within our control. The General Education Committee would like the results of the Assessment Days to be more readily used to inform changes in programming.

Although we have used reported assessment results to inform potential changes to the general education rubrics at the system level, we have not been as aggressive at creating internal change. Some of the artifacts we encounter are bereft of much of the detail our rubrics evaluate. This means that our committee does a great deal of prescreening of artifacts before our Assessment Days. We will be working with our academic departments to produce artifacts that address the rubrics. As more members of the college come to see the value of ePortfolios, it may be that multiple assignments can be submitted so it is to our advantage if more students submit whole ePortfolios rather than small segments of them. Although all faculty are welcome, few adjunct instructors attend our Assessment Days, and we would like to increase their numbers. As we have embarked on ePortfolios, we have single-mindedly focused on viewing a cross-section of the students at a point in time. Our paper artifact collection only allowed this type of assessment, but our electronic collection can support us in doing something more exciting for a community college, longitudinal assessment. We hope to have a sufficient amount of artifacts that will allow us to assess students over time, using multiple classes over their years at the college. We will just have to keep using the technology and continue to pursue our goals.

References

ABET. (2009). *Accreditation policy and procedure manual.* ABET, Inc. https://www.abet.org/wp-content/uploads/2015/04/appm-2010-2011.pdf

Accreditation Council for Business Schools and Programs. (n.d.). *ACBSP accreditation overview.* https://www.acbsp.org/page/accreditation-overview

Barret, H. C., & Wilkerson, J. (2004). *Conflicting paradigms in electronic ePortfolio approaches: Choosing an electronic portfolio strategy that matches your conceptual framework.* https://electronicportfolios.com/systems/paradigms.html

Commission on Institutions of Higher Education. (2011). *Standards for accreditation* [Educational standards]. New England Association of Schools and Colleges.

National Association for the Education of Young Children. (2018). *NAEYC early learning program accreditation standards 7 assessment items.* NAEYC. https://www.naeyc.org/accreditation/early-learning/standards

National Center for Education Statistics. (n.d.). *Part 6: Maintaining and supporting your technology.* https://nces.ed.gov/pubs2005/tech_suite/part_6.asp

Pedersen, S., & Williams, D. (2004). A comparison of assessment practices and their effects on learning and motivation in a student-centered learning environment. *Journal of Educational Multimedia and Hypermedia, 13*(3), 283–306. https://search.proquest.com/docview/205853785?accountid=36783

Watson, C. E., Kuh, G. D., Rhodes, T., Light, T. P., & Chen, H. L. (2016). ePortfolios—the eleventh high impact practice. *International Journal of ePortfolio, 6*(2), 65–69. http://www.theijep.com/past_6_2.cfm

11

ASSESSMENT AND TECHNOLOGY USE AT A GRADUATE HEALTH UNIVERSITY

Melanie Davis, Jordan Farris, Jill Matejcik, Forrest Bollow,
Lise McCoy, Aaron Hunt, and Ammar Musawi

Established in 1892 by Andrew Taylor Still, A.T. Still University (ATSU) is the founding institution of osteopathic healthcare. Osteopathic healthcare is a unique form of American medical care developed in 1874 by Dr. Still, in which osteopathic physicians take a "whole person" approach to caring for patients. Instead of treating specific symptoms or illnesses, they regard the body as an integrated whole consisting of mind, body, and spirit.

ATSU has an average annual enrollment of over 3,700 students from 35 countries. Students who attend ATSU are graduate students seeking a professional degree in a health sciences field who are committed to serving underserved communities and treating patients as a whole person rather than as a body with a series of symptoms. Simply put, ATSU students choose to come here because they are passionate about the university's mission. ATSU has more than 977 employees dedicated to its not-for-profit mission. ATSU has two campuses, one in Mesa, Arizona, and one in Kirksville, Missouri. ATSU also has an online school and offers multiple online programs. Locations also include a facility in Santa Maria, California; a clinic in St. Louis, Missouri; and affiliations with community health centers across the nation. This means that although ATSU is one university, the demographics and culture within our campuses and student body have the potential to be vastly different at times.

Balancing the changes in medicine throughout the past century while also challenging itself to maintain distinction in serving the underserved, ATSU has generated a rich history of leadership, both in healthcare and cor-related research. ATSU remains dedicated to the founding tenets of osteo-pathic medicine while intentionally integrating innovative technology and changes in science into the curriculum. Making evidence-based decisions is for not only the practitioner but also the educator and administrator. Through a culture of assessment, ATSU strives to develop students who will be the very vision of whole-person healthcare. Inspired to influence whole person healthcare, ATSU graduates contribute to the future of integrated care while also leading with a selfless passion in the communities they serve.

ATSU, a private, not-for-profit university, has to be judicious in its distribution of funds; therefore, programs and faculty often seek external grants and funding to implement innovative changes. Innovative educational changes often include technology and assessment, requiring universities to seek external funding sources. These external funds often support the impor-tant time it takes programs to collect evidence about the effective uses of technology accompanied with plans to integrate specific technologies success-fully. With external funding to support those processes, three of our schools have gone from traditional curricula to innovative and technology-driven curricula, relying on real-time assessment results to identify and address pat-terns of student underperformance before it is too late to do anything about them. Real-time assessment gives students the opportunity to learn from and correct their mistakes immediately, allowing them to truly master content. Focusing on three of our schools, in this chapter we will describe what real-time assessment looks like at a graduate health sciences university; how the intentional integration of technologies benefits students as they are learning and demonstrating their professional skills and attributes; and what correlat-ing benefits are noted by faculty and institutional leaders. The first school is the Missouri School of Dentistry and Oral Health (ATSU-MOSDOH). The type of technology faculty have incorporated is the KaVo Mannekin Simulator. The second school is the Arizona School of Dentistry and Oral Health (ATSU-ASDOH), which uses SimMan technology and provides a more in-depth look into real-time assessment. The third and final school we will discuss is the School of Osteopathic Medicine in Arizona (ATSU-SOMA), which uses digital case scenarios in medical education.

ATSU-MOSDOH

ATSU-MOSDOH is located in Kirksville, Missouri, and is dedicated to increasing access to oral healthcare for the most vulnerable populations by addressing the critical shortage of dentists in Missouri and throughout the United States. Offering a doctor of dental medicine, ATSU-MOSDOH features an innovative curriculum, simulation technology, state-of-the-art facilities, service-learning experiences, and leadership training. Only the second dental school in Missouri, ATSU-MOSDOH's goal is to graduate dentists who have a desire to become caring, community-minded healthcare providers, serving populations in need while also maintaining an educated and interactive presence within their professional community.

Students spend their first and second year in the classroom, studying the basic sciences and principles of patient care, along with complete dental simulation exercises at the Kirksville campus simulation clinic, known as the Sim clinic. The first 6 months are focused on biomedical didactic courses. The curriculum then moves to a more modular format, in which students spend 2 weeks completing a course. For almost all of these courses, students gain skills and knowledge through working in the Sim clinic. In courses with skills that cannot be taught solely in the clinical setting, like extraction of a tooth or history of oral pathology, students pair their simulated experiences with didactic coursework. During the third and fourth years, students transition to the clinical environment by providing patient care at a clinic in St. Louis (St. Louis Dental Center) under the supervision of ATSU-MOSDOH clinical faculty and staff. Students have the opportunity to return to the Kirksville campus to work in the Sim clinic; however, due to geographical distance between the clinical and preclinical campuses, they seldom do. To solve that problem, students are provided with portable mannequins they can install on dental chairs, enabling them to practice on the clinic floor.

Simulation Clinic

The 7,000+ square foot simulation clinic (Sim clinic) in Kirksville has 48 student workstations, each equipped with a KaVo Mannekin Simulator, which is a simulator consisting of the head and torso of a dummy that can be adjusted into different levels and positions. This adjustability enables all students to attach upper and lower arches (jaws) that have plastic teeth, allowing students to perform procedures. Additionally, each student has a unit that includes all the instruments and equipment a dentist would use in a practice, as well as a flat-screen display monitor (e.g., LED dental light and standard dental instruments). An instructor's station at the front of the clinic provides space for faculty members to demonstrate techniques that can be broadcast directly to each individual student station via these display monitors. The faculty screens also broadcast to the entire room so students can see and interact wherever they are working or walking. When one student's question is being answered, every student receives the response. In addition to student and faculty workstations, the simulation clinic houses four dental operatories (where dentists typically perform tasks away from patients) with digital x-ray units, a sterilization center, a dispensary containing everything a student might need to complete a procedure from A to Z, and a wet lab consisting of eight sinks and stainless steel work spaces.

Before students begin a project in the Sim clinic, a lecture helps them better understand the requirements for a particular skill or procedure by providing the students with solid scientific background on the procedure they will be performing. The students then practice in the Sim clinic and apply the knowledge learned in lecture. Each course has a number of projects students will complete.

The first few projects are not graded in the traditional sense but merely monitored and evaluated. Students are given as much time as needed and may ask questions of faculty while completing projects. Students evaluate themselves using a rubric to assess how well they believe they did on a particular project. This self-reflection (formative assessment) is a valuable learning tool for students. Once a student has completed an assessment, that student asks faculty for feedback. The faculty point out areas needing improvement, after which a student then has the chance to complete the suggested improvements. Finally, the faculty complete the summative assessment and assign a grade. Faculty measure students with a pass or fail based on whether or not the student was able to apply the evaluated knowledge. ATSU-MOSDOH decided to use a pass/fail grading system earlier in the course to help students focus on the learning rather than on the grade. At the completion of each course, ATSU-MOSDOH also incorporates Sim clinic progress exams during which the students do not receive faculty instruction or assistance. These exams provide data for student competence in a given procedure, curricular evaluation, and faculty reflection.

Toward the end of students' first 2 years, approximately 4 months before they go to St. Louis and actually start treating patients, the time they are given to complete projects becomes limited to 3 hours. This change correlates to the amount of time students will have to complete a progress exam, the time they will have for a morning or afternoon session at the St. Louis Dental Center, and best practice for patient care in the field.

The final assessment in the Sim clinic is the Objective Structured Clinical Exam/Objective Structured Practical Exam (OSCE/OSPE). This exam consists of 12 stations, and each station assesses students' competence in a specific field of dentistry. Students are required to perform different tasks within a 10-minute period. Some stations are faculty proctored and are graded on the spot using a carefully designed rubric. Standardized patients are used in this assessment to evaluate students' communication skills and critical thinking capabilities. Other examples from the assessment include, but are not limited to, taking an x-ray on a mannequin, making impressions, performing digital dentistry, and evaluating dental procedures. This exam evaluates competence in various procedures and is a requirement for becoming a third-year dental student who is then able to see and treat patients.

To complete the assessment cycle, faculty meet regularly throughout the semester to discuss the projects that were completed in the Sim clinic. Questions such as the following may prompt faculty to make changes: How do you think that session went? What went well? What could we improve upon? What were the students' responses in your group? The ATSU-MOSDOH curriculum committee also meets with the course directors and reviews the course evaluations. If there are any concerns noted, the committee asks the directors what they have done to address noted concerns. For example, one course evaluation revealed there were two difficult courses offered at the same time. Students noted this schedule was very stressful and made it difficult for them to achieve the mastery they desired. The committee noted the concern and made immediate change to the next year's course schedule in an effort to alleviate the concern.

ATSU-MOSDOH uses a variety of assessment techniques such as projects carried out in the Sim clinic, small group activities, patient encounters, and progress exams. The curriculum also consists of a variety of assessment activities including formative and summative assessment, both of which occur at many points as students progress through the dental program. MOSDOH assesses student performance utilizing technology through the Sim clinic. Faculty and staff maintain a consistent cycle of assessment as they strive to continually improve teaching and learning.

ATSU-ASDOH

ATSU-ASDOH is ATSU's pioneer school for dentistry, paving the way to fully claim whole person healthcare as part of their mission and strategic plan. Located in Mesa, Arizona, ATSU-ASDOH serves a diverse student body and patient population. ATSU-ASDOH provides students with experiences in a Sim clinic along with time in the main dental clinic, orthodontic clinic, and advanced care clinic.

ATSU-ASDOH prides itself on innovation within its curriculum. An example of innovation within its curriculum is use of the SimMan (registered trademark of Dental Simulation Experiences), which provides students the opportunity to experience real-time simulations of medical emergencies before working on live patients. Medical emergencies can and do happen in dental settings. SimMan scenarios help students learn how to handle emergencies with faculty guidance. During the first and second years, SimMan is incorporated into the Clinical Dentistry courses to guarantee that first-year students have one encounter involving taking patients' vital signs and second-year students have one encounter with medical emergencies. Students often report gaining confidence in their ability to handle a medical emergency after these SimMan encounters. ATSU-ASDOH students typically get to experience SimMan four to five times over the course of their 4 years at ASDOH. Students often begin an encounter confident that they can handle a situation and quickly realize they know less than they thought. Students are given a survey prior to and after taking part in the encounters to measure their level of comfort and confidence in their ability to handle a medical emergency. While the SimMan encounter provides immediate, real-time assessment, the surveys provide feedback the faculty and administrators can use to strengthen the experience for their students and the program's curriculum.

SimMan

SimMan interactions require two to four students to participate in scripted scenarios. The scripts have been written by ATSU-ASDOH faculty. The SimMan is voiced by faculty in a separate room, who watch and gauge responses through a two-way mirror and the use of microphones. Responses depend on how the participating students react to the scripted scenario. Students are given the opportunity to observe the SimMan scenarios they are not directly involved in, and the whole group debriefs at the end of the scenario. Classmates may comment on the choices their participating peers made and provide constructive feedback. By debriefing after the simulated experience of a medical emergency in a real-time setting, students are provided the opportunity to self-reflect and further develop their critical thinking skills.

During the debriefing ATSU-ASDOH faculty provide real-time feedback related to the following areas: Did students understand and apply the previously covered lessons? Did students make accurate and confident choices for their patients? If not, did the students who observed their classmates catch the mistakes made? By including faculty as part of this simulated experience, both the students and the faculty receive immediate feedback on the successes or failures of their lessons and learning.

SimMan gives students the opportunity to see how medical emergencies play out and experience some of the anxiety an emergency situation can cause to the medical professionals involved. Students are able to assess and correct their own knowledge and behaviors in a safe, guided, real-time encounter before they potentially come across a similar situation with a real patient. There is a distinct difference between recalling information in a sterile academic testing environment and applying it in a dynamic simulation experience that forces accurate recall, critical thinking, and on-the-spot decision-making. In a medical emergency, the consequences are more real than they are on an exam. If students fail to ask the right questions, they may miss very important information about the patient's overall health. These clues could be the very key to disaster in the dental chair: a heart attack, an asthma attack, or even an allergic reaction to anesthesia.

A Vignette: Observation of SimMan Encounter

Imagine walking into the SimMan classroom. One finds team tables facing one main screen and the instructor's podium. The three instructors mill around the room as students fill their seats. The students of ATSU-ASDOH have a uniform, wearing the same color scrubs as the rest of their cohort. They are comfortable with one another, calling out first names and laughing at inside jokes. They seem excited to begin their first SimMan experience. Two students are running late, and they all joke how these two tend to run late after the lunch hour.

When the two students finally arrive, class begins. Only two instructors remain in the classroom now; one has left to take her station behind the two-way mirror, which allows for direct observation as her students interact with the SimMan. This view allows the instructor to time her reactions appropriately, making the SimMan experience more real for the students. The two instructors who remain in the classroom begin the introduction to this simulated, real-time assessment experience. They explain the technology of SimMan and the classroom to the students. At this point in students' careers at ATSU, they have had the opportunity to meet with cohorts ahead of them. They have heard about SimMan but have yet to interact with him one-on-one. Their nerves stem from the knowledge that two or three of them must be the guinea pigs today. As the lead instructor details technology, the students eagerly shift in their seats, awaiting the true experience.

Directly in front of the students is a large screen that displays the SimMan located in the "clinic." The clinic is just through the door located to the left of the student tables. In this clinic, there is very little other than the essentials: a dental chair, the SimMan reclining in the chair, two counters, oxygen, a defibrillator, two rolling stools for the students, and one stationary chair for the observing instructor. From the perspective of the large screen in the classroom, students can also see the two-way mirror that sits just behind the head of the reclining SimMan. The students are aware of the two-way mirror and know the instructor who is leading the scenario. To enhance the viewing and participation, the clinic room has two high-tech microphones hanging from the ceiling. These microphones feed to the instructor behind the two-way mirror and to the rest of the students in the classroom. SimMan has his own microphone, which acts as his voice.

Lying in front of every student on their table is a piece of paper detailing today's scenario. The scripted scenario we observe is about a middle-aged man with a heart condition. The leading instructor now asks for two volunteers. The students, all nervous and new, fall silent. The instructor takes the opportunity to play along with their nerves and jokes that the first two students who should volunteer should be the two students who were late to class. The entire classroom erupts in nervous laughter and turns to the back of the classroom. The late students accept their humorous punishment and take their place as volunteers.

Because this cohort is composed of first-year students, they have not had much experience with the actual clinic and real patients. As the two students walk into the simulated clinic, the rest of the classroom observes them on the large screen. They are as nervous as their volunteered peers, wiggling in their seats and whispering to one another. The lights have dimmed, and the lead instructor has left to speak with the observing instructor and her students. The observing instructor is the one who will sit in the simulated clinic with the two students as they fumble their way through the scripted experience.

The leading instructor has ensured that the two students know where the hanging microphones are and has asked they speak directly into them so their observing peers can hear. He has reassured them of the openness and safe environment this simulated experience offers. They are to feel safe and comfortable to make mistakes, but, most importantly, they are encouraged to stop and ask questions at any time. First-year students are allowed this leniency in the scripted experience, whereas the second- and third-year students are held to a higher standard of independence and accountability.

Today's SimMan immediately follows a morning lecture where these first-years in their dark blue scrubs have just heard about medical emergencies in the dental setting. Prior to entering the SimMan classroom, the students complete a pre-experience survey asking how they would rate their ability and comfortability in handling an emergency situation. After their simulation experience, they are given a post-survey, asking the same questions. The two students who we now see interacting with SimMan on the large screen have introduced themselves as Dr. [She] and Dr. [He]. Their fellow students giggle at this, not having had the pleasure of introducing themselves as doctors yet. SimMan responds begrudgingly. It seems this character chosen by the instructors is not very thrilled to be at the dentist's office. The students stall, unsure of themselves and their simulated experience. The observing instructor quietly suggests to direct their attention to SimMan, to treat him as a human and address his eyes when speaking to him.

The two students, now Dr. She and Dr. He, promptly adjust their rolling stools to face their patient. This change in stance has given them confidence, seen in the way they quickly fall into their formulated list of questions for their patient: How have you been feeling lately? What kinds of food have you been eating? Any major concerns you'd like to tell us about? SimMan seems rather tight-lipped, not wanting to divulge too much information. Every answer SimMan gives ends with a complaint about the direct environment: "Is it hot in here? I should just leave. This chair is making me dizzy. Your questions are confusing."

The main classroom has now fallen silent in the darkened room; all eyes are facing the front, indicating the anxiety classmates feel for their peers' abilities to comfort their patient and solve the case. A few of the students lift their piece of paper detailing the patient's medical history (as written by him), most likely wondering if they missed a clue. They did. Today's SimMan has a heart condition, and he didn't include very much about his medical history. Medical history is self-reported. Doctors know only as much as they receive from the patient, which is why the one-on-one interaction between doctor and patient (also referred to as interpersonal skill) is key to being a successful doctor as well as to improving a patient's health and wellness.

The two students are caught in their own nerves. Only the programmed list of questions settles their nerves and guides them forward. This simulated experience suddenly feels very real. SimMan is not responding as they expected him to, but instead, is pressing them to think on their feet—to go off-script. The two students are now concerned with making their patient comfortable. They move the dentist's chair up, then down again. They simulate turning a fan on, then off again. Nothing is making their patient more comfortable; now they are uncomfortable. Even their peers are uncomfortable. The two students pause and ask the observing instructor if they can call for an ambulance; they believe their patient is having a heart attack.

The observing instructor quietly says, yes, of course the students should be able to call for an ambulance, but have they tried oxygen yet? Have they asked about what kinds of medications their patient is using? Is SimMan showing the tell-tale signs of cardiac arrest, or is he having a panic attack? The observing instructor sees the two students are thinking and returns to observe as they begin to switch their tactics. As it turned out, SimMan was having a panic attack. The golden answer to today's simulated scenario was "nitrous oxide." The dentists could have given their patient nitrous oxide to help calm him. This would also allow the patient to still drive home afterward. The collective body of first-year students breathes, "Ahhhhhh" in unison. The instructor reminds his first-year students of their morning lecture regarding nitrous oxide and its appropriate applications during emergency scenarios. Hands begin to fly up, asking the leading instructor further questions about the differences between panic attacks and cardiac arrests, asking the proper procedure and response times for an ambulance. This simulated experience has directly tied their in-class lecture and homework to a real-time experience. The combination has the students buzzing with curiosity, but what is most observable is the students' willingness to be vulnerable in their questions, to admit they do not know and they want to know more. Even the instructors have changed their body language, mirroring the excitement and eagerness of their students. The answers the instructors are giving are more honest, revealing, and vulnerable. The instructors are using examples from their own lives, openly showcasing their own mistakes and the steps they took to change their practice in order to become better doctors for their patients.

This debriefing has done more for education and cohort bonding than any lecture could have, but the key is in the deliberate and intentional planning that goes on behind the scenes. ATSU-ASDOH has collected pre- and post-surveys since the initial decision to use SimMan as part of its curriculum. Over the years, the school has found more strategic ways to tie the didactic curriculum to the clinical curriculum, developing stronger character profiles and scripted scenarios to best complement current students' knowledge and skill sets. In addition to monitoring, assessing, and enacting change to its own curriculum, ATSU-ASDOH places value in creating the most successful environment for this simulated classroom. In the past year, the school has undergone remodeling to properly serve the scenario, their students, and their instructors. Updating technology and intentionally building a better-suited simulated clinic have provided the student body with an innovative, real-time assessment, disguised as a safe zone, to practice their future clinical interactions.

Can SimMan actually die? Yes, but never on a first-year, and never as the end-goal of an exercise. Essentially, the only way SimMan can die is if a third-year student has completely forgotten protocol. With the guidance of three instructors and the support of their peers, most students do not fumble so far as to fatally fail their patient. Even so, emergency scenarios are real. Students must be trained and able to respond proficiently. SimMan is a safe place to practice an emergency scenario, but SimMan is still scripted as true to life as possible, complete with begrudging responses and distaste for the doctor, too.

ATSU-SOMA

ATSU-SOMA was developed in response to a need expressed by the National Association of Community Health Centers (NACHC). The aim of the educational program is to produce leaders in medicine who will take the foundation of a broad education in medicine to improve health through patient care and educational research. It prepares physicians to practice compassionate clinical medicine of the highest standard and to identify and solve fundamental questions in the mechanisms, prevention, and treatment of disease.

The Learning Context: National Priorities for Medical Education

Students arrive to medical school equipped with 4 years of undergraduate baccalaureate "pre-med" training, but it takes a minimum of 7 more years to become a fully accredited, practicing physician. For the first 2 years of a typical medical school curriculum, students receive basic science instruction. During the second 2 years, students participate in clinical rotations (family medicine, internal medicine, obstetrics-gynecology, pediatrics, psychiatry, and general surgery), guided in their patient encounters by clinical instructors called preceptors. During clinical encounters, preceptors closely monitor trainees to protect patient safety (Eva, 2005; Gawande, 2009).

Over this long horizon of learning, through years of protracted studying, medical students can become complacent, passive learners if the learning environment does not include structured, interactive, multimedia skill practice. Medical students need to learn to contribute strongly as members of clinical healthcare teams (Buring et al., 2009; Weaver et al., 2014). This implies that healthcare students need to learn to collaborate well prior to encountering patients. Finally, experts recommend deliberate practice for medical students to master medical cognition and clinical diagnosis (Gawande, 2009; Patel et al., 1986). Thus, we have identified three areas for innovation in medical education: learning engagement, teamwork, and deliberate practice in clinical reasoning.

During the past 20 years, medical educators have been exploring digital learning through decision-making games, role-plays, and virtual patient simulations. There are many reasons for these digital choices, including their potential for increasing students' fluency with technology, self-assessment of clinical reasoning, engagement with problem-solving, and teamwork, as discussed in the following sections.

Technological Fluency

Medical science is rapidly changing due to scientific advances and new technologies (Mabry, 2011). According to experts in the field of medical information technology, in the near future, physicians will be aided by artificial intelligence and rely more heavily on cognitive extension devices such as smart phones and other electronic devices for rapid information queries (Farrell, 2011; Ferrucci, 2010). This implies that the focus of higher education should shift away from rote memorization of content toward critical thinking and creative thought processes, supported by the intelligent use of technology (Mishra et al., 2012).

Self-Assessment of Clinical Reasoning
As the field of medicine grows more complex, medical schools must find more efficient ways to train students to make effective, accurate clinical decisions. For physicians, the measure of competence is the ability to diagnose and manage patients (Ericsson, 2004; Norman, 2005). Simulations provide a low-risk context for practicing clinical encounters prior to interactions with human patients (Nishisaki et al., 2007; Ziv et al., 2003).

Engagement With Problem-Solving
Modern educators concur that active, learner-centered instructional approaches are more successful than lecture (Cullen et al., 2012; Tagg, 2003; Wieman, 2007). Others emphasize that students require 21st-century skill sets with a strong focus on thinking and communication (Kereluik et al., 2013; Senge, 1990; USC Rossier, 2011). The current generation of students grew up playing independent and group video games. Given their fluency with learning through the internet and through simulation, they are accustomed to self-directed learning (Kron et al., 2010; Oblinger & Oblinger, 2005).

Engagement With Teamwork
Virtual games and simulations benefit medical students because they provide them with learning spaces that allow them freedom to experiment, process evidence, and collaborate in authentic scenarios (Gee & Jenkins, n.d.). Twenty-first-century scientists will need to demonstrate the ability to assess high volumes of bio medical and contextual data quickly through the filter of well-established problem-solving schemata (Bird, 2010; Wieman, 2007).

Teaching Technological Fluency, Self-Assessment of Clinical Reasoning, Engagement With Problem-Solving, and Engagement With Teamwork Through Digital Healthcare Scenarios
Over the past 10 years, in an effort to increase students' technological fluency, self-assessment of clinical reasoning, engagement with problem-solving, and engagement with teamwork, faculty of our medical school have experimented with a variety of technology-enhanced learning media. The progression evolved from simple mobile and electronic quiz games, toward complex

case studies and simulations. This section will highlight a medical education project with virtual patient simulations.

To provide students with adequate preparation for clinical years, medical education traditionally includes practice with patient case scenarios in years one and two of medical school. Case practice helps students apply basic medicine principles to patient cases, often called *clinical vignettes*. These scenarios, when viewed on a computer screen, are known as virtual patient (VP) cases (Poulton et al., 2009). The American Association of Medical Colleges (AAMC) reported that 60% of medical schools are employing at least one type of screen simulation (Passiment et al., 2011). Medical schools all over the world are experimenting with digital case studies and VPs (Bland & Ousey, 2010; Cook & Triola, 2009; Ellaway et al., 2008). Authors produce these learning tools in a variety of digital formats: mobile apps, learning modules, VPS and brief vignettes. Some case studies focus on a theme, such as "interdisciplinary teamwork."

Collaborative Development of Digital Case Studies

In 2010, ATSU-SOMA formed a faculty learning community, based on the principles of innovation and communities of practice, called the Technology-Enhanced Active Learning (TEAL) team. Meeting monthly for 4 years, the learning community's goals were to develop new learning tools, implement the tools, and test the tools using action research or design-based research methods, using iterative cycles. We conducted a literature review, selected a few key technology projects, and applied for grants. The formation and evolution of this learning community was instrumental in our forward motion of innovation. During these years, we reviewed the principles of medical cognition (the science of medical decision-making; Patel et al., 2004) and schema theory (condensing knowledge through bundled concepts and schemata; Anderson & Pearson, 1988) in order to develop games and simulations for medical education. Box 11.1 outlines our process for developing, implementing, and evaluating new digital case scenarios.

Learning Benefits of Digital Case Studies or Scenarios
Over the course of our literature review, we found seven benefits of fusing digital case studies or scenarios into medical education curricula

1. *Engagement*: Placing students in the driver's seat by making key decisions during the scenario
2. *Collaboration*: Fostering teamwork among students from a variety of disciplines

BOX 11.1.

The Process for Developing, Implementing, and Evaluating New Digital Case Scenarios

1. Forming a *community of practice* (i.e., learning community, steering committee)
2. Identifying the problem of practice
3. Applying for project funding
4. Selecting content standards
5. Selecting dependent variable (outcomes) and research questions
6. Conducting a literature review for developing new lesson content
7. Narrowing the content domains
8. Selecting the learning medium
9. Formatting lesson content into the new digital format
10. Piloting the new digital case studies
11. Reviewing learner performance results
12. Assessing faculty and student perception of value of learning
13. Revising the digital case study to improve learning

3. *Real-world application*: Allowing for virtual worlds or elements of realism not typically provided in paper case studies
4. *Clinical reasoning*: Supporting student decision-making in a formative, safe failure mode, or a summative, assess performance mode
5. *Distance training*: Offering online accessibility, for ease of use with distributed learners in remote locations (e.g., in our case, students logged on from 11 community health centers and completed the digital cases online)
6. *Swift feedback*: Providing immediate feedback to students, who learn from mistakes in real time
7. *Learning analytics*: Tracking student analytics through a learning analytics dashboard (LAD) or learning management system (LMS); students and professors can log onto the dashboard to review progress and results

The Learning Exercise

During the first and second year of medical school, course directors include about one Virtual Community Health Center project per month during small group case practice as discussed in Box 11.2.

BOX 11.2.
The Project (2014–Present)

SOMA medical students train at or near community health centers in their second, third, and fourth years of medical school. This academic mission calls for flexible, immersive, and blended trainee education that is sensitive to the social determinants of health and emphasizes team-based, compassionate, preventive, and long-term care at education health centers.

Interested in interactive learning and formative assessment, a team of ATSU-SOMA faculty formed the TEAL team, a faculty learning community based on the principles of innovation and communities of practice. Meeting monthly for 4 years, the team's goals were to develop new learning tools, implement them, and test them using action research or design-based research methods, using iterative cycles. TEAL conducted a review of literature, selected a few key technology projects, and applied for grants. The formation and evolution of this learning community was instrumental to the forward motion of innovation. During these years, TEAL reviewed the principles of medical cognition and schema theory in order to develop games and simulations for medical education. We also selected a training platform, Envision Community Health Center with 27 individual virtual patients, for student use (Figure 11.1). The purpose of this training platform was to orient medical students to working with patients in community health centers.

TEAL authors developed the library of 27 digital cases using a software by Decision Sim. These cases currently run in an online case player by Medical Joyworks. Following a self-directed learning approach, osteopathic medical students assume the provider role, evaluate a patient, make meaningful choices, and explore the consequences of these choices. This approach allows for situated cognition, as well as legitimate peripheral participation, a process in which medical students orient into the professional role of physician in a peripheral (safe and risk-free) environment. Student learning is scaffolded via the feedback provided in each case module, and a debrief exercise that follows the case study allows for personal and group reflection.

Through these exercises, students learn to care for patients by managing each part of the patient encounter. These include

- collecting a detailed patient history, including social determinants of health;

Figure 11.1. A scene from a virtual case about limb pain.

Note. The patient has fallen off a skateboard, and injured his wrist.

- conducting a physical examination, including an osteopathic structural examination;
- ordering laboratory and imaging tests;
- suggesting a presumptive diagnosis; and
- recommending a treatment and follow-up plan.

Figure 11.1 illustrates a scene from a virtual case study.

After studying topics in a given course, students complete an assigned case. Students individually access the online case through the Envision Case Player (registered trademark by Medical Joyworks). Later, they meet to discuss the case with their small group team, facilitated by their clinical faculty. The entire sequence of completing the case study and debrief questions, followed by small group case discussion, takes approximately 1 hour. The sequence is illustrated in Figure 11.2.

Figure 11.2. The learning sequence.

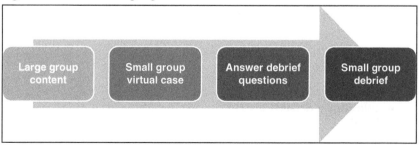

Box 11.3 identifies the features of our current Virtual Community Health Center case studies that were not addressed by other virtual patient case scenarios at the time we developed our case studies. These seven features, we believe, prepare our students to address the needs of our diverse population and remain current with developments in technology in their areas of specialization.

BOX 11.3.

VCHC Case Features

Each case module includes seven important aspects of care that were—at the time of development—not addressed by other virtual patient case scenarios.

1. **Community Health Center (CHC) Setting**
   VCHC cases are set in a virtual world. Once the trainee begins the case at the CHC, they are part of the healthcare team at the CHC. Within each case, a virtual preceptor provides advice.

2. **Family Connections**
   Each patient in each case study belongs to one of 10 families in the patient panel. Several case studies focus specifically on patient and family interactions. Consistent with CHC patient population statistics, the VCHC patient panel reflects a variety of age groups, ethnicities, and modern lifestyles, such as adoptive parents, single parents, same-gender parents, multi-ethnic families or extended families.

3. **Healthcare Team Members**
   In an effort to stimulate clinical reasoning and professionalism, students worked in teams during these exercises. Collaboration during clinical casework is considered to be a sound approach to fostering the development of clinical decision-making. Further, we hoped the opportunity for peer discussion would strengthen specific skills associated with interprofessional teamwork, such as respect and equal contribution. A range of providers and team members work at the CHC: receptionists, MAs, NPs, dietitians, pharmacists, specialists, nurses, translators, social workers, behavioral health, dentists, and so on.

4. **Deliberate Practice With Clinical Reasoning Through Clinical Decision Flow Charts**
   Trainees practice clinical reasoning using clinical decision flow charts, which are called schemes.

(Continues)

BOX 11.3. (*Continued*)

> **5. Electronic Health Record**
> Each case is equipped with a Centricity Electronic Health Record, a real-world feature that allows students to acclimate to new health information technology ahead of true clinical practice.
> **6. Social Determinants**
> Virtual patients present to the clinic with chronic or acute health-care conditions and complex social determinants of health, such as little or no health insurance, low income, low education, homelessness, or as new immigrants. Debrief exercises encourage the students to think about the social determinants that shape healthcare decisions and outcomes.
> **7. Osteopathic Principles and Practices (OPP)**
> VCHC case studies integrate osteopathic considerations, including relevant history, osteopathic structural examination, an osteopathic case consultation, and osteopathic manipulation therapy (OMT) videos.

Conclusion

As a graduate health sciences university, ATSU's assessment needs may vary from the typical 4-year undergraduate institution. With two culturally unique campuses, one coastal facility, and a large online community, ATSU values innovation and technology, with a critical eye to need. To address these needs adequately, ATSU became an early adopter of real-time assessment technology. Knowing our graduates will enter a high-tech industry, we at ATSU see the importance of incorporating technology into the curriculum. As the student body changes with the new millennium, we are also teaching the importance of determining the true value and need of changing technology. Will this shiny, new gadget help your patient? Or will it harm the clinic's budget by throwing a new, and possibly unnecessary, step into your daily routine as a clinician?

The Sim clinic at ATSU-MOSDOH provides students with the opportunity to practice techniques and procedures while receiving immediate feedback from instructors. Further, it allows instructors to evaluate not only student comprehension but also curriculum and instruction as students are learning, not after they have graduated. So often, it is the students who have graduated who teach a program how to become better educators. With real-time assessment technology, ATSU is able to address its students where they are as learners and correct mistakes before they graduate. Timely use of assessment results encourages students to actively participate in their education and even to assume accountability for their education.

ATSU-ASDOH's SimMan provides students with a real-time experience where they must apply recently gained knowledge of medical emergencies. Because knowledge is a scale of perception, offering a simulated experience for students to put their perception to the test is a safe way of teaching medical emergencies in a clinical scenario. SimMan gives students the awareness of their own mistakes while also giving them confidence to move forward as a student, to ask those vulnerable questions. Students not only evaluate themselves but also their peers provide feedback, as well. These learning experiences can be invaluable to long-term comprehension as well as to interprofessional and interpersonal skills.

ATSU-SOMA uses the Virtual Community Health Center as an innovative technology approach. The potential educational advantages of this approach include increased engagement, enhanced collaboration, real-world application, clinical decision-making, distance training, learning analytics, and swift feedback. The longer we incorporate technology with real-time assessment, the more we appreciate the value of that integration and its positive impact on student learning outcomes.

Real-time assessment experiences provide instructors with the opportunity to offer students immediate feedback, but the subtle success of real-time assessment for instructors and programs is the ability to evaluate their own instruction in real-time. The long-term benefits for a program that is able to assess and apply change to its curriculum for the students it currently has are triple-fold: their cohort has direct access to innovation, their faculty and instructors see success and feel valued, and their program sees higher board scores. Long-term benefits like these are better seen when looking at 3- to 5-year trends, but a cohorted program does see the benefits happening in real-time, as well. The confidence and professionalism of their student body is sustainable in a way that other programs can only hope to enforce via guidelines and syllabi. When students take accountability for their education and when faculty take initiative in innovative lesson planning, programs will see their ultimate goals come to fruition: preeminence in education and life-long learners in their students.

Perhaps one could safely assume every university desires to be or views itself as being preeminent and innovative. Certainly, every university hopes to inspire its graduates to be the very best in their field, the most desirable employees. How does a university prove it is accomplishing these grandiose goals, though? At ATSU we rely on data as the evidence of our success. Feedback is a valuable part of the data that support our university's claims to preeminence in education, but we don't rely fully on self-reported claims.

Institutional mapping provides us with the foundation for reliable student success. Real-time assessment is innovative in both technology and teaching, but it is also entwined into educational planning. Perhaps educational planning sounds old-school with all of this real-time assessment talk, but by attaching our institutional goals to the lesson plans and syllabi before the students ever engage in the real-time assessment, teachers and their programs are able to track their students' successes on the university scale. We do not track our students in the sense of failure or success, we track our programs' intentional and innovative education. Now, teachers and programs can see the immediate successes of their students, and the university can see the annual successes of its programs and their students.

At ATSU we believe our commitment to the integration of learning technologies into our curricula enables us to be more flexible in this ever-evolving world of education. But flexibility has been achieved by defining and solidifying our institutional goals. Having a foundation at the university level allows our programs and their teachers to build on the core values in new and valuable ways. Knowing who we are as a university was the first innovative step in education. It allowed ATSU to reach higher and farther, to test and try new forms of education, and to say confidently—through mapping and technology—that preeminence is more than a golden word used to flash on the school website. Preeminence is achievable through the simplest form of innovation: intentional education. With intentional education and innovative technologies, ATSU found real-time assessment. By bookending real-time assessment with data, we see the power of innovative education in our students; in the future of medicine; and in our educators, building their school's curriculum one course at a time.

References

Anderson, R., & Pearson D. P. (1988). A schema-theoretic view of basic processing in reading comprehension. In P. Carrell, J. Devine, & D. D. Eskey (Eds.), *Interactive approaches to second language reading* (pp. 37–55). Cambridge University Press.

Bird, A. (2010). Eliminative abduction: Examples from medicine. *Studies in History and Philosophy of Science Part A, 41*(4), 345–352.

Bland M., & Ousey, K. (2010). *The effectiveness of simulation in preparing student nurses to competently measure blood pressure in the real-world environment: A comparison between New Zealand and the United Kingdom (pilot study)*. The National Centre for Tertiary Teaching Excellence.

Buring, S. M., Bhushan, A., Brazeau, G., Conway, S., Hansen, L., & Westberg, S. (2009). Keys to successful implementation of interprofessional education: Learning location, faculty development, and curricular themes. *American Journal of Pharmaceutical Education, 73*(4), 60. https://doi.org/10.5688/aj730460

Cook, D. A., & Triola, M.M. (2009). Virtual patients: A critical literature review and proposed next steps. *Medical Education, 43*(4), 303–311. https://doi.org/10.1111/j.1365-2923.2008.03286.x

Cullen, R., Harris, M., & Hill, R. (2012). *The learner-centered curriculum.* Jossey-Bass.

Ellaway, R., Poulton, T., Fors, U., McGee, J. B., & Albright, S. (2008). Building a virtual patient commons. *Medical Teacher, 30*(2),170–174. https://doi.org/10.1080/01421590701874074

Ericsson, K. A. (2004). Deliberate practice and the acquisition and maintenance of expert performance in medicine and related domains. *Academic Medicine, 79*(10 Suppl), S70–81.

Eva, K. W. (2005). What every teacher needs to know about clinical reasoning. *Medical Education, 39*(1), 98–106. https://doi.org/10.1111/j.1365-2929.2004.01972.x

Farrell, J. (2011, May 11). *IBM Watson: A brief overview and thoughts for healthcare education performance improvement* [Paper presentation]. Medbiquitous Conference, Baltimore, MD.

Ferrucci D. (2010). *Build Watson: An overview of deep QA for the Jeopardy! challenge* [Paper presentation]. PACT10 Proceedings of the 19th International Conference on Parallel Architectures and Compilation Techniques, Vienna, Austria.

Gawande, A. (2009). *The checklist manifesto.* Metropolitan Books.

Gee, J., & Jenkins. H. (n.d.). *Games, learning, and the looming crisis in higher Education.* The 33rd Pullias Lecture. Los Angeles: University of Southern California, Rossier School of Education. Retrieved from http://www.youtube.com/watch?v=FmcgMK46nfg

Kereluik, K., Mishra, P., Fahnoe, C., & Terry, L. (2013). What knowledge is of most worth: Teacher knowledge for 21st century learning. *Journal of Digital Learning in Teacher Education, 29*(4), 127–140. https://files.eric.ed.gov/fulltext/EJ1010753.pdf

Kron, F. W., Gjerde, C.L., Sen, A., & Fetters, M. D. (2010). Medical student attitudes toward video games and related new media technologies in medical education. *BMC Medical Education, 10*(50). https://doi.org/10.1186/1472-6920-10-50

Mabry, P. L. (2011). Making sense of the data explosion: The promise of systems science. *American Journal of Preventive Medicine, 40*(5 Suppl. 2), S159–161. https://doi.org/10.1016/j.amepre.2011.02.001

Mishra, P., (2012). Rethinking technology & creativity in the 21st century: Crayons are the future. *TechTrends, 56*(5), 13–16. https://doi.org/ 10.1007/s11528-012-0594-0

Nishisaki, A., Keren, R., & Nadkarni, V. (2007). Does simulation improve patient safety? Self-efficacy, competence, operational performance, and patient safety. *Anesthesiology Clinics, 25*(2), 225–236. https://doi.org/10.1016/j.anclin.2007.03.009

Norman G. (2005). Research in clinical reasoning: Past history and current trends. *Medical Education, 39*(4), 418–427. https://doi.org/10.1111/j.1365-2929.2005.02127.x

Oblinger, D. G., & Oblinger, J. O. (2005). *Educating the net generation.* EDUCAUSE.

Passiment, M., Sacks, H., & Huang, G. (2011). *Medical simulation in medical education: Results of an AAMC survey.* Association of American Medical Colleges.

Patel, V., Arocha, J., & Zhang, J. (2004). Thinking and reasoning in medicine. In K. H. Holyoak & R. G. Morrison (Eds.), *Cambridge handbook of thinking and reasoning,* (pp. 727–750).Cambridge University Press.

Patel, V. L., & Groen, G. J. (1986). Knowledge based solution strategies in medical reasoning. *Cognitive Science, 10*(1), 91–116. http://csjarchive.cogsci.rpi.edu/1986 v10/i01/p0091p0116/MAIN.PDF

Poulton, T., Conradi, E., Kavia, S., Round, J., & Hilton, S. (2009). The replacement of "paper" cases by interactive online virtual patients in problem-based learning. *Medical Teacher, 31*(8), 752–758. https:// doi.org/10.1080/01421590903141082

Senge, P. (1990). *The fifth discipline.* Doubleday.

Tagg, J. (2003). *The learning paradigm college.* Wiley.

USC Rossier. (2011, April 14). Pullias lecture: "*Games, learning, and the looming crisis in higher education*" [Video]. YouTube. http://www.youtube.com/watch?v= FmcgMK46nfg

Weaver, S. J., Dy, S. M., & Rosen, M. A. (2014). Team-training in healthcare: A narrative synthesis of the literature. *BMJ Quality and Safety, 23*(5), 359–372. https:// doi.org/10.1136/bmjqs-2013-001848

Wieman, C. (2007). Why not try a scientific approach to science education? *Change: The Magazine of Higher Learning, 39*(5), 9–15.

Ziv, A., Wolpe, P. R., Small, S. D., & Glick, S. (2003). Simulation-based medical education: An ethical imperative. *Academic Medicine, 78*(8), 783–788. https:// doi.org/10.1097/00001888-200308000-00006

Bora Aytun, BS in business and BS in communication equivalencies, is a 30-year veteran of building technology-based solutions, including B2B product development for the TV broadcast industry; TV and video production; software product development; and, in the last decade, game development for training and higher education. He has been serving the organizational training space as the CEO of MAVI Interactive (MAVI) since 2008. Aytun and his team's key contribution to the training industry is making immersive skill development products accessible to all, removing the prohibitive cost barriers. MAVI's approach is developing immersive training systems with modular data structures that can reliably deliver engaging skill development scenarios as well as data-driven performance evaluation. MAVI uses advanced competency mapping techniques and creative experiential learning design, bridging the gap between subject matter expertise and job performance. MAVI's work has been recognized by industry organizations and customers worldwide for its singular focus on behavior modification solutions that leverage natural learning principles, designed to "train the brain" and affect behavior change.

Kem Barfield, EdD in educational leadership and management, Capella University, is the dean of academic and student affairs at Three Rivers Community College. He previously served as the associate dean of academics and director of educational technology, where he managed the distance learning program, institutional research program, and tutoring center and supports all aspects of the academic program. He had a career as a submariner in the U.S. Navy and developed curriculum for all submarine schools in the country. Throughout his 20 years in higher education, he has worked in a multitude of areas, including strategic planning, guided pathways, enrollment management, accreditation, climate assessment, veterans' issues, graduation, advising and counseling, continuing education, and student issues or other issues. In all areas, he has used technology to solve problems, expand access to information, and increase institutional knowledge. At Three Rivers Community College, he has worked in concert with faculty and staff co-leaders to move the assessment process from a small paper-based program to a digital one, an effort aimed at not only assessing but also supporting the assessment learning community at the campus. Additionally, he provides workshops to faculty and staff on the use of technology, including social media.

Daniel Belenky, PhD in cognitive psychology, University of Pittsburgh, is director of learning science research at Pearson. His team synthesizes and conducts research to help build more effective learning technologies. Prior to joining Pearson in 2014, he was a postdoctoral fellow in the human-computer interaction institute at Carnegie Mellon University. In his PhD program he studied how student motivation interacts with (and is impacted by) innovative instructional methods. His current research projects explore how insights from cognitive psychology and behavioral science can be used to improve learner outcomes at scale.

Forrest Bollow, EdD, University of Missouri-Columbia; EdS, Northwest Missouri State University; and MA in secondary administration, Northeast Missouri State University (now Truman State University), is the university data manager at A.T. Still University of Health Sciences (ATSU). His focus is on creating and sustaining institutional processes within the university, primarily in relation to assessment and accreditation. Bollow's projects are also highly specialized to address and support the needs of the program and course level. Bollow enforces maintenance, revisions, and archiving of ATSU's institutional data. Before joining ATSU, Bollow spent 28 years in K–12 public education, serving as a teacher, a coach, and an administrator.

Adriana Botha, MEd in educational psychology, University of Johannesburg, and PhD in information systems, University of Pretoria, is head education consultant in the faculty of engineering, built environment, and information technology (EBIT) at the University of Pretoria (UP). Her area of expertise revolves around curriculum development and student success. Her present research interests are in the field of institutional and program level assessment. Previously she worked in New Zealand as an educational psychologist for the Ministry of Education. On her return to South Africa in 2010, she joined the local higher education landscape when she was appointed at Sefako Makgatho University of Health Sciences (SMU) as project manager for the improvement of graduate throughput. The UP appointed her in 2014 to the Department for Education Innovation as instructional designer. Here she honed the skill of implementing and facilitating eLearning in EBIT. She is presently completing her PhD studies in information systems with a focus on developing a learning management system-based framework for quality program review in higher education.

Emily Cole, PhD in educational leadership and policy from the University at Buffalo, State University of New York, is an independent mixed methods and action researcher. With interests in studying and improving culturally responsive educational systems, Cole recently completed an advanced certificate in program evaluation from Claremont Graduate University. She is lead author of an upcoming book, *Action Research: Principles of Practice* (Routledge). Cole has served as a co-principle investigator in Exploring Emerging Technologies for Lifelong Learning and Success (a massive open online course; see more using the hashtag #EmTechMOOC) since its inception. As an adjunct instructor at the University at Buffalo, Cole became proficient in educational technologies through the SUNY Tools of Engagement Project, later becoming a fellow in the project.

Melanie Davis, DHEd, A.T. Still University (ATSU) and MA in teaching English to speakers of other languages, Southeast Missouri State University, is director of the Office of Assessment and Accreditation for ATSU. She manages her team to foster best practices and ensure ATSU's quality higher education through developed processes in assessment and accreditation. Davis initiated many of the processes in place at ATSU addressing these concerns and is an active leader in educational assessment. She is a member of several committees related to assessment, accreditation, and planning, chairs the university-wide Assessment Committee—Resources subcommittee, and is principal investigator of the Cultural Climate Study Project. Davis worked in K–12 education for 13 years, first in the classroom and then as a curriculum and assessment administrator. She then joined ATSU, where she has worked since 2009. Davis is an evaluator for the American Osteopathic Association's Commission on Osteopathic College Accreditation and was recently trained as team chair. She has given several presentations on assessment and accreditation topics at conferences such as HLC's Annual Conference, Association for Institutional Research Forum, Assessment Institute at IUPUI, Tk20/Watermark Conference, and the Society of Teachers of Family Medicine Conference on Medical Student Education.

Kristen DiCerbo, PhD in educational psychology, Arizona State University, is chief learning officer at Khan Academy, where she is responsible for driving and communicating the teaching and learning strategy for Khan Academy's content and products, as well as ensuring pedagogical coherence and research-based design in their offerings. Previously she served as vice president of learning research and design at Pearson, where she led a team of researchers and learning designers conducting new research in learning and assessment and translating research insights into the design of digital learning environments. DiCerbo's personal research program centers on the use of games and simulations to understand what learners know and can do. Prior to joining Pearson, DiCerbo was a school psychologist in a local school district in Arizona and then a researcher with the Networking Academies at Cisco.

Jordan Farris, BA in English literature with a focus on education, Arizona State University, is the assessment specialist at A. T. Still University of Health Sciences (ATSU) in Mesa, Arizona. Her primary role is to serve the Office of Assessment and Accreditation, a department committed to assuring best practice and quality education. Farris also serves as a member on a handful of university committees and actively participates in the university accreditation process for the Higher Learning Commission (ATSU's regional accrediting body). She has attended multiple conferences for assessment and/or accreditation, having submitted and presented on selected topics for the Watermark conference each year of her employment with ATSU.

Katrina Fulcher-Rood, PhD in communicative disorders and sciences, University at Buffalo, State University of New York (SUNY), as well as a certified speech-language pathologist, is an assistant professor at SUNY Buffalo State. Fulcher-Rood is a qualitative researcher with expertise in surveys, interviews, and think-aloud research methodology. Her research focuses primarily on examining the diagnostic decision-making process of speech-language pathologists employed in school-based settings. In addition, she investigates the ways individuals with complex communication needs use speech-generating devices to overcome their technological limitations. She is a Tools of Engagement Project (TOEP) Phase 2 awardee, has served as a TOEP Fellow, and is on the current #EmTechMOOC assessment team.

Jamey Heit, PhD in literature, theology, and the arts, Glasgow University, is founder of Ecree, a technology company that specializes in a proprietary, interactive writing tool for students and teachers. A lifelong learner and lover of technology, he believes technology plays an essential role in solving big problems and insists that it is part of a broader solution, rather than a quick fix to a temporary challenge. He has taught in a variety of higher education disciplines. By credit hours, Heit has over 25 years of teaching experience across disciplines and has graded more than 30,000 papers (yes, he counted!). During his time in the classroom, Heit saw limits in his ability to help students consistently improve their writing. So, in 2014 he left academia and founded Ecree. Heit is on a mission to nurture a generation of better writers and thinkers with widespread access to easy and adaptive writing software. With the Ecree technology, he's found a way to provide consistent, timely, and quality feedback to students to ensure they develop lifelong skills for success.

Jennifer H. Herman, PhD in higher education, University at Buffalo, State University of New York, and MA in international training and education, American University, is executive director of the Center for Excellence in

Teaching and Research and associate professor of practice in health professions education at Simmons University. She has developed, facilitated, and overseen hundreds of research-based faculty development programs and provides structured support for curriculum design at all levels. In her faculty role, she teaches courses on teaching, assessment, learning theory, and curriculum development for the health professions education certificate of advanced graduate study and doctoral program. Her publications include *Creating Engaging Discussions: Strategies for "Avoiding Crickets" in Any Size Class and Online* (Stylus, 2018; with L. Nilson).

Aaron Hunt, PhD in public health with specialization in global health, University of Nevada, Las Vegas, and MPH, University of Nevada, Las Vegas, is the program coordinator for a primary care training enhancement program at A.T. Still University of Health Sciences (ATSU), School of Osteopathic Medicine in Arizona, funded by the Health Resources and Services Administration (HRSA). Since 2018, Hunt has been contributing to the development of new cases and management of the Virtual Community Health Center, which is an innovative virtual tool for simulated case-based medical education. In addition, he has experience working for HRSA- and National Institutes of Health-funded HIV/AIDS prevention programs in both the United States and Nigeria. His current research focuses on improving maternal child health outcomes and reducing health disparities through the use of mobile health technologies.

Jessica Kruger, PhD in health education, University of Toledo, and MS in health education, University of Michigan-Flint, is a clinical assistant professor in the Department of Community Health and Health Behavior, School of Public Health and Health Professions at the University at Buffalo, State University of New York. She is a health educator whose research focuses on consumption and addictive behaviors, health behavior decision-making, and pedagogy in public health. She collaborates with a wide variety of community-based organizations and advises students at the Lighthouse Free Medical Clinic in Buffalo. Kruger is coeditor of the *Journal of Student-Run Clinics* and continues to promote the importance of public health within free medical clinics. She is also a member of the SUNY Exploring Emerging Technologies for Lifelong Learning and Success (#EmTechMOOC) assessment team.

Danielle Leek, PhD in communication studies, University of Iowa, is the director of academic innovation and distance education at Bunker Hill Community College in Boston, Massachusetts. Her background includes over 15 years of teaching in higher education, specifically communication studies and business. Prior to working at Bunker Hill Community College,

Leek served as the director of professional learning at Campus Compact and associate professor of communications at Grand Valley State University.

Tian Luo, PhD in instructional technology, Ohio University, is an associate professor of instructional design and technology at Old Dominion University. She worked previously as an instructional design professional in both higher education and corporate settings. She currently serves as an associate editor-in-chief for the *Journal of Information Technology Education: Research*. Her research interests center on teaching and learning with and through social technologies and media, as well as designing social media-supported learning environments. Her broader research interests include instructional design, online learning, gamification, open educational resources, and learning analytics.

Peggy L. Maki, PhD in literature and linguistics, University of Delaware, writes, speaks, and consults with higher education organizations and institutions on the process of assessing student learning, an internally motivated and shared commitment to currently enrolled students' equitable progress toward achieving high-quality learning outcomes. She has consulted at over 610 institutions in the United States and abroad and has written books and articles on assessment for more than 20 years. Her previous book, *Real-Time Student Assessment: Meeting the Imperative for Improved Time to Degree, Closing the Opportunity Gap, and Assuring Student Competencies for 21st-Century Needs* (Stylus, 2017), challenges institutions to prioritize the use of chronological assessment results to benefit enrolled students compared with the more common practice of prolonged assessment cycles that generally benefit future students. She served as the former American Association for Higher Education's (AAHE) senior scholar on assessment; a consultant in the Association of American Colleges & Universities' (AAC&U's) annual General Education and Assessment Institutes; and a member of several advisory boards, including one for the Lumina Foundation. Currently, she serves on the National Institute for Learning Outcomes Assessment's (NILOA) advisory board. She is the recipient of a national teaching award, the Lindback Award for Distinguished Teaching.

Jill Matejcik, BS in human communication, Arizona State University, is the accreditation specialist at A.T. Still University of Health Sciences (ATSU) in Mesa, Arizona. Matejcik also divides her time among a handful of university committees that foster communities of best practice in the areas of assessment and accreditation. Matejcik has been with the university since 2014, working as the education specialist for Arizona School of Dentistry and Oral Health (ASDOH). Her role within ASDOH often contributed to the major projects and goals of the university's Office of Assessment and

Accreditation. Prior to working for the university, Matejcik acquired nearly 10 years of experience in education.

Lise McCoy, EdD and MTESL, both from Arizona State University, is director of faculty development at New York Institute of Technology, College of Osteopathic Medicine. She directed and codirected faculty development and technology-enhanced active learning at A.T. Still University (ATSU) of Health Sciences' College of Osteopathic Medicine from 2014 to 2019. A higher education specialist with more than 35 years of experience, McCoy is known for her scholarship in the field of medical education innovation, virtual patient simulation, active learning, and interprofessional teamwork. A graduate of Arizona State University's Education Leadership and Innovation, she has a passion for action research, communities of practice, learning-centered instruction, and education technology. McCoy has taught master's and doctoral level courses in contemporary teaching and learning concepts, education research, and strategies for inquiry. An experienced researcher, McCoy has been the principle investigator on many grant projects and served on several national committees: the 2020 Beyond Flexner Conference Steering Committee (2019), the American Medical Association's Accelerating Change in Medical Education Consortium (2016–2019), and the American Association of Colleges of Osteopathic Medicine's Undergraduate to Graduate Medical Education Faculty Development Committee (2017–2020).

Pauline Salim Muljana, PhD student in instructional design and technology (IDT), College of Education and Professional Studies, Old Dominion University, focuses her research on investigating how learning analytics informs instructional design to foster learning behaviors and strategies associated with academic success. Before joining the IDT program, she held instructional design responsibilities for 12 years at California State Polytechnic University, Pomona, that included design and development of courses with various delivery modes and multimedia learning objects, as well as facilitation of faculty workshops on instructional strategies, course design, and effective technology integration.

Ammar Musawi, MDS in prosthetic dentistry, University Malaya, and BDS from Baghdad University, is an associate professor and the director of pre-clinical education and simulation clinic at A.T. Still University's Missouri School of Dentistry and Oral Health (ATSU-MOSDOH). Musawi started his career in academia in 2010; he is a member of the American Dental Education Association (ADEA) and the International Association of Dental Research (IADR). He has conducted multiple research projects and mentored students in many of his research projects.

Ruth Newberry, PhD in English, Duquesne University, joined Blackboard in 2014 with over 25 years of higher education experience in teaching, faculty development, educational technology leadership, administration, and assessment and curriculum development. As a principal education consultant, she provides consulting for Blackboard's Assessment & Accreditation Solution to assist clients with institutional and program assessment projects, as well as on competency-based education solutions. Previously, she was a director of educational technology for 14 years at Duquesne University and prior to that spent 11 years as a lecturer in Duquesne's School of Leadership and Professional Advancement. She was involved in two Middle States self-studies and was a Middle States Team reviewer. She has facilitated workshops for the Online Learning Consortium, is Quality Matters certified, and is an EDUCAUSE Leadership alum. She presents at national and regional conferences and has completed more than 100 successful assessment and accreditation engagements across North America, the Middle East, South Africa, Latin America, and Asia Pacific. She is based in Pittsburgh, Pennsylvania.

Matthew Olson, EdD in leadership in education, University of Massachusetts Lowell, is currently dean of liberal arts at Middlesex Community College in Bedford and Lowell, Massachusetts. Olson previously served as director of online learning at Middlesex for 17 years. His long-term interests focus on the relationship between new digital technologies and student learning. Olson has vast experience in technological professional development for faculty. He has written and presented on the topic of online teaching and learning in numerous local, national, and international venues.

Greg V. Placencia, PhD in industrial and systems engineering from the University of Southern California, is an assistant professor in the Industrial and Manufacturing Engineering department at California State Polytechnic University, Pomona. He currently teaches Fundamentals of Human Factors Engineering, Fiscal Implications in Technical Decision Making, Advanced Human Factors in Engineering Design, and Human Systems Interaction. His research interests include human engineering; human–systems interaction; and adapting macroergonomics to health care, human trafficking, education, and other nontraditional disciplines.

Jing Qi, EdD in educational leadership and policy studies, University of Vermont, serves as learning analytic and learning management system specialist at Dartmouth College. Prior to joining the Dartmouth information technology and consulting team, Qi served as the director of institutional research and information management at public institutions. Qi has been working in the field of institutional research and instructional technologies for many years. Using her solid background in computer science, extensive experience in statistics, and strong interest in data visualization, she integrates the core elements of learning analytics and educational technology in the exploration of analytics in instruction and learning.

Rachel Rigolino, MA in English language and literature/letters, SUNY New Paltz, and BA in English literature, Vassar College, is coordinator of the Supplemental Writing Workshop Composition Program at SUNY New Paltz. She has taught full-time in the English department since 1999 and is the recipient of a 2014 SUNY Innovative Instruction Technology Grant (IITG), which her team used to develop online resources for teaching writing across the curriculum. She has been instrumental in the content refinement of both the Tools of Engagement Project at SUNY and #EmTechMOOC.

Robin Robinson, MA in technical and professional writing, Northeastern University, is the director of education technology and eLearning at Framingham State University (FSU). She is responsible for implementing strategies to integrate technology throughout the curriculum and facilitating related continuous academic improvements based on quality standards and generally accepted best practices regardless of the course delivery modality. On-campus Robinson leads an educational technology collaborative team; is the cofacilitator of the FSU Quality Matters course design initiative; is an active member of ITS Leadership Team and the Center for Excellence in Learning, Teaching, Scholarship and Service (CELTSS). Robinson also is an adjunct instructor for FSU, UMass Boston, and the Boston Public Schools Pathways Program. She presents at regional and national conferences.

Peter Shea, MA in English education and a graduate certificate in instructional design and technology, University of South Florida, is an instructional designer and currently serves as director of the Office of Professional Development at Middlesex Community College in Bedford and Lowell, Massachusetts. He is an advocate for highly immersive learning experiences and the use of learning analytics to inform instructional design. Currently, he is working on the promotion of interactive open educational resources (iOER). In the past, Shea has worked as a book reviewer for *eLearn* magazine and coauthored a chapter in the book, *Transforming Virtual World Learning: Cutting-Edge Technologies in Higher Education* (Emerald Publishing, 2011). He manages a Facebook group for instructional designers in education which has over 5,000 members from around the world. He also serves as the chief hub administrator for the Massachusetts Community Open Educational Resources (OER) Hub.

Gina Sipley, PhD candidate in digital literacy studies at Hofstra University and MA in English from Syracuse University, is the coordinator of emerging educational technologies at Nassau Community College, State University of New York, where she is also a tenured assistant professor in the department of Critical Reading and Academic Advancement. She was awarded first place for the most pedagogically intriguing use of educational technology in the SUNY Tools of Engagement Project (TOEP) and volunteers as an Uber Fellow for the SUNY Exploring Emerging Technologies for Lifelong Learning and Success (#EmTechMOOC; http://suny.edu/emtech). Sipley has been recognized with an Open SUNY Effective Practices Award and was twice the recipient of the Nassau Community College award for Excellence in Teaching Students with Disabilities. She is a first-generation college graduate of SUNY Binghamton University.

Roberta (Robin) Sullivan, MAH interdisciplinary degree in education and communication design and MLS in information science, University at Buffalo, State University of New York (SUNY), is a teaching and learning strategist with education services with the university libraries at the University at Buffalo. She conducts research regarding innovative digital pedagogy and helps students, faculty, and other stakeholders explore and implement established and emerging technologies to support teaching and learning. Sullivan leads the SUNY Exploring Emerging Technologies for Lifelong Learning and Success (#EmTechMOOC; http://suny.edu/emtech), a global learning opportunity to create 21st-century citizens equipped for today's technology-driven society. Sullivan has been recognized through a SUNY Chancellor's Award for Excellence in Professional Service, a SUNY Faculty Advisory Council on Teaching and Technology (FACT2) Excellence in Instructional Support award, and three Open SUNY Effective Practice Awards.

Cherie van Putten, MEd in adult education, Penn State University, is an instructional designer for the Center for Learning and Teaching at Binghamton University. She facilitates workshops for faculty and serves as a resource for faculty who want to pursue online and hybrid courses. Her areas of interest include faculty development, creating learning communities, nontraditional learners, and distance education delivery. Van Putten has served as co-principle investigator on both the Tools of Engagement Project (TOEP): On-Demand Discovery Learning Professional Development and #EmTechMOOC (Emerging Technologies for Lifelong Learning and Success; http://suny .edu/emtech). She is the recipient of two SUNY Faculty Advisory Council on Teaching and Technology (FACT2) Excellence in Instructional Support awards and two Open SUNY Effective Practice Awards.

real-world benefits from, 49,
91–92, 115–18
relevant to, 10–13
requirement gathering by, 229–31
SimMan as, 270, 274–78,
286–87
simulation-based science
assessment and, 86–87, 279–80
sites for, 82
students and faculty targeted for,
127
student surveys on, 110
AT system goals in, 223
task software as, 24–26
taxonomy of current, 64–81
teams integrating, 10
tutoring and, 65, 69
tutoring and adoption of, 131
types of, 23
virtual world and, 132
VR and, 132
web meetings, 116–17
websites and resources on, 82
learning tools, 125
lecturing
inefficiency of, 47
interactive and breakout features
in, 83
learning versus, 280
Lederman, Doug, 1–2
licensing, 32, 81, 103, 114
lightweight directory access protocol
(LDAP), 265
LMSs. *See* learning management
systems

massive open online course
(MOOC). *See also* hybrid
MOOCs
cMOOCs as connective, 104
definition of, 103–4

distance learning for, 103
Edx and, 104, 210
faculty and, 6–7, 99, 105
metacognition and self-regulation
in, 9, 57, 88, 90–92, 94–95
of SUNY, 51–52
xMOOCs as extended, 104
Medical Joyworks, 283–84
messaging systems, 30
metacognition
engagement and, 81, 85, 156,
176
self-regulated learning and, 9, 57,
88, 90–92, 94–95
MetaTutor, 91
Middlesex Community College,
129, 131–32
Missouri School of Dentistry
and Oral Health
(ATSU-MOSDOH)
assessment by, 273
formative assessment at, 272
KaVo Mannekin Simulator at,
270–73
student work at, 271–72
Mitchell, Ted, 57–58
mixed reality (MR), 48
mobile design, 75
MOOC. *See* massive open online
course
Moodle, 101
formative analytics using,
159–62
summative analytics in, 168–71
MR. *See* mixed reality

NACHC. *See* National Association
of Community Health Centers
narrative technologies, 53, 64
adaptive learning-based
technologies and, 209